CASSELL STUDIES IN PASTORAL CARE AND PERSON
AND SOCIAL EDUCATION

D0228158

VISION OF A SCHOOL

Books in this series:

R. Best (ed.): *Education, Spirituality and the Whole Child*

R. Best, P. Lang, C. Lodge and C. Watkins (eds): *Pastoral Care and PSE: Entitlement and Provision*

G. Haydon: *Teaching about Values: A Practical Approach*

P. Lang (ed.): *Pupils Can Be People Too: Affective Education in Europe*

P. Lang, R. Best and A. Lichtenberg (eds): *Caring for Children: International Perspectives on Pastoral Care and PSE*

O. Leaman: *Death and Loss: Compasionate Approaches in the Classroom*

J. McGuiness: *Teachers, Pupils and Behaviour: A Managerial Approach*

J. McGuiness: *Counselling in Schools*

S. Power: *The Pastoral and the Academic: Conflict and Contradiction in the Curriculum*

P. Whitaker: *Managing to Learn: Aspects of Reflective and Experiential Learning in Schools*

CASSELL STUDIES IN PASTORAL CARE AND PERSONAL
AND SOCIAL EDUCATION

VISION OF A SCHOOL

The Good School in the Good Society

Jasper Ungoed-Thomas

CASSELL

London and Washington

Cassell
Wellington House
125 Strand
London WC2R 0BB

PO Box 605
Herndon
VA 20172

First published in 1997

British Library Cataloguing-in-Publication Data

A catalogue record for this book is available from the British Library.

ISBN 0–304–33655–6 (hardback)
    0–304–33646–7 (paperback)

Typeset by BookEns Ltd, Royston, Herts.
Printed and bound in Great Britain by Biddles Limited,
Guildford and King's Lynn

Contents

Series editors' foreword   vi

1   What is a good school?   1
2   Respect for persons   10
3   A curricular crisis of identities   12
4   Persons: being and becoming   18
5   Education's ideals of a person   31
6   The personal school   52
7   The whole truth   59
8   The true curriculum   74
9   Justice and responsibility   99
10   The school: institution and community   126
11   Justice and the government of education   134
12   The good school in the good society   154

References   157
Index   165

Series editors' foreword

The title of this series is 'Studies in Pastoral Care and Personal and Social Education'. As editors we have sought to ensure that the books included in it represent as broad as possible a view of what these areas are concerned with. Consequently, some books in the series focus directly on aspects of pastoral care and PSE, whilst others involve topics which have an identity of their own but have significant implications for, or relationships with, pastoral care and PSE. This book adds a new dimension to the series, for it both focuses on pastoral care and PSE and roams widely over broader issues which are rich in implications for schools' pastoral work.

Vision of a School is a book whose arguments all those involved in pastoral care and PSE would do well to consider, but its message is significant for a much wider audience; indeed it has something important to say to everyone involved in education today, be they teachers, politicians or parents. It sets out to answer one of the most fundamental, but hitherto inadequately answered, educational questions: 'What is a good school?' It does this in a rigorous, scholarly and above all convincing way. Though its arguments are often in opposition to key elements of the new political and theoretical orthodoxy, the rational, measured and analytical way in which they are presented makes a welcome change from the ill-considered and dogmatic assertions which are typical of contemporary debate.

The new educational orthodoxy has been influenced as much by the concept of the *failing* school as by that of the *effective* school. Both types of school have been characterized in terms of inputs and outcomes, effectively using what in research is described as the 'black box' model, where the concern is solely for the relationship between inputs and outcomes and not for the actual processes going on in the institution concerned. Where consideration has been given to processes, this has tended to be at a simplistic and mechanistic level, and still closely tied to outcomes. A good example is the current emphasis on whole-class teaching. This is based at least in part on the fact that this approach is used in Pacific Rim countries which achieve high levels of success in terms of measurable outcomes but does not seriously address the other implications of the way teaching and learning are organized and carried out.

Although there is an undeniable need to promote the development of effective schools and revitalize failing ones, much of the current approach is narrow, naive and inadequate. Narrow in its use of a 'black box' approach, inadequate in the way that many significant variables are ignored, and naive in the assumption that all that failing schools need to do is emulate what is done in effective ones. More seriously, the approach promotes a very limited view of the purpose of education and perceives the role of school from a predominantly economic perspective. In our view, the most serious omission is the way this perspective all but ignores the underlying question of what we might mean by a 'good school' in the first place.

In our view there is an increasingly worrying vacuum at the centre of current educational thinking. Indeed, it may be that the term 'thinking' is in itself inappropriate, for the vacuum is in part the result of a decline in rigorous analysis and reflection, encouraged by those politicians, pedagogues and quango officials who systematically denigrate both theoretical and empirical research in education. The failure to address the issue of what we mean by a good school is a failure which could have the most serious effects for the way in which education develops into the next millennium.

The publication of Jasper Ungoed-Thomas's book is therefore particularly timely, for it both offers a convincing case for what a good school ought to be and provides an impetus for renewed debate of this important question.

Of course, Jasper Ungoed-Thomas's 'good school' is concerned to produce well-educated students, but his view of what being 'educated' means is far broader and more holistic than that which informs the school effectiveness movement discussed above. He is not rejecting the aims of this movement however. On the contrary, he argues that a confident and shared vision of a good school is essential if we are to identify good performance and promote good practice. But by returning to first principles he shows up the superficiality with which the pursuit of this aim is so often treated.

His analysis of what features would go to make up a good school is insightful and systematic. He begins with the identification of several significant areas of study within education: in the 'personal school' (Chapter 6) pupils will learn to understand themselves and the sorts of worthwhile people they can become; in the whole school curriculum (Chapter 8) there is concern for various forms of understanding, exploration and expression; in the school as an institution pupils learn to appreciate fair rules, the need to behave in an acceptable way and to discipline themselves (Chapter 9); in the school as a community they learn to contribute to school and wider community (Chapter 10). These areas are of course highly significant for those concerned with pastoral care and PSE.

Jasper Ungoed-Thomas goes on to argue that the good school has readily recognizable moral and intellectual traits that can be related to the areas of study outlined above. Of these, he sees the most significant as respect for persons, truth, justice and responsibility, which he calls *the first virtues of education*. Thus: respect for persons is the first virtue of the personal school; truth is the first virtue of the whole school curriculum; justice is the first virtue of the school as an institution; responsibility is the virtue of the school as a community. Clearly, this analysis is of great significance in a much wider educational field than that of pastoral care and PSE.

Throughout the book we are reminded that 'education is concerned with encouraging respect for persons, self and other ... [and that] ... schools cannot hope to do this effectively unless they are clear about the ideas of a person which they value' (p. 31). This theme is developed in Chapter 5 where the various ideals of the person which exist in our society and influence our schools are discussed. These include the 'Christian' person, the 'classical' person, the 'rational' person, the 'humanist' person and the 'economic' person. His examination of these models fills an important gap in the literature of PSE, but it is again clear that what the author has to say is of importance to a far greater audience than those directly concerned with this aspect of the curriculum.

Jasper Ungoed-Thomas is not just concerned with the good school but also with the good society in which the school exists. As we have seen, the good school is, for him, one which successfully reflects in its teaching and learning the qualities of respect for persons, truth, justice and responsibility. He believes that these are the first virtues of education and central to its affective dimension. He argues that they are both ends in themselves and means towards achieving the aims of the school. Notably he believes that the nature of the good school should not be 'read off' from a particular view of the 'good society' but, having established the qualities of a good school, it becomes possible to infer the kind of educational system which might promote it. For Jasper Ungoed-Thomas, an education system to which the comprehensive ideal and the comprehensive school are central is the most appropriate environment for the development of good schools.

Offered a choice between the fashionable concept of the 'effective school' and the model of the 'good school' offered in this book, we know which we would encourage parents to choose for their children. For an education which goes beyond the purely economic and is of real benefit in equipping children for Life (with a capital 'L'), we commend Jasper Ungoed-Thomas's vision to all those with a concern for education – and that should be everyone!

We hope that the ideas in this book reach as wide an audience as possible for they have the potential to make an important and positive contribution to current debate and to the future development of education.

CHAPTER 1

What is a good school?

'Nobody,' wrote Kingsley Amis in his memoirs (1992, p. 127), 'can really put his head into our (or probably any other) educational arrangements without a twinge of fear for the survival of the nation.'

Be that as it may, there certainly are those who, whether or not they have taken the trouble to take a good look at schools, express hyperanxiety about the state of education. From journalistic Cassandras to political axe-grinders, cries of alarm fill the airwaves and emerge in print.

And whatever their reactions, the world appears to be full of people who are interested in, or concerned about, what is going on in schools. Schools may have their problems; but lack of attention is certainly not one of them.

The general hue and cry has led to certain matters, in particular, being pursued with especial vigour. For instance: What sort of evidence reliably indicates how good a school is? How can one assess whether a school is good, bad or indifferent? How can a school be improved, that is, become better? Should the national system of education be reorganized; and if so, along what lines? These, and similar questions are, self-evidently, of immediate practical importance.

There is, however, another, deceptively simple question, which also needs to be asked – one which has received rather less attention. This is:

What *IS* a good school?

Initially, the answer must be that it is one which reflects, or is consistent with, a notion of what a good school is.

Do we have a common idea of the good school? In other words, is there a shared vision of the good school which encompasses comprehensives, secondary moderns, grammar schools, City Technology Colleges, public schools, primary schools, prep schools, and so on?

Or are there differing, even idiosyncratic, ideas of the good school? Are different types of school, perhaps in certain cases, even individual schools, all trying to become good schools in the light of ideals which are discrete, disparate, even mutually incompatible?

Or do we, in fact, have only a vague idea, or ideas, of what we understand when we talk of good schools?

The answers to these questions seem to me to be pretty clear. We lack any confident, shared vision of what a good school is. Insofar as we have any ideas of what a good school is, they tend to be specific to particular types of school. However, in general, we have little more than rather ill-formed notions of what we mean when we refer to a good school.

One could suggest various reasons for this state of affairs. We have, for instance, spent very little time and effort considering what we mean by a good school. Other issues have, perhaps understandably, taken priority. And, anyway, we may have been happy to assume that we all know what we are talking about, to stick closely to the pragmatic, and to avoid anything which smacks of the theoretical.

But surely the main reason is to be sought in the nature of our society. In a pluralist liberal democracy there are different, at times antipathetic, social, religious, political and ethnic groups, each evolving and subscribing to sets of values which differ to a greater or lesser extent. In turn, such values are liable to generate various expectations of education. The result is, on the one hand, dispute and confusion, and on the other a lack both of consensus and of clarity. Such circumstances are hardly conducive to the emergence of a clear vision, or even visions, of the good school.

All this does matter. For unless we have a clear notion of what we understand when we talk of a good school, we cannot hope to be in a strong position to identify what indicates good performance, to seek out good features of high quality education, to develop ways of making schools better, or to judge how best to organize the national education system. Analysis, management and leadership of education only acquire substantial meaning in the context of a view of what a good school is.

Furthermore, if we are poorly placed, as we are, to consider what contributes to making a good school, and to identifying its characteristic features, then quite serious practical difficulties are likely to arise and indeed do. While other factors, no doubt, make their contribution, our lack of agreed understanding of what a good school is surely helps fuel disputes over such matters as the role of public tests and examinations as indicators of a good school, and the best ways of inspecting or evaluating school performance. Since there is uncertainty, or disagreement, over what on earth it is we actually believe to be good, it is almost inevitable that we can become confused about what represents achievement, about how and what to assess, about how to interpret relevant evidence, and about what weight to attach to any judgements made.

A vision of the good school

In this book, I shall discuss a vision of the good school.

This is not a vision that came to me, as visions are conventionally supposed to, in a moment of sudden illumination. Would that it had! Little by little, over time, jigsaw-like, a notion of the good school has gradually crystallized and taken form in my mind.

This vision is, if not entirely down to earth (that would quite possibly represent a contradiction in terms), at least close to earth. It is as someone actively involved with schools, whether as student, teacher, parent, governor, inspector or voter, that I have struggled to be able to understand and perceive the real nature of a good school.

The vision, accordingly, arises from, and closely relates to, actualities. It came into existence because I was looking for a comprehensive idea which could help both to make sense of and to provide an inspiration for, the multifarious educational activities which I observed and in which I was involved. While these activities were often sustained by good intentions, too frequently in practice they appeared, to me at least, confused, confusing and static.

What I have to say is intended as a contribution to a discussion which is already beginning, albeit sometimes in rather different terms. For it has become very evident that we need a clearer sense of moral purpose in education, whether in some schools or in society more generally. To date, the most significant recent thinking on this theme has probably come from the National Forum for Values in Education and the Community, established by the Schools Curriculum and Assessment Authority (SCAA). What it has to say (National Forum, 1996) is consistent with much of the argument I shall develop, particularly as concerns key values to do with self, relationships, society and the environment.

The vision I shall explore I see as being akin to a working hypothesis. It is a model whose real worth and viability can only properly be tested in debate and practice. Accordingly, it must take its chances in the educational market-place. If it proves to have some validity and usefulness, so much the better. At the least, I hope it may provoke thought.

And so, I ask, what is a good school?

The good school is a community of learning.
It produces well-educated young people.

This much is clear.

But what about the detail?

The good school contains, and recognizes, various **fields of education**. These overlap, and interconnect, but nevertheless are readily identifiable (see Figure 1.1 for a diagrammatic outline of the analysis of the good school given in this chapter).

In the good school, the most significant fields of education are:

- *The personal school* (people, or persons, in the school);
- *The whole school curriculum* (courses of study concerned with the teaching, learning, investigation and application of selected elements of organized knowledge and systems of thought);
- *The school as an institution*; and
- *The school as a community.*

Within the good school there are a range of **worthwhile practices** which are both inherent in education and which contribute to the achievement of the school's aims and purposes. Groups of these activities relate particularly, though not exclusively, to each major field of education.

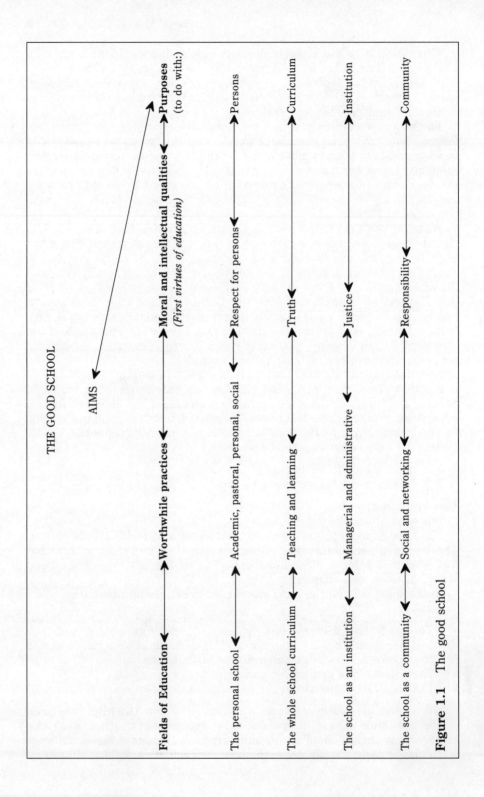

THE GOOD SCHOOL

Fields of Education ←→ **Worthwhile practices** ←→ **Moral and intellectual qualities** ←→ **Purposes**
(First virtues of education) (to do with:)

AIMS

The personal school ←→ Academic, pastoral, personal, social ←→ Respect for persons ←→ Persons

The whole school curriculum ←→ Teaching and learning ←→ Truth ←→ Curriculum

The school as an institution ←→ Managerial and administrative ←→ Justice ←→ Institution

The school as a community ←→ Social and networking ←→ Responsibility ←→ Community

Figure 1.1 The good school

The worthwhile practices include:

- *Academic, pastoral, personal and social education* in the personal school;
- *Teaching and learning* in the whole school curriculum;
- *Managerial and administrative matters* in the school as an institution;
- *Social and networking matters* in the school as a community.

Through worthwhile practices:

In *the personal school*, students will learn to understand themselves, their abilities and the sorts of worthwhile persons they could become. They will also learn to cope sensibly with authority, relationships with fellow students and staff, and with conflict.

In *the whole school curriculum*, students will learn to think; to study; and to remember, organize and present information, in writing, graphically, numerically and orally. They will also learn to understand, explore and express themselves through spiritual, artistic and physical experience. As appropriate, they will learn how to apply their knowledge.

In *the school as an institution*, students will learn to observe and discuss fair rules and to understand their nature and necessity; to behave well; and to discipline themselves.

In *the school as a community*, students will learn how to participate fully and contribute positively as members of the school and wider community, not least through extra-curricular activities; to practise democracy; and to prepare for citizenship.

Teachers and other staff, through pastoral, teaching, organizational and administrative practices, will support and promote the worthwhile practices of students in the various fields of educational practices, and throughout the school.

The good school has readily recognizable **moral and intellectual qualities**, or, more specifically, traits. Of these, the most educationally significant are:

- *Respect for persons* (self and others);
- *Truth*;
- *Justice*; and
- *Responsibility*.

In the good school, each of these qualities is associated with, particularly but not exclusively, a specific field of education, together with that field's related worthwhile practices. In such circumstances, the traits may be called the necessary **first virtues of education**.

- *Respect for persons is the first virtue of the personal school.*
- *Truth is the first virtue of the whole school curriculum.*
- *Justice is the first virtue of the school as an institution.*
- *Responsibility is the first virtue of the school as a community.*

A school possesses virtues where it is consciously organized, both as a whole and in its various fields, to encourage the development in students of particular moral and intellectual traits. (See Rawles, 1972, p. 3 for a discussion of the idea of first virtues, especially with reference to truth and justice; see Steutel and Spiecker, 1997, for an incisive discussion of the possible distinctions and relationships between moral and intellectual virtues.)

As for students, they possess virtues where their characters are consciously organized in such a way that they display traits of character, and hence dispositions to act, that are positively valued. Students, like schools, should at the least show signs of, and a commitment to, developing those virtues that are intrinsic to education. The first virtues of the student and of the school correspond with each other, and indeed are mutually supportive.

In the good school, students display, and are encouraged to display, respect for self and others, respect for truth and truthfulness, a sense of justice and a sense of responsibility.

The first virtues of education are not the only relevant virtues. Other moral and intellectual virtues are educationally important. For example, a good school will encourage, and students will display, patience, perseverance and self-control, as well as open-mindedness, respect for rational argument, and so on. Nevertheless, all these qualities, however and wherever exercised, are, in the final analysis, supplementary to and supportive of the first virtues of education – respect for others, truth, justice and responsibility.

Nor do the first virtues of education apply exclusively to their immediately related fields of education. For example, a sense of responsibility can help students manage their learning effectively. Similarly, a sense of justice can help to develop community spirit. And so on.

The possession and development of the first virtues of education, in schools and in students, are necessary for two reasons.

First, it is a good in itself that schools should be moral places, and that students should become moral beings.

Secondly, a virtuous disposition, together with, hopefully, ensuing educationally valued behaviour, whether in institutions or persons, is essential if the practices of schools are to lead to success. (For a detailed discussion of the relationship between virtues and practices, see MacIntyre, 1985, chapter 14.)

In the school, arrangements to promote respect for self and others are crucial in enabling students to acquire a personal sense of worth, and to help them to deal positively with fellow students and those in authority.

Truth is an essential trait of organized knowledge and systems of thought. The curriculum must enable students to verify facts, to establish the coherence of propositions, and to consider the extent to which revealed truth may be considered reliable.

Justice is a vital aspect of all institutions, including schools. If the formal and informal rules and arrangements of a school are fairly conceived and implemented, then it can function efficiently as an institution. Further, in such a school students can learn about justice from the way the system works.

Responsibility is a key feature of the school as a community. Practical preparation for citizenship and democracy, together with social and extra-curricular activities, can only thrive where responsibility is effectively practised.

Correspondingly, in students, respect for self and others promotes the ability to relate appropriately with others; concern for truth contributes to academic understanding; a sense of justice encourages an awareness of the nature and significance of fair rules and arrangements and a commitment to sustaining and developing them; and a sense of responsibility provides a moral foundation for learning about democracy and citizenship.

The need for schools and students to display the first virtues of education becomes very apparent if one considers what would be likely to happen if these virtues were disregarded.

Where the school does not adequately incorporate procedures and does not promote attitudes requiring respect for self and others, there is liable to be a lack of concern to meet students' personal and learning needs. Teachers will often be suspicious of, and unwilling to cooperate with, colleagues; they may show contempt for students, may shout at them and may ignore their learning needs. As for students, if they have low self-esteem, they are hardly in a good position to perform well. And where they do not respect others, they are liable to disrupt, bully and taunt.

If the curriculum is structured without a concern for truth, then the content and skills being taught and learned will, morally, intellectually and practically, be of negligible use to students, or indeed to society.

Where rules and procedures are arbitrary or inconsistent, and where staff and students act unfairly towards one another, then those who work in the school are liable to feel alienated and resentful. This is hardly a good environment in which to work productively, or in which to learn about the workings of a just institution.

Similarly, where the networks of the school community are uninspired by any sense of responsibility, there will be little feeling of shared concern, or of common endeavour. A school of isolates, self-centred and self-regarding, would be ill-placed to encourage education in democracy and citizenship.

In fact, a school which fails to encourage, and where students do not practise, the first virtues of education cannot but be a bad school. It does not provide the conditions necessary for effective learning, and it neglects the moral education of its students.

Clearly, moral and intellectual virtues in students are essential to the effective and efficient carrying out of the worthwhile practices of a good school. Unfortunately, few if any students arrive at school in a fully virtuous state. With luck, they will have, whether inborn or acquired, an inclination to contribute to their own, and the general, educational good. But this will need encouragement.

So if the practices of education are to flourish, good teachers will be concerned not only to teach particular skills and abilities, but will also realize the importance of teaching the educational virtues. They will do this by example (that is, by virtue of the sort of people they are), through the myriad of daily school circumstances. They will also do it through precept, that is by explicitly focusing with students on the educational necessity of certain sorts of good behaviour if particular practices are to be successfully carried out. Specific lessons, courses or other planned activities to do with matters such as the practice of moral reasoning, the exploration of social and moral issues or the development of virtues could also be of value. But, they certainly could not be sufficient in themselves. In the good school, moral education pervades the whole enterprise.

Worthwhile educational practices, together with their related first virtues imply, and help to define, the *aims* and *purposes* of the good school.

In the good school, all particular purposes relate to the major fields of education, and are subsumed under aims for the whole school. The latter, at the least, reflect the requirements stated in the Education Reform Act of 1988 (Sections 1, 2a and 2b).

The **aims** of the good school are to promote the full and balanced spiritual, moral, social, cultural, artistic, mental and physical development of students at the school and of society; and to prepare students as fully as possible for the opportunities, responsibilities and experiences of adult life. More particularly, the good school aims to educate students as moral beings who are respectful of themselves and others, who are truthful and concerned with truth, and who are fair-minded, and responsible.

The **purposes** of the good school are:

- In relation to *practices concerned with the personal school*: to encourage full and balanced personal development; to provide informed and caring guidance, welfare and pastoral care; and to promote respect for self and others.
- In relation to *practices concerned with the whole school curriculum*: to ensure that students achieve to the best of their various capabilities, and show serious regard for truth. The school intends to ensure this through the provision of a broad, balanced, coherent and relevant curriculum, characterized by truth; together with specific objectives, for particular subjects, courses and topics, and for the development of related skills and attitudes.
- In relation to *practices to do with the school as an institution*: to ensure that students are well-behaved, self-disciplined and fair-minded; that there are just rules; and that there are effective, efficient and equitable leadership, management and organisation.
- In relation to *practices to do with the school as a community*: to ensure that students learn to participate as full and responsible members of the school, and wider, community; and that they are well prepared, through experience as well as through the curriculum, for their role as citizens in a democracy.

Good schools will differ from each other in the detail of particular practices, aims and purposes. But they will have in common a recognition of the importance of each of the key fields of education, and of the need to identify integrally related purposes.

Above all, however, the good school will acknowledge the vital importance of the moral qualities of respect, truth, justice and responsibility. And it will succeed in ensuring that its educational practices incorporate, and its students display, those virtues.

In the following chapters, I will explore the necessary first virtues of education. I will discuss how in the good school these may influence arrangements and activities in the major fields of practices. I will consider how the national system of education could best support the development of the good school. Finally, I will draw the threads together by offering a vision of the good school in the good society.

CHAPTER 2

Respect for persons

If we are to teach, learn and exercise respect for persons we need in the first place to have an informed grasp of what we mean when we talk of respect.

The idea of respect once came with strong connotations of deference. Those who occupied positions of power or prestige, or who were members of the higher social classes, expected respect as of right from those in more humble situations than themselves. Likewise, adults looked for a similar sort of respect from the younger generation. Anyone told to 'Show a little respect' understood immediately what was meant. However, that secure and hierarchical world, profoundly missed by some, despised by others, is disintegrating around us. Before long all that is likely to remain are stray, no doubt occasionally spectacular, outcrops of obsolescent custom.

Our deeper understanding of what is meant by respect is illuminated by those religious and philosophic traditions which, in different accents, in different times, and formulated for different audiences, explore and justify in their own particular terms the proposition that we should learn to value and respect persons because, in the final analysis, all life is inviolable.

Theologically, in Judaism and Christianity, such arguments are rooted in the concept of human beings as created in the image of God, and for Christians more specifically, in the scriptural commandment that we should love our neighbours, and, moreover, love them as we love ourselves. Other major faiths, in the context of their own doctrines, develop similar approaches.

Philosophically, the thinking which perhaps resonates most powerfully today is the Kantian view that persons are citizens of a 'Kingdom of ends', a Commonwealth where persons are not purely subjective ends, whose existence has a value for us only as means, but where they are also objective ends, or beings, whose existence is an end in itself, for which no other end can be substituted. A person as an end has 'an intrinsic, unconditioned, incomparable worth or worthiness' (Paton, 1958, pp. 35, 91).

It is on such foundations that contemporary discussion of the meaning of respect for persons is grounded. Modern thinkers generally suggest that respect is a disposition required on account of the essential nature of persons as human beings. Iris Murdoch (1992, p. 365), for example, argues that we should value persons, 'not because they are created by God or because they are rational beings or good citizens, but because they are human beings'. Similarly, Ronald Dworkin in *Life's Dominion* (1993, p. 24), his work on issues relating to abortion, suggests that all human life can be seen as sacred, as having intrinsic value, and that one major reason why so many people have reservations about abortion is that they believe it 'denies and offends the sanctity or inviolability of human life'.

What can we call behaviour which originates from the virtue of respect? Certainly, sometimes, respectful. But the actions we observe, or have in mind, may not fully be described by the term 'respectful'. Genuine and deep respectfulness may result in conduct which might, quite reasonably, be considered caring, or concerned, or loving. For, the fact of the matter is that respect provides a moral basis for engagement with, for commitment to, persons.

The essential understandings of respect which we have inherited are powerful. But they are also general. The concept is quite heavily dependent upon its object for any specifity. Only when we begin to get a focused notion of what it is we wish to respect does the idea of respect emerge with sharp-edged definition. And this is where the real difficulties, at least for education, begin.

CHAPTER 3

A curricular crisis of identities

Martin Buber (1961, p. 148), opening a lecture on 'What is man?', recalled that a certain Rabbi von Przysucha, one of the last great teachers of Hasidism, once said to his students, 'I wanted to write a book called Adam, which would be about the whole man. But then I decided not to write it.' The rabbi's title, together with his synopsis, suggests questions about gender, spirituality and corruption, just the sort of value-laden, powerful and emotive issues which almost invariably arise sooner or later in any consideration of personhood which is more than superficial. It is perhaps hardly surprising that the good rabbi, who no doubt like many teachers was a cautious individual appreciative of a quiet life, decided that discretion was the better part of valour.

However, if we wish to encourage respect for persons in education, it would be as well not to follow the rabbi's example. Both logically and in practice, it is difficult if not impossible to teach, learn about or exercise respect for persons in the absence of a secure grasp of what one is supposed to be respecting. Accordingly, we need to be clear about what we mean when we talk of persons.

Schools, however, are currently facing a curricular crisis of identities.

The crisis is manifest because too few of those with responsibility for education have much more than an implicit notion of what it is they, and others, mean when they talk of persons. At worst, where such unexamined views are inconsistent with each other, they may lead to conflicting perceptions and actions. Even at best, they are seldom likely to be sufficiently coherent to make any worthwhile contribution to the definition of educational thought and practice.

In such circumstances, there is an ever-present danger that the actions of many of those who provide education, whether politically, professionally or as representatives of local communities, will ultimately come to be informed by little more than an enfeebled and token sense of humanity. This is hardly a satisfactory way in which to try and develop a system of education in which respect for others is likely to flourish.

The crisis arises, not so much on account of flaws intrinsic to education, as because of the difficulty which schools can find in evolving effective responses to powerful external forces. In particular, the sense of personal authenticity within a school can be undermined by the historic and continuing attacks on that view of the centrality and moral worth of the individual which has been characteristic of mainstream Western thought.

The attack on the centrality of persons

We are faced with a modern feeling of loss of certainty over the place and nature of persons. There is a suspicion of having come adrift. We have our being in a climate of anxiety provoked by those questions which, over time, have challenged the centrality of persons, and have also led, both directly and indirectly, to a shrouding, even to a decomposition, of the notion of personhood.

While this atmosphere is general, it is also one to which education, by its very nature, is particularly sensitive. Schools need to move into a position from which they can have a reasonable opportunity of dealing with the underlying historical and cultural aspects of the crisis of identities which they face. An essential first step is to clarify the nature and extent of the attack on belief in the centrality of persons.

Paradoxically, questioning of the pivotal position of the individual originated in the Renaissance. On the one hand, of course, the period saw the emergence of a confident humanism. The concern of the ancient classical world with the individual was rediscovered. The medieval Civitas Dei, a universe divinely decreed, ordered and guided, was deconstructed; and citizens of the divine commonwealth, not necessarily any more children and servants of God, were freed if they so pleased, to enjoy personal freedom, unguided by inner immutable essence or external doctrine.

On the other hand, the newly liberated intellect was now at liberty not simply to celebrate, reflect upon and explore its own significance. It was also able to turn its full attention upon questioning its place in whatever scheme of things might be discovered to exist.

There emerged the successive assaults, now deeply familiar but still retaining a capacity to unsettle and provoke, upon all the major assumptions which enabled persons to be placed centre stage in whatever particular piece of explanatory narrative, theological, philosophical, scientific and so on, was being represented. Copernicus and Galileo, disrupting the harmony of the spheres, despatched the Earth, together with all its creatures, away from its place at the fulcrum of the universe. Darwin appeared to demonstrate that the human species, far from being the end and instrument of divine purpose, was simply the product of a mindless evolutionary process of natural selection, of adaptation, of survival of the fittest. Hegel argued that self-conscious persons, far from being free-standing, independent members of their communities, could only become fully real and individualized in the larger whole of society, itself a greater individual being, of which all humans were lesser parts or moments. Metaphysically, and in due course politically, persons became not arbiters but ciphers. Finally, Karl Marx proposed that individuals were no longer the admittedly often beleaguered, at times tragic, but ultimately controlling arbiters of history. Rather they were little more than victims, or at best participants, in an inevitable, dialectically determined sweep of inevitable happenings.

Accompanying the dispersion of persons, there developed a sustained and prolonged questioning of their interior coherence and stability. The unpredictability of human behaviour, the apparent absence of any unifying personal identity, the seemingly multifarious natures of single individuals were all observed and explored. Such perceptions could lead to attempts to reestablish the integrity of the person, for example through the workings of the rational mind or of the divine spirit; or they could result in acceptance of the inevitability of disintegration. Either way, the effect was unsettling at best; pessimistic, even nihilistic, at worst.

Doubts over the oneness of persons began to be expressed as the early humanist confidence of the Renaissance waned. Montaigne (1991, p. 5, 1:1), kept returning, almost obsessively, to reflecting on 'Man ... an object miraculously vain, various and wavering,' and upon 'The natural inconstancy of our behaviour and our opinions.' In similar vein the Catholic and Jansenist, Pascal (1966, p. 64, section 131), exclaimed, 'How many natures lie in human nature!', and 'What sort of freak then is man! How novel, how monstrous, how chaotic, how paradoxical, how prodigious! Judge of all things, feeble earthworm, repository of truth, sink of doubt and error, glory and refuse of the universe!' Meanwhile, Pascal's near contemporary Descartes (1968b, p. 127) was ruminating that, 'The whole of my life may be divided into an infinity of parts, each of which depends in no way on the others.' And later, in the English empirical and sceptical tradition, Hume (1978, 1, iv, 6), pursuing a similar theme, was to say that there was not 'Any single power of the soul which remains unalterably the same'; while as for the mind, 'There is properly no simplicity in it at one time nor identity in different [times].'

Over time, such thoughts have gradually extended their influence, until now we are hardly surprised to come across them in academic philosophy and popular culture alike. In today's world it seems many of us, whoever we may be, have difficulty in knowing what to make of ourselves or of others. Thus, we can find Derek Parfit (1985, pp. 216–17), an Oxford Fellow of All Souls, writing that 'We are not separately existing entities, apart from our brains and our bodies, and various interrelated physical and mental events ... It is not true that our identity is always determinate ... Personal identity is not what matters.' More prosaically, Denis Healey (1989, p. 570), contemplating his experience of politics, reports that 'Human behaviour is infinitely diverse'; even Mick Jagger, interviewed in the *Observer* (10 January 1993), reached a similar conclusion, though perhaps by a rather different route: 'People seem to find it hard to accept that you can be several people almost at the same time. I refuse to believe that everybody's just got these tiny constricted little personalities and that they can only behave in one kind of way.'

Under pressure persons of necessity, or even as a matter of choice, could attempt to ensure survival through the adoption of certain sorts of identity indicative of their destabilized situation. They might simply present themselves, or be perceived, as anxious, resentful, insecure. As

Dollimore (1989, p. xxx) has pointed out in his study of Renaissance drama, the playwrights, having 'Subverted the idea of a divinely ordered universe ... also subverted its corollary the unified human subject ... Hence the Jacobean anti-hero: malcontented, dispossessed, satirical and vengeful.' And, one might add, eventually hence also the alienated theatre of Brecht, and the marginalized world of the existential Outsider.

Alternatively there was the possibility not of becoming defined in contradistinction and antagonism to conditions of existence understood as unacceptable or as unreal, but of retreating into the sort of private identity, or even identities, which were now becoming a genuine choice. As George Eliot (1994, p. 537) perceived, from her still morally secure position in what Leavis was to categorize as 'The Great Tradition', there were indeed those to whom a world on and of their own could offer a real temptation. 'We have all,' said Mrs Cadwallader to Dorothea in *Middlemarch*, 'to exert ourselves a little to keep sane, and to call things by the same names as other people call them by.' Dorothea, supported by a world which for the most part remained comfortably centred, in both divine and human terms, did indeed exert herself, and successfully. But there would be others, living in less privileged circumstances, who would not be so fortunate. Private identities could lead to psychosis, to personality disorder; even to multiple personalities, to the three faces of Eve.

When defiance or escape could not adequately sustain personal meaning, the effort to endure and secure a sense of identity might collapse or even never be attempted. Individuals might appear as overwhelmed by the sheer unmanageableness of unstable, mutant, transient and multiple elements. They could, like Louis MacNeice, in his poem 'Snow' (1935) conclude that:

> World is crazier and more of it than we think
> Incorrigibly plural.

They could find themselves in sympathy with Shakespeare's Antony (*Antony and Cleopatra*, IV. xii, 3–22):

> Sometime we see a cloud that's dragonish,
> . . .
> That which is now a horse, even with a thought
> The rack dislimns, and makes it indistinct,
> As water is in water ...
> ... now thy captain is
> Even such a body: here I am Antony,
> Yet cannot hold this visible shape ...
> ... there is left us
> Ourselves to end ourselves.

Or they might identify with the less heroic figure of Decoud in Conrad's *Nostromo* (1963, pp. 409, 411–12) who 'caught himself entertaining doubts of his own individuality. It had merged into the world of cloud and water, of natural forces and forms of nature.' Decoud, seeing the universe as no more than 'a succession of incomprehensible images', shoots himself, and vanishes 'without a trace, swallowed up in the immense indifference of things'.

Imagined, or actual, instances of the inability of particular individuals to cope with existence prefigured and accompanied the development of assaults, increasingly systematic and assertive, directed at the viability of the notion of the person as such. In the first place, both socially and psychologically, the significance of consciousness was diminished. 'It is not,' said Marx, 'the consciousness of men that determines their being, but ... their social being that determines their consciousness.' (Preface to a critique of political economy', 1859, in McLellan, 1977, p. 389). Freud and Jung, through their postulation of the underworld forces of the id and the collective subconscious, while not exactly disempowering consciousness, at the least located it in a threatened situation.

From this point on, analysis of what was now increasingly seen as a crisis, developed in detailed pessimism to the point where it became difficult to distinguish diagnosis of what was generally agreed to be an identity-threatening condition from forecasts of imminent demise. Adorno talked of the 'withering of the subject', its shrunken consciousness, its loss of awareness, spontaneity and truth (see, for example 1973, pp. 60–76). Barthes (1977, p. 143) refers to 'a dispersion of energy in which there remains neither a central core nor a structure of meaning. I am not contradictory. I am dispersed.' For R. D. Laing (1960, p. 47), the predicament of the person lay not so much in diminution or diffusion as in being voided of content. He talked of implosion, of 'the full terror of the experience of the world as liable at any moment to crash in and obliterate all identity, as a gas will rush in and obliterate a vacuum. The individual feels that like the vacuum he is empty. But this emptiness is him.'

The ground was prepared for Levi-Strauss's (1966, p. 247) rallying cry, 'The ultimate goal of the human sciences ... [is] ... not to constitute but to dissolve man.' For Foucault (1970, p. 387), the achievement of that objective was thought to be well within reach: 'Man is an invention of recent date ... likely soon to be erased, like a face drawn in the sand at the edge of the sea.' While the poet John Ashbery, even more optimistic, or pessimistic depending on one's point of view, considered that the foretold demise of the individual had, to all intents and purposes, arrived, 'Just being a person does not work any more' (quoted in Murdoch, 1992, p. 151).

And now, there is deconstruction. As Iris Murdoch (1992, p. 202) has pointed out, Derrida joins with Wittgenstein and Heidegger in rejecting the philosophical concept of the autonomous 'I'; while structuralism and Marxism, in her vivid phrase 'Hold hands under the table' in a shared concern, through attacking the individual, not to explain the world but to change it.

Derrida, in particular, challenges the 'metaphysics of presence' (see for instance, *Writing and Difference*, 1978). Proceeding from Wittgenstein's and Saussure's argument that language depends upon, and develops from, internally related groups of concepts, he proceeds to propose that all language is a vastly complex multi-dimensional network or system of signs, a structure of 'primal writing', 'archi-écriture', which unavoidably transcends the parochial words of any individual. In fact, language speaks the person, and humans do not have the capacity or responsibility for generating meaning in any other than a trite or trivial sense. Persons cannot validly articulate and interpret experience derived from an inner, owned, flow of consciousness. And this holds equally true for real life, whatever status that may now enjoy, and for fictional existence.

Authority, and a sense of what is truly real, reside not with ordinary persons, however imagined, but with the modern clerisy of critics. It is only these latter day hierophants who have the gift of interpreting 'le jeu des signifiants', of deconstructing the text, of finding real meaning in the transcendent, or alternatively in the deep metaphysic of language.

For all theoretical and practical purposes the person is effectively gutted by post-structuralism. In the universe as revealed by Derrida virtually the only beings of worth are the critics, and it would be little short of blasphemous to describe them as anything so earthbound, so mundane, so relentlessly contingent, so troubled, and so ordinary as mere persons.

CHAPTER 4

Persons: being and becoming

Schools are hardly in a position where they can credibly deny or ignore the thinking which considers a person as decentred. They find themselves in a situation where such notions are not only influential, but where, in certain instances, they may appear to evoke contemporary experience in persuasive and convincing tones. Moreover, schools have to sustain their existence within the cultural climate of the times. This is not a period in which a few, selected, self-confident certainties about what it means to be a person readily thrive.

Conversely, however, schools cannot make any substantial educational use of notions which see persons as having minimal capacity for choice, or as being disintegrated, or as finding themselves existentially overwhelmed by the social or historic circumstances in which they find themselves. The nature of such individuals is manifested not in coherence but in dispersion, not in progress but in dissolution, not in responsibility but in capriciousness. This is not an idea of humanity with which education can readily work, nor one which it can realistically help to develop towards a condition capable of inspiring respect.

So what should be the overall approach of schools?

Education, by virtue of its purposes and its procedures, is inescapably committed to certain general propositions concerning the nature and purpose of being human. Schools really have little choice but to accept: first, that persons are able to improve in ways generally agreed to be worthwhile; secondly, that different ideals of a person can emerge, and that these have to be treated as potentially worthy of respect; thirdly, that persons have, in however limited a way, some capacity and freedom to chose what sort of person they wish to become; and finally, that the way persons develop is open to influence. A school which failed to subscribe to any of these postulates would be training, indoctrinating or child-minding its students: it would not be educating them.

Certain consequences follow from the above.

First, schools have to teach now, as they predominantly have in the past, within, and with reference to, the major Western traditions of perceiving, understanding and interpreting persons. That is to say, they need to work in the context of an inheritance which sees persons as conscious, inward, private, capable of exercising freedom and responsibility, and, if not necessarily situated at the fulcrum of their universes, certainly significantly placed within them. This is an approach which is not only consistent with the nature of education, but which, for many, represents an idea of what it means to be human which continues both to make sense and to command respect.

Secondly, with substantial reference to the received systems of thought, schools need to have confident notions of what a person is; of what it is in the being of persons which enables them, when young, and throughout life, to develop and progress; and of what are the ideals of being a person which education can, and should, help students to achieve.

Thirdly, schools need to provide students with an understanding of those particular views of the human being as a unified subject which should inform all teachings and activities to do with persons. Any failure to help students consciously to experience and learn about this tradition would be a failure in enabling them to understand the personal, social, cultural and historical situation in which they find themselves.

However, teaching predominantly within, and about, the main Western notions of what it means to be a person is not an alternative to providing young people with the means to understand the full complexities of modern views of a person, and of how they have reached their present point; it is, rather, a necessary precondition to it. As schools become more secure in reflecting in their activities concepts of a person as centred, so they become better placed to provide students with a firmer base from which, as they grow older, they can explore or at least try and come to terms with, notions and feelings of decentredness. Ideas of decomposition cannot properly be grasped in the absence of some prior knowledge of what is composed.

The centred person

When we talk of the Western tradition of the person, what, in particular, are we likely to have in mind? How can we best describe the more significant characteristics of the centred person?

Each centred person, in its particularity, is itself the substantiation of a universal, an instance of a given human nature. It is 'l'uomo singulare, l'uomo unico, l'uomo universale' of the thinkers of the Renaissance. As Samuel Johnson put it, there is 'Such a uniformity in the life of man ... that there is scarcely any possibility of good or ill, but is common to humankind' (quoted in Dollimore, 1989, p. 73).

The centred person is a whole, or to put it more accurately, of her or his nature has the capacity and desire to achieve wholeness.

The condition of being as an entity is fundamentally moral. A person develops as a whole through a willed, sustained and continuing effort to become at one with a particular founding and guiding principle, identified most usually as the divine, the rational or, more generally, the good.

To be moral, persons must be capable of exercising choice. They will be autonomous, or endowed with free will. It is within their power, indeed it is of their nature, to recognize and align themselves with the magnetic poles of good or evil, and with different points in relation to those poles. Through the quotidian decisions required in the life of each individual humans create themselves as more or less moral beings.

Ethical thought and behaviour can only properly arise where persons have the capacity, not merely to observe external phenomena, but to evaluate and judge them in the light of an inner sense of reality. Hence, as Iris Murdoch (1992, p. 294) has pointed out, 'The concept of the individual as it has been developed... since Homer *requires* the idea of consciousness, inwardness, privacy, separate worlds.' Each centred person, in this perspective, could be said to inhabit his or her own universe; or, at the least, to have their own unique, perhaps even idiosyncratic, perspective on a shared universe.

Ideas of difference and interiority were, in due course, to help fuel exploration of the person as decentred. However, within the family of concepts which nurture the notion of the centred person, perhaps their main effect was to contribute to the generation of various sibling concepts of the individual.

From the resulting debates and controversies arose those by now well-worn issues which have become the familiar landmarks of any serious consideration of the nature of persons. Thus, for instance, it is asked, are persons exclusively, or somehow in compound, material, spiritual, rational? How far are they autonomous and self-creating, or to what extent are they influenced by their environment, whether social or physical? Are they fundamentally flawed, even intrinsically evil, or are they naturally good? Are they basically driven by altruism, or by self-interest, or to differing degrees by both?

We can, if we so wish, trace the evolution of such thinking through every significant period of Western thought; from the classical era of Aristotle and Plato, through the early Christian and medieval writing of Augustine and Aquinas, to the Enlightenment works of Hobbes, of Descartes and Kant, and of Locke and Rousseau.

Finally, we can follow the apotheosis of the individual through its high noon of nineteenth-century romanticism and bourgeois triumphalism to the dark uncertainties of the twentieth century. In the latter, we can identify the destructive tensions between the Nietzschean *Übermensch*, and Vaclav Havel's (1989, p. 57) reincarnated liberal individual, with its 'Human predisposition to truth' which, even in totalitarian regimes lies ready to break through 'the orderly surface of lies'; and between the existentialist hero of Sartre (1948, p. 29) who 'is responsible for what he is', and who not only 'chooses himself', but in so doing 'chooses for all', and the Kafkaesque victim of labyrinthine and malign bureaucracy.

What a person is

So centred persons can not only be understood as having certain general, shared characteristics. They can also be seen as displaying various differences. And these differences can matter. They have the power to confer contrasting identities and senses of personal meaning. They can evoke commitment. And they are more than capable of provoking controversy.

All this poses challenges for schools. When they consider what it means to respect persons, is any understanding they may have of what centred persons have in common sufficiently specific to be educationally useful? On the other hand, do any differing views of what it means to be a centred person have sufficient mutual consistency to provide an educationally viable set of ideals, or models?

We therefore have to ask very specifically, looking for detailed answers: should one respect all persons? Every One? The centred, whatever the particular identity? Even, perhaps, the disintegrated?

Presumably one would respect, in the fullest sense of the word, a Nelson Mandela or a Mother Teresa. On the other hand, one might pity a disorientated, empty person, a Lee Harvey Oswald; or one might fear someone who gained their identity through a greater whole, a totalitarian state, for example, an Eichmann. But respect?

A genuine respect for others is, of course, only likely to develop where there is a securely grounded belief that such respect is deserved.

Equally evidently, lack of respect can come from rebellious, alienated or anarchic attitudes. However, a failure to feel or show respect can also be symptomatic of a real uncertainty about what should be worthy of respect in people.

There are two aspects of the concept of a person which, like the chains in a double helix, are mutually linked. The first of these is concerned with what all persons, of necessity, are; what has been called a *status* concept (Thatcher, 1990, p. 123).

The second is to do with what persons are capable of *becoming*, in different ways, for better or worse. This latter notion has threaded into it an idea of the *ideal*; it is not, however, identical with it since persons can develop along lines which are not always or universally agreed to be desirable.

Respect for status, for what all persons intrinsically and inescapably are, should be absolutely unconditional. This applies equally to persons whether on their own or as members of groups.

However, respect for what persons intend to become, are becoming, or have become, is not usually, and should not be, unconditional. Whether respect is given or withheld should be influenced by a view about how a person is developing; and about what sort of person an individual seems to be, seems to wish to be, or seems likely to become.

I consider the status and the becoming of persons in this chapter. In the next chapter, I discuss ideals, and particularly educational ideals, of a person. Throughout I refer predominantly, but not exclusively, to the traditions of thought concerned with notions of the centred person.

What, then, can be said to constitute the status of a person? For a start, it makes sense to follow the *Oxford English Dictionary* definition, itself supported by ordinary usage, which understands a person to be an 'individual human being, man, woman or child'.

The concept of person includes the ideas of 'self' and of 'other'. It is, in normal usage, quite acceptable to refer to oneself and to others as persons. Persons have subjectivity and objectivity.

The task of seeking to establish what a person is can, accordingly, be approached by following two initially distinct but ultimately converging paths. First, through personal reflection upon one's own nature. Secondly, through observation of the characteristics of others.

The importance of self-knowledge has long been emphasized. 'Know thyself,' commanded Socrates, in Plato's *Timaeus*. Some, however, have expressed reservations. Chekhov (1964, pp. 100–1) was one of many who, while accepting the importance of the axiom in principle, wondered how easy it was to put into practice: 'Know thyself is excellent and useful advice; the pity is the ancients did not think it necessary to show us the way to avail ourselves of this advice.'

Today if we wish to look inwards we may well consider ourselves to be better placed than Chekhov was. After all, are we not armed, even enlightened, by the insights and findings of modern psychology?

For contemporary sensibility, it is perhaps especially through exploration of our own subjectivity, and through encountering reports of the subjective histories of others, that we become most acutely aware of what it essentially means to be a person. More particularly, it is within the psyche of the individual self that we may look to see defined and played out in its fullest actuality the drama of the present-day person. It is here, above all, that we can find the conflict between multiplicity and unity, dispersion and integrity.

And, as one contemplates what the future might bring, it is through considering the struggles of the subjective individual that one may perceive a perspective of optimism. As persons seek to survive and make sense of experience, it appears that there are those who can not only identify what is happening, but who can begin to synthesize and integrate, to relate plurality within schemas of wholeness.

'Which self?' asked Katherine Mansfield (1977, p. 205) in her journal, 'Which of my many – well, really. That's what it looks like coming to – hundreds of selves?' But, she did not accept legion as inevitable. 'There are signs,' she wrote, 'that we are intent as never before on trying to puzzle out, to live by, this own particular self ... our persistent yet mysterious belief in a self which is continuous and permanent.'

Under other stresses, in very different conditions, Brian Keenan, as a hostage, found himself having to explore, through traversing his own spiritual terrain, his understanding of what a person essentially is. He found how difficult, even fearful, it can be to travel the way of self-knowledge. 'How little a person knows what is in himself. To see all the fissures and cracks, to throw light into the dark cavities, to see the landscape of a mind and recognize no part of it but know that it is yours is a fearful and disturbing thing,' (1993, pp. 80–1).

He came upon other selves pursuing their own existences within the contours of what he believed to be 'myself'. 'During my captivity I ... was forced to confront the man I thought I was and to discover that I was many people.' These other people were, doubtless, potentially psychologically disruptive. However, for Brian Keenan, that preeminent element of his personality which he identified as 'myself' proved to have both the desire and the capacity to integrate the other selves within an harmonious whole.

'I had to befriend these many people, discover their origins, introduce them to each other and find a communality between themselves and myself,' (p. xv).

Above all, however, during the course of their prolonged crisis, it became apparent, not only to Brian Keenan, but also to his fellow hostages, that the critical characteristic of being a person was the attribute which enabled one to be open to, aware of, the experience of transcendent otherness, the Good. It was this which was crucial to being and to surviving as a person. 'There was a sense of self greater than me alone, which came and filled me in the darkest hours (p. 204) ... In searching through the complex panorama of our past one thing emerged again and again: our relationship to and understanding of love underlay everything else' (p. 271).

If we turn from looking at personhood through self to considering it through observation of, and reflection about, others, we may well find that there is a gain in clarity of definition. But, arguably, this is obtained at the expense of depth of insight.

Given that persons are by definition human beings it is evident that creatures other than humans cannot be counted as persons. There have been various attempts, for instance in a collection of essays by Richard Dawkins and others, *The Great Ape Project* (Singer and Cavaliaeri, 1994), to extend the definition of persons to include all the major primates. Such proposals have been put forward partly on grounds of genetic similarity, but mainly as a way of trying to ensure that the rights of persons can be claimed on behalf of, for instance, chimpanzees and gorillas, so providing for them some sort of ethically grounded defence against neglect or ill-treatment.

Views of this sort have considerable moral, if perhaps less compelling logical or scientific, strength. However, while they do not convincingly demonstrate that the meaning of the term 'person' should be stretched ever wider, they do properly remind us of two important matters. Namely, first, that members of other species do, as Mary Midgley (1995) has demonstrated convincingly and in detail, share many characteristics with human beings. And, secondly, that any discussion of respect for persons should not, in whatever sense, be taken to imply lack of respect for other forms of life, or indeed for the physical environment. It can be persuasively argued that these deserve consideration fully as much as persons. It is just that the rationale for such respect rests on arguments different from, albeit related to, those which justify respect for persons.

On the other hand, no human can be excluded, on any grounds, from the status of person. It has been suggested, for example by Glenn Langford (1978), that one can distinguish between being a human being and being a person. As Richard Pring (1984, p. 13) has pointed out, while this 'on the surface appears to be simply wrong', it can in fact be interpreted as highlighting some 'important conceptual truths', for instance that a foetus may be regarded by some as not yet a person. Nevertheless, all attempts to identify humans and persons separately ultimately fail to counter the view that any identification of such a difference is liable to give unjustifiable authority to the treatment by some humans of others as morally inferior. If we can look on any other individuals or groups as non-persons, then we may feel we can legitimately regard them as subhuman, and treat them accordingly. It is therefore, as Ralph Ruddock (1972, p. 203) has put it, 'in all cases... ethically imperative that a recognisably human individual should be accorded the status of a person'.

It follows that personhood cannot, in any sense, be racially exclusive. In the realm of persons there can be no subtle discrimination, and certainly no apartheid.

All persons have life, and consciousness is an essential attribute of being a person. Such a state may be more or less clear and focused, it may be heightened or dulled, it may be dispersed or intermittent. The nature of consciousness remains fully as much a matter for debate and research now as when John Locke (1947, p. 26) asserted that the mind is 'white paper, void of all characters, without any ideas'. Nevertheless, persons as such have forms of consciousness which inanimate entities, clouds and rocks, for instance, do not.

No one, however, can be declared a non-person on grounds of lack of rationality or intelligence. The educationally severely sub-normal, the senile, the chess champion, the crossword expert and the professor, they are equally persons.

Of course, this is not to deny that the faculty of reason is not a vital, and in its ability to speculate in abstract terms, an exclusive, human attribute. How one views its role is open to debate, and is closely related to any ideal one may hold of persons. Thus, a variety of functions may be assigned to reason, in relation to the will, to instincts, to drives, to motives, to emotions, and, more generally, to the whole complex structure of the human personality. Reason may be viewed as integrative; as identifying priorities among internal desires, and choices between external possibilities; as a slave, or ruler, of the passions; as informing the will, or as marginal, even irrelevant to the workings of the will; etc., etc. One pays one's money, and makes one's choice between the solutions on offer from various schools of philosophical and psychological thought. The crucial point, however, and the one which must not be obscured by the complexities and niceties of the debate over the nature and function of reason, is that rationality, while a necessary attribute of persons in general, is not a defining characteristic of persons individually.

As humans, persons are embodied. Scientifically, humans have a chemical and biological basis. Their nature is encoded in their genes and DNA. 'Chemistry is us!' as a *Guardian* correspondent put it (14 September 1993). However, it does not follow that one has to accept a reductionist approach to the human as organic machinery. The material nature of humans is no more, and no less, than one necessary criterion of being as a person. Philosophically, it has been argued by Strawson (1959, pp. 101–2) that a person is a type of entity such that predicates ascribing corporeal characteristics are applicable to a single individual of that type (equally with predicates ascribing states of consciousness).

More ambitiously, the body may, as Peter Brooks (1993) has suggested, citing Rousseau's *Confessions* as the seminal work, be seen as a prime determinant of life's meanings, and intertwined with the new notion of personal identity. It may even nowadays be placed, as Michel Foucault (for instance in 'Nietzsche, genealogy, history', 1977) has argued it should be, at the centre of all our concerns as the fundamental material of experience upon which are constructed the various structures and norms of Western society.

However, the influence of our inherited culture has tended to distort, minimize or relegate (for example through the mind/body dualism endemic in Western philosophy) issues to do with the significance of the body. This has perhaps been particularly true of the sorts of questions which deal with gender and sexuality. Persons are female or male; are sexual creatures; have at one time or another erotic energies and appetites, libidinous impulses and orientations. Despite the detailed analysis and exploration of such matters in recent years, it can still be true, not least in education, that discussion of personhood is carried out as if all persons were male, or as if sexuality was, at best, a peripheral issue. Any such approaches devalue the status of persons.

Persons exist in a social environment.

The social environment generates culture. In particular, it generates the ability of persons to create, share and reflect upon knowledge and values across groups and over generations.

Persons have access to complex systems of non-verbal and verbal communication. It is, above all, through the use of networks of symbols, signs and abstract and concrete terms that persons sustain and develop society and culture. It is through their vocabulary that persons explore, discover, make sense of and construct their scientific, mathematical, aesthetic, moral, religious and spiritual universes.

From time to time persons may withdraw, for longer or shorter periods, voluntarily or otherwise, from society. However, in even the most extreme cases, individuals will, even if only in infancy, have lived with, depended on and interacted with other humans.

The social nature of persons, of their environment, and of how these all relate to each other, is interpreted according to various traditions. These not only differ, but may be mutually antagonistic. Nevertheless, what they have in common is an acceptance, ranging from the reluctant to the enthusiastic, that persons are social creatures insofar as, at the least, they are directly or indirectly dependent upon the society of others for individual and collective survival.

The interpretation of what a person is which is perhaps least likely to accept any necessary social component is what David Marquand (1988, p. 214) has identified as a 'reductionist model of human nature'. This he sees as influenced by 'The reductionist materialism of the seventeenth and eighteenth centuries – that just as the world is made of solid lumps of matter, so is society made up of sovereign, atomic individuals.'

In such a view, which to some degree underpins a capitalist, *laissez-faire* interpretation of society, humans are the first premise and any social organization is derivative. The humans in question may, as in Hobbes's eyes (1946, p. 81), be competitive, fearful and dangerously quick to take offence; or, as in Locke's eyes, rational, capable of cooperation and, possibly, also capable of altruism. Nevertheless, even for reductionists, humans, whatever they themselves or others might like them to be, cannot of their nature be entirely solitary creatures. For the isolate is threatened, or diminished, cannot prosper and ultimately is extinguished.

The most significant alternative tradition is inclined to see persons more as social beings, less as lone riders; that is to say, as individuals who acquire identity and value primarily as contributing and dependent members of communities. This view, for Western culture, originates with Aristotle (1905, p. 29) who considered that 'he who is unable to live in society, or who has no need to because he is sufficient to himself, must be either a beast or a God'. Rousseau shifted the emphasis towards the significance of society as an entity, believing that 'We begin properly to become men only after we have become citizens.'

Modern enquiries into the social nature of persons, while conducted in the language of various disciplines, come to similar conclusions. Ethology, the science of animal behaviour, sees humans not as solitary beasts, but rather as creatures who, of their nature, need to live in complex and differentiated social organizations, and who, as such, have only been able to develop their unique capacities through membership of larger and smaller groups. 'If it were not for a rich endowment of social instincts, man could never have risen above the animal world', wrote Konrad Lorenz (1966, p. 246). While Mary Midgley (1995, p. 130), discussing the human species, has concluded that 'insofar as there is one "compelling force", it is sociability'.

More particularly, social anthropology and social psychology have, between them, contributed to, in Raymond Williams' words (1965, p. 98), 'an enormous strengthening of the tradition which emphasized the extent to which individual personality is formed by social processes'. The result of this is perhaps best summarized in the words of David Hargreaves (1975, p. 5): 'A person's self develops in relation to the reactions of other people to that person and ... he tends to react to himself as he perceives other people reacting to him. The self system is not merely a function of a person's manipulation of the environment, but a function of the way a person is treated by others. The self is a social product.'

This sort of thinking raises a crucial, if familiar, question, and one not seriously at issue in the reductionist tradition of the person as individual atom. How far can persons, if they are seen to be integrally involved in social processes, be said to be autonomous or independent beings? Raymond Williams, for one (1965, p. 117) saw 'danger in certain trends in the new sociology which isolate the group, the society or the culture as an absolute point of reference'. His own, surely convincing, conclusion was that the autonomous self should be seen as growing within a social process which radically influences it, but which nevertheless gains a degree of autonomy that 'makes possible the observed next stage, in which the individual can help to change or modify the social process that has influenced and is influencing him' (pp. 100–1).

There is a third, less familiar, approach. While this equally takes for granted the reality of a necessary social dimension to the experience of the person, it attempts dialectically to synthesize the two contrasting traditions of the individual as a self-contained entity within society, and the individual as participant member of community, or even as an integrated unit of a greater whole. For Martin Buber (1961, p. 244), 'The fundamental fact of human existence is neither the individual as such nor the aggregate as such...what is peculiarly characteristic of the human world is above all that something takes place between one being and another the like of which can be found nowhere in nature.' Buber describes this 'something' as 'the reality of the mutual relation between man and man' (p. 15).

Persons are complex and protean. They metamorphose, physically, socially, psychologically. In different times and places they appear in various forms, roles and guises. As the attacks on the centred person have argued, these characteristics may be both cause and effect of confusion and destabilization. Either way, they can contribute to the undermining of whatever unifying force, principle or psychological function may be present in the self.

On the other hand, the possibility of achieving human authenticity arises from this same capacity to change appearance and identity. The Renaissance humanist, Pico della Mirandola, in his 'Oration: on the Dignity of Man', has the Creator tell Adam that he has been deliberately made without fixed identity, 'neither of heaven, nor of earth, neither mortal nor immortal' (Cassirer *et al.*, 1948, p. 225). An amorphous condition allows the possibility of persons exercising free will, and of choosing the sort of persons they wish to become. To be able to create a particular identity, working with the material of one's original nature, is a necessary aspect of what it means to be human. It gives to the individual responsibility for what she or he is to become, for better or for worse.

The person as narrator in a quest

So we have had a preliminary look at some of the main traditions of thought with reference to which persons can be located. We have a view of what all persons necessarily are. And we recognize that we require a notion of the ideals of being a person towards which an individual might strive.

The next major step, therefore, is to consider the ideals of a person. However, there is another question which must be addressed first.

What sort of a person does one need to be to be able to progress from actual 'is' to desired 'ought'?

In one sense, such a question has always been at the heart of moral and religious concern about the good life.

However, any problems to do with the pilgrimage involved in becoming a worthwhile sort of person were conventionally seen as arising from weaknesses inherent in personal psychology, rather than from any ambiguities or complexities to do with ideals of a person.

In traditional perceptions of Western thinking it was mostly accepted that, while there might be a range of ideals of personhood, ultimately these could usually be interpreted as, if not necessarily entirely consistent one with another, at least sharing a common core of being. Above all, the person was seen as incorporating an essential self. It was this, effectively, which enabled all individuals, whatever the nature of the self to which they aspired, or which they were, to cohere, to achieve oneness. In these circumstances, it was generally taken for granted that, by exercising various spiritual, intellectual or physical disciplines, a person could, if typically only after great struggle and often at the cost of considerable suffering, make progress from what he or she was towards ends which were readily identifiable, and were mostly, if not always, believed by society to be desirable. The question of whether one needed to be a particular sort of person to be able to develop scarcely arose. One did, or at least accepted that one should try to do, one's utmost to control, educate and perfect one's given being.

Now, however, the situation is different. Today persons are presented with a plurality of ideals; and these, whatever they may be, are liable to be perceived as fundamentally different from each other. For we have moved from an era which preferred to emphasize commonality to one which would rather highlight, and make a virtue of, difference.

So the question inevitably arises. If persons can have contrasting, possibly mutually incompatible ends; if persons are internally diverse, possibly to the point where they are in danger of ceasing to cohere; if these things are so, then how may persons be interpreted as whole individuals with the capacity to progress towards a desired, and morally justifiable, condition of human being?

One idea which meets this requirement is that of the person as a narrator in quest. The attention given to the particular aspects implicit in this notion can vary. Thus, Alasdair MacIntyre (1985) emphasizes the unity of the person. Ricoeur (1988) and Rorty (1991) seem perhaps more concerned with ambiguity. Wilna Meijer (1995) focuses, rather, on expectations and their relationship to experience. Nevertheless, all share a concern to assert the possibility of the progress of persons as actually or potentially coherent beings towards particular identified ends.

So what might be the distinguishing features of the person as narrator in quest?

Being in quest requires, fundamentally, that individuals seek to develop as, and into, particular sorts of worthwhile person.

However, individuals may not, as yet, be sure what their ideal is or should be. This may be because they are still in the process of trying to discover it; or because, while involved in the activity of discovering, they have not been able to decide between various ideals which they can envisage, all of which appear to have value in some sense or other.

In order to distinguish and to follow an ideal which seems to them worthwhile, persons need various skills and qualities. They must have intentions; be able to discriminate between differing intentions, the long and the short term; and have the capacity to put the intentions in an order of priority. Having decided upon their first priority, their ideal, they must intellectually be capable of choosing, and emotionally capable of committing themselves to striving to become, a particular sort of person. And they must have the will and tenacity to enable them effectively to pursue their goal.

A person in quest is on a journey. With any luck, there will be times when direction is clear, and progress smooth. But, as tends to happen all too frequently with any journey, there may also be misleading directions, wrong turnings, dead-ends and confusion. The problem is, how can a person in quest, potentially destabilized, or actually dispersed, by erratic internal and external happenings, build a reliable sense of identity? For, if self is in a state of inner disunity, then pursuit of a purpose of being can become virtually impossible.

To some extent, the very identification of an ideal gives meaning to the individual. Indeed, it can be that which predominantly provides a sense of authenticity. I can become integrated, gain integrity, by virtue of a vision of the worthwhile person I am aiming to become, or aiming to become more fully.

But this, in itself, is not sufficient. For it does not really provide me with the wherewithal to identify, analyse, cope with the challenges, crises, metamorphoses, which threaten the achievement of my ideal. And if I am still struggling to discover my goal then, self-evidently, a notion of my ideal cannot help me to secure a belief in the reality of what I am, because I am as yet possessed of little more than the inklings of any such vision, if that.

It is now that the idea of a narrator becomes helpful.

Persons as narrators tell the story of their own lives. But persons are not only observers of the relevant events. They are also the subjects. Each is the central character in the unfolding drama. And the dominant theme of the action is quest, the actor as being in quest.

As a narrator, the attribute of which I am in greatest need is the ability to reflect upon happenings. As in a modern novel, I may interpret the developing saga from different perspectives. I may take account of the views of others. I may come to accept that facts are, as a rule, contingent; the present ambiguous; the past a shifting landscape whose features may appear to change as I move on, and as I come to understand more, or remember less. I may not only interpret, but I may well reinterpret both the marginal detail of my life and, perhaps in moments of personal crisis, those beliefs about my existence which I have previously taken for granted, or at the profoundest level, accepted as true.

Nevertheless, it is through a sustained and continuing ability to create for myself a realistic, viable, responsive network of meanings that I can keep in play a notion of a person whose experience and self-image cohere as a unity. This unity will be multi-faceted; it will evolve; it will reflect and refract numerous passing phenomena. But, ultimately, it can cohere. And if it fails to cohere, then the person will be at risk of ceasing to quest, of disintegrating, of breaking down.

The making of a viable self, through the act of quest and the creativity of the narrator, is a drama which occurs in what Alasdair MacIntyre calls 'settings'. Persons do not arrive on an empty stage, devoid of scenery. Far from it. While they have their own starting points, they join an eddying flow of people, events, surroundings. They inherit histories; present environments of family, community, nation; and shared aspirations. They are on set with others, each of whom is narrating a story in which she or he plays a focal part.

Persons are constrained by conditions, over time and simultaneously, to play a variety of roles. Roles are not, of course, identical with persons. Indeed, where identification occurs, the integrity of the person is at risk. What roles do is to remind us that the actor has to function in relation to others, and the narrator to interpret a world where persons cannot but operate, amongst other things, as social beings.

Each person, in fact, is at once limited and enabled in their opportunities for development by a kaleidoscope of given and potential contingencies. Whether as narrator or actor a person needs the ability to make sense of, and to make a safe way through, the given circumstances of his or her existence. If these are dismissed, or misunderstood, or neglected, then the survival of self is in danger. Thus, as well as the ever-present threat of inner dissolution, as when an individual fails to find order in the lived existence, there arises external danger: the menace of annihilation through collision: the arrogant or ignorant person splintering against the rocks of external reality: and, always, the possibility of becoming the victim of random, chance occurrences.

The narrator in quest is searching for the good, and thus for a sustainable version of personal truth. He or she is intent on becoming a true person. In consequence, the chronicle which unfolds must essentially be enacted and interpreted as a moral history. The central person must be a person who is responsible for his or her actions; who is ready to be answerable to others; and who can give an intelligible account of, and justify, what has been done, is being done, or is being planned to be done. Such a person cannot be an isolate, but will have the will and the ability to contribute to the dialogues, spoken and unspoken, intimate and public, of what Michael Oakeshott has called 'the conversations of mankind'. In the last resort, the person as narrator continuously elucidates a moral purpose and a coherent being, and in the light of that developing understanding, the person as actor makes a sane progress through the contingencies of existence to the desired ideal of self.

CHAPTER 5

Education's ideals of a person

So education is concerned with encouraging respect for persons, self and other. And schools cannot hope to do this effectively unless they are clear about the ideas of a person which they value.

We have now reached the point where we can attempt to answer the question: what are, and should be, those valued ideas? Or, to put it another way, what are the models or ends of a person which education should consider worthy of respect?

The ideals of a person which a school can justifiably hold are, as already argued, in certain respects predicated by the nature of education. In practical terms, they are also generally limited to such inherited and current notions of a person as a society may approve: education is not in the business of promoting values significantly at odds with or detached from the community it serves. Only marginally, if at all, are schools in a position to make any unilateral declarations of independence over models of persons.

However, there is a range of such models. They vary from those which were once almost universally revered to those which are respected by some but by no means all of the individuals and groups who together constitute our pluralist society. Of the latter, it is prehaps the ideals of the principal religions represented in Great Britain which evoke the most powerful sentiments. The extent to which any of these ideals will influence a particular school will depend on the leadership of the school, and on the views of the communities it serves.

There is room for argument over what are the key, culturally inherited ideals of a person which influence schools. I would propose that they are the Christian, the classical, the rational and the humanist. Schools are also, increasingly, likely to be influenced by current notions of what it means to be an economic person. Finally, I would also suggest that schools have a working model of what persons ought to be. This draws upon inherited ideals, but is predominantly influenced by contemporary thinking.

The Christian person

Schools in the United Kingdom have traditionally been dominated by the Christian and the classical ideals of a person.

The Christian ideal is refracted through debate, and controversy, over questions about the nature of God, Jesus Christ, and human beings as persons. Nevertheless, the Christian idea of what a human being should be, as a person, continues to retain power and meaning for many in British society, and not only for active members of the Christian churches.

Much of Western Christianity sees the whole person as an 'anima naturaliter religiosa'. One feature of this view, given more or less emphasis according to doctrinal position, is of persons as capable of ill-doing; not simply on account of their circumstances, although these may indeed play a part, but on account of the sort of beings persons necessarily are.

For St Augustine the whole of humanity was a 'massa peccati', a mass of sin, its flesh weak, its reason fallible, its will perverted. A similar message was subsequently developed by others. John Donne (1955, p. 202, lines 193–4), for example, Anglican Dean of St Paul's as well as metaphysical poet, wrote in 'The anatomy of the world: The first anniversary':

> For, before God had made up all the rest,
> Corruption entered, and depraved the best.

John Calvin (1949, *Institutes* II, 3, 5), with the insight of a modern psychologist, noted that people not only had an ineradicable tendency to do wrong, but in fact often chose to do so and got pleasure from it: 'Man sins ... by liking and strong inclination.'

In recent times, on both historic and domestic scales, events and behaviour continue to occur for which the Christian belief in the fallen nature of humans provides, at the least, a plausible explanation. William Golding, himself a Christian, whose ideas were radically influenced by his experience of war and by the Holocaust, came to the conclusion (as quoted in the *Guardian,* 21 March 1993) that: 'Human beings do have a strand – or element if you like – of real malignancy. I think we ignore it at our absolute peril.' And those closely concerned with certain crimes of murder can be heard struggling, with the deepest reluctance, towards similar views. Following the conviction of two men and two women, all younger than 30, for burning to death a girl of 16, having held her captive for a week and tortured her, a detective inspector said: 'Psychological reports say that these are absolutely sane individuals. It's frightening that they are such ordinary people. There is nothing special about any of them' (*Guardian*, 18 December 1993).

Unqualified pessimism about human nature is ultimately nihilistic. For Christians, however, it is counterbalanced, indeed in the last resort outweighed, by what are seen as greater truths. While the orthodox view of a person is constantly being reintepreted, the characteristic lineaments are clear enough. 'We are,' as Cardinal Basil Hume (1991, p. 4) has expressed it, 'made in the image and likeness of God and are created ultimately so that we might share the life and love of God for eternity. We are a unique whole, a physical reality which is also an immortal spirit.'

Thus, identity is created, in accordance with divine will and law. 'Man is man,' said T. S. Eliot (1951, p. 485), 'because he can recognize supernatural realities, not because he can invent them.'

Furthermore, the person is an amalgam of the material and the immaterial. A human being is referred to by Thomas Browne (1977, p. 103) in his essay 'Religio medici', as 'that amphibious piece between a corporeal and spiritual essence', who has to live 'in divided and distinguished worlds'. Kierkegaard makes a similar point when he talks of the human that holds together the infinite and the finite.

The distinction between soul and body has at times been identified, or confused with, that between good and evil. It is notorious that this can lead to the expression of fear, anxiety, hostility towards the body. It also, and with potentially equally disastrous results, may result in refusal to accept that spirituality may have its dark side. While this can be a contentious issue, it is at the very least arguable that malevolence may have spiritual, as well as emotional or physical, sources (see, for instance, Hans Kung, 1978, p. 369, on the Christian New Testament belief in evil spirits).

Much of modern theology is concerned to suggest notions of a person which, while not necessarily denying traditional or orthodox views, can transcend them in such a way as to indicate solutions to some of the dilemmas which they may raise. Thus, it is argued that a person is a unity 'logically and objectively prior' to distinguishable elements of matter and spirit (Rahner, 1966, pp. 161–2). This proposition, while succeeding in keeping body and soul distinct, at the same time, through synthesizing them in the concept of a person, makes it more likely that they will be seen as having a necessary mutual relationship, rather than one of potentially endless conflict.

To the modern mind the idea of a person as, in the last resort, an effect of God is one which, at the least, can raise difficulties. This orthodox view, even allowing for the doctrine of free will, may appear to limit the independence of the individual, and so appear to deny a certain dignity to persons.

And there are, of course, all those doubts raised in popular and theological debate concerning 'the death of God'. Don Cupitt (1980, p. 164), for instance, suggests that mankind is emerging from its mythological childhood. As it does so, the self appears more like a self-defining relation, freeing itself of the myth of the divine as essential reality. 'We should not suppose God to be a substance and independently existing being. No external object can bring about my spiritual liberation ... Only I can free myself. So the religious imperative that commands me to become spirit must be regarded as an autonomously authoritative principle that I impose upon myself.' Such an approach has inevitably provoked serious anxieties about where this leaves the idea of an omnipotent divine presence. Nevertheless, it does illustrate one possible way of constructing a religious concept of a person which takes account of contemporary concerns.

Ultimately, in religious terms, 'a fully achieved ... spiritual subject' must be a person who has a transcendental purpose, and who is so developing that such an aim may be increasingly realized. What then is, to a Christian, the meaning of fulfilment for a person? The first answer which can be offered is that sanctification, a growth in holiness, is what we are about. Such a view can be supported by Bonhoeffer's statement that: 'The Christian goal is ... pure and simple ... to be as Jesus was.' The second, in St Augustine's words (*De Trinitate*, I, 17), is that: 'The contemplation of God is promised us as being the goal of all our actions and the everlasting perfection of all our joys'; or, as St Thomas Aquinas (1939, p. 172) put it more briefly: 'Man's ultimate happiness lies in a supernatural vision of God.'

It is the nature of Christian personal, spiritual and religious experience which often fascinates. It intrigues, at least in part, because of the paradoxes it seems to suggest. It does not, for instance, appear to be exclusive, but it seems to involve forms of perception and enlightenment reported by followers of other faiths and traditions: there seems to be, in Aldous Huxley's phrase, a 'perennial philosophy'.

Further, in what could be interpreted almost as a contradiction in terms, it is reported that spiritual fulfilment as a person may be accompanied by an obliviousness of self. For Eckhart there is the 'empty soul', for Simone Weil the 'decreated person', and for Pascal (1966, p. 309), 'the world forgotten, and everything except God'.

Spiritual experience may be reflected in a certain personal maturity and integrity. This comes about, according to John MacQuarrie, because as persons go out from or beyond themselves, the spiritual dimension of their lives is deepened, they become more truly themselves, and they grow in likeness to God, who is Spirit. MacQuarrie (1972, p. 45) also goes on to suggest that where, on the other hand, a person increasingly 'turns inward and encloses himself in self-interest, the less human does he become. This is the strange paradox of spiritual being – that precisely by going out and spending itself, it realizes itself.'

The classical person

The person was, for the Greeks, an object of the greatest fascination. In *Antigone*, Sophocles wrote (1947, p. 135):

Wonders are many on earth, and the greatest of these is man.

As in their natural landscape, the Greeks saw themselves illuminated with great clarity. This was no Northern European scene, with its changing shades and chiaroscuro, no Shakespearean universe where one might observe psychological humours and subtleties. Here dominant traits stood out in sharp relief, with clear-cut and dramatic contrasts between light and dark.

Greeks portrayed themselves as cunning and self-interested; as courageous, aggressive and ruthless; as highly intelligent and endlessly talkative; as curious and observant; as proud; and as dangerously susceptible to overconfidence. These were people who, given the choice, would combine jaw-jaw with war-war, emerge as victors, and then go home and write it all up in the most factual, detailed and objective style they could manage.

The Greeks lived in a world which, they believed, was overseen and visited by Gods. These beings were, for the most part, amoral, self-centred and unscrupulous. Not infrequently they might interfere in the mortal scene, simply for fun, or in pursuit of their own interests. Occasionally the results were beneficial, but more often than not they caused trouble. These Gods, however, did not really dominate the proceedings. Rather, they personified the unpredictability and callousness of fate. They also displayed, in vivid colours, some of the more dramatic characteristics of the Greeks themselves. Greeks had created a universe which, in its essentials, was anthropomorphic; and in which, whatever the difficulties, persons were free agents.

The Greek ideal of a person was essentially masculine, and reflected a society in which males dominated. It is true that women (albeit acted by men) were given parts of great power in Greek drama. And female Gods were very far from being mere bystanders. Nevertheless, particularly in Athens, women were socially and legally underprivileged. While modern research has modified this picture, it has not altered it in any really significant respects.

Not only were women relegated to hearth and home, where like Socrates' wife they were no doubt often unhappy, but they appear to have played little more than a reproductive part in the relationships between the sexes. In the odes of Pindar, in the dialogues of Plato, it is love between men rather than between men and women which is considered the more natural and the more noble. Here was an environment where, according to Kenneth Clark (1956, pp. 65–6), it was the male rather than the female nude which was regarded as 'a more normal and appealing subject'. This was perhaps only to be expected, given that women went about covered from head to toe while men, divesting themselves of the short cloaks they usually wore, would strip naked for sport.

It was, however, the power, and in particular the destructive power, of the emotions which perhaps most fascinated the Greeks when they observed and tried to make sense of human personality. And here, at least, there was full sexual equality. Women and men alike could be the victims of passions which ran out of control, bringing harm or annihilation to themselves, and to those with whom they came into contact.

Whether one turns to drama, to philosophy or to history this theme repeats itself. Euripides shows Medea, betrayed by her husband Jason, murdering, in addition to Jason's new wife and children, her own children. This last happening was invented by Euripides, who altered the original myth so as to show the utter and self-defeating devastation which unleashed passion was capable of causing. In *The Republic* Plato (1955, p. 345) remarks that: 'Even in the most respectable of us there is a terribly bestial and immoral type of desire'; while Thucydides (1972, p. 245), reflecting on the effects of war, reveals a similarly bleak outlook: 'With the ordinary conventions of civilized life thrown into confusion, human nature, always ready to offend even when laws exist, showed itself proudly in its true colours, as something incapable of controlling passion, insubordinate to the idea of justice, the enemy of anything superior to itself.'

It was, for the Greeks, a matter of the utmost practical importance to find an ideal of a person which could help in the control or sublimation of the worse passions, while at the same time legitimating and strengthening the virtues. That they never fully succeeded perhaps helps to explain the rapid disintegration of their civilization.

How, then, was a person to develop in a way which was both morally desirable and socially acceptable? For Plato, all emotions except proper pride were classed as appetites and subjugated to those powers of reason which, if properly used, helped an individual to achieve wisdom through a knowledge of the true and the good. However, for such persons reason became at once dominant and threatened: for the emotions make unruly subjects.

At the height of Athenian civilization, before the time of Plato and when it was at its most self-confident, it was generally accepted that the emotions and reason should work together. At best, this would result in a harmonious equilibrium of psychological forces, in a balanced personality.

Equally importantly, inner concord would manifest itself in completeness. The Greeks valued the idea of a whole person. The ideal of wholeness was reflected in all spheres of life, from the artistic to the political. Kenneth Clark identifies the Hermes of Praxitiles as representing, in its strength, grace, intelligence and physical beauty, 'the last triumph of the Greek idea of wholeness'.

And it was expected that an individual would make use of his full range of gifts, not simply for personal benefit, but for the good of the *polis*. The citizen whom Athenians respected was an all-rounder. Like Socrates, he should be able to fight, argue, play an active political role, philosophize, and so on. Mere specialists were held in low esteem. Officials and bureaucrats were usually slaves.

The Greeks had a particularly strong belief in the importance of the person achieving excellence, *arete*. This conviction, although not necessarily incompatible with the ideal of balance, was certainly distinct from it. While the ideals of both wholeness and excellence involved the notion of a person as an individual entity and as a social being, achievement of excellence was, in the classical perception, dependent on securing the recognition and approbation of society in a way that becoming a balanced person was not.

The ideal of *arete*, originating in the heroic age of Homer, was almost infinitely adaptable. For the Athenians it was a teleological concept. Persons were born with certain natural capacities. Their ultimate purpose was to develop these as fully as was humanly possible. In particular, abilities should be displayed, tested, refined and strengthened primarily through action. To Greeks it was despicable to let faculties lie idle, to evade challenges, to seek out a quiet life. 'Il faut cultiver son jardin' is not a phrase likely to have been uttered in classical Greek. The person who aroused admiration was one who fought with all his power, in full view of his peers, to be true to himself, and to achieve his full potential.

A Greek came to excel primarily through the exercise of power. This involved the ability to make the most of one's capacities and opportunities; more specifically, it meant employing the skills of political manoeuvre to help one on one's way in whatever fields one desired to succeed. This preoccupation was reinforced by the religion of the Greeks which, in C. M. Bowra's (1957, p. 59) phrase, displayed a 'cult of power'.

The greatest prize which society offered for the achievement of excellence was fame. This the Greeks desired with an inordinate passion. They longed to transcend mortality; but beyond the grave humans were mere shades. Only the Gods were immortal, and to aspire to join the Gods was blasphemous. However, while life in another world was not on offer, one could, through great deeds, hope to live on, celebrated, in the memory of this one. To reach this end many of the greatest of the Greeks directed their very considerable resources and vitality. 'The best seek one thing above all others: eternal fame': so wrote Heraclitus, the early Greek philosopher (quoted, with references, by Karl Popper, 1966, vol. 1, p. 17). And, a century later, Plato, in *The Symposium* (1951, p. 17), was making the same point: 'It is desire for immortal renown and a glorious reputation ... that is the incentive of all actions, and the better a man is the stronger the incentive.'

Tragically, as the Greeks understood only too well, the longing for fame carried within it the potential to destroy both personal and social balance. Ambition and self-assertion, the usual fuel of any drive for fame, could in principle be guided by reason. In practice, they often proved to be highly volatile elements which might erupt at any time into ruthless behaviour and unjustifiable risk-taking. A need to excel could degenerate into an urge to dominate, even to humiliate, others.

The Greeks had a sense of wholeness, not only of persons and their activities, but more widely, of existence. They sought not simply underlying realities, but rather one single sustaining essence. The quest for ultimate unity increasingly came to influence, and in due course to dominate, the Greek view of the person.

The reality which was sought by the Greeks could readily be identified with the Good, and with Truth, which it encompassed. Its apprehension could be seen as the main purpose of human existence. According to Plato (1955, p. 269), 'Good is the end of all endeavour, the object on which every heart is set, whose existence it divines ....'

If one was to have any chance of aiming successfully for such a goal, one needed to develop as a person along certain lines. Persons must have the intellectual capacity to search for the truth. They must also display the moral qualities of respect for understanding of reality, combined with the persistence to acquire the necessary knowledge. 'Unflinching thought,' said Parmenides, the early Greek philosopher, 'must lead to truth' (quoted in Burn, 1990, p. 142).

The rewards for being, or becoming, such a person lay in the journey as well as in the ultimate arrival. For the pursuit of Truth and Goodness itself gave a sense of satisfaction. One was both motivated and rewarded for following the path towards wisdom. 'Of the three types of pleasure,' said Plato (1955, p. 357), 'the pleasantest is that which belongs to the element in us which brings us knowledge, and the man in whom that element is in control will live the pleasantest life.'

Whatever the benefits might be, the way of wisdom was more likely to be travelled by the few than by the many. Indeed, Plato's idea of what a person should become was developed to a large degree in critical response to the culture of Athenian democracy and the sort of personality and behaviour which it appeared to encourage.

Consequently, just as Athenian civilization was beginning to decline, Plato's philosophical perspective led to a turning inward of attention, and to a view of the person which was in contrast to the hitherto dominant ideals. Where they had been activist, and incorporated elements of both the heroic and the democratic, Plato's perspective was predominantly concerned with spirit and the life of the mind. It offered a moral and intellectual vision of what a person should aspire to be; it was elitist in tendency.

The rational person

During the Enlightenment, or the 'Age of Reason', persons were, above all else, beings defined by their capacity to think. The intellectual foundations on which this image of a person were built was substantially the work of Descartes.

The Cartesian stance 'Cogito ergo sum' is individualist. The process of thinking is carried out unassisted, alone. Identity is established with little or no help from others. Relationships have no significant role to play; meaning comes from an inner world.

But Descartes was not only an individualist; he was also a dualist. Because being a person is equated with having the ability to think, any function the body might have is seen as subordinate and not significant. Physical care and exercise are only worthwhile insofar as they ensure that effective functioning of the thinking processes is not impeded. As for feelings and emotions, material and somatic as they substantially are in origin, they need to be kept in check. Spiritual, moral and aesthetic awareness arise from the workings of the mind.

Of the various attributes of the rational person, the ability to make choices emerged as the one with perhaps the most far-reaching practical implications. A person was an individual with the capacity to decide what to think, or even feel, and say on whatever topic engaged his or her interest, be it, to use J. S. Mill's words (1979a, p. 138), 'practical or speculative, scientific, moral or theological'. Persons also had the capability to decide upon the 'tastes and pursuits' which appealed to them. More fundamentally, persons could determine what sort of person they wished to become; although their room for manoeuvre in this respect was inherently limited by the nature of reason itself. 'The end of man,' said von Humboldt (quoted in Mills 1979a, p. 186), 'or that which is prescribed by the eternal or immutable dictates of reason...is the highest and most harmonious development of his powers to a complete and consistent whole.'

Such a person was essentially autonomous. Consequently, she or he greatly prized the idea of liberty. In the absence of either freedom of conscience or of action, any sense of personal independence would atrophy, while the capacity to make choices would be stunted for lack of opportunity to exercise it. At the very least the rational individual required a circumference of inviolable personal space.

Rational persons had the capacity to take ethical decisions, and to act morally. All moral concepts originate *a priori* and entirely in the reason. Moral worth existed, according to Kant (quoted in H. J. Paton, 1958, p. 84), where persons acted according to objective moral necessity, without ulterior motive. 'Act only on that maxim through which you can at the same time will that it should become a universal law': thus ran the categorical imperative. Rational persons might not always act morally. They were not necessarily inclined by nature to be virtuous, although Kant, like other contemporary thinkers, was ambivalent about this. On the one hand he could comment that 'Out of the crooked timber of humanity no straight thing was ever made'; on the other hand he could write that humanity was 'not basically corrupt, but capable of improvement'. In any case, the capacity to choose meant precisely that. And without doubt the rational person both could and should opt to become a moral person.

The idea of a person as a rational being could command, paradoxically, strong emotional commitment. It was perhaps only to be expected that it would achieve more than a cult, almost a religious status. Isaiah Berlin (1969, p. 138) has argued that rationalism 'is a form of secularized Protestant individualism in which the place of God is taken by the conception of the rational life, and the place of the individual soul which strains towards union with Him is replaced by the conception of the individual, endowed with reason, straining to be governed by reason and reason alone and to depend upon nothing that might deflect or delude him by engaging his irrational nature'.

The rational faith attracted followers because of its intrinsic appeal. It also came, from the nineteenth century onwards, to provide some reassurance for those fearful of the excesses of romanticism. Rationalism could be turned to in the hope that it might offer at least some form of protection from emotional turbulence, and above all from belief in the moral, even spiritual, value of opening oneself to such turbulence. 'My respect for reason as the rock of refuge to this poor exaggerated sur-excited humanity increases and increases,' wrote Mathew Arnold to his friend Arthur Hugh Clough (quoted in Lowry (1932), pp. 116–17).

The main attacks against the rationalist notion of a person were undoubtedly fanned, but by no means exclusively fuelled, by resentment at the presumption of setting up an ideal which undervalued, neglected, or even ignored the religious. A major criticism was that the spiritual capacity of the individual to be aware of the numinous, to encounter Other, was effectively denied. The profundities, the wonder, the awe, even the fearfulness of existence were sanitized and tidied away. In their place emerged an ultimately arid preoccupation with the thinking self as the scale by which everything must be weighed and valued.

Criticism along these lines was widespread. It came from various quarters. Creative artists, theologians and intellectuals alike had their say. According to Samuel Taylor Coleridge (quoted in Clark, 1956, p. 22):

The intelligible powers of ancient poets,
The fair humanities of old religion,
The Power, the Beauty, the Majesty,
They had their haunts in dale or piny mountain
... all these have vanished.
They live no longer in the faith of reason.

Much the same point, albeit from a very different perspective, was made by Cardinal Newman (1982, p. 165): 'Knowledge, viewed as knowledge, exerts a subtle influence in throwing us back on ourselves, and making us our own centre, and our minds the measure of all things ... A sense of propriety, order, consistency and completeness gives birth to a rebellious stirring against miracle and mystery, against the severe and the terrible.'

Similar doubts could even be heard from Reason's own congregation. Reflecting on his early life, particularly in the Cambridge of G. E. Moore and Bertrand Russell, in his memoir, *'My Early Beliefs'* (quoted in Annan, 1990, p. 323), Maynard Keynes recalled, 'I can see us as water spiders gracefully skimming, as light and reasonable as air, the surface of the stream without any contact at all with the eddies and currents underneath ... We practised a thin rationalism ignoring both the reality and the value of the vulgar passions.'

The humanist person

Humanism is a broad church. It can appeal to those with an orthodox scientific view of the universe, as well as to those interested in the personal nature of heightened perception and of immanent, even transcendental, spiritual experience. It allows Huxley to speak unto Huxley, Aldous to Sir Julian.

Humanism sees itself as having much in common with other life stances. Like members of the major world religions, many humanists consider that they belong to a faith community. Like rationalists, which numbers of them also consider themselves to be, they value the role of reason. And, in common with many believers and non-believers alike, they subscribe to a morality which is ultimately grounded in a belief in the inviolability of human life. Humanists are inclined to consider, and with some justification, that they seek the common ground, that they work for consensus not division.

However, as an explicit, and reasonably coherent and consistent system of ideas and values, humanism does, of course, have its particular defining characteristics. If everyone accepted these, we would all be humanists. Since we are not, there are those who disagree, more or less strongly, with what humanists stand for.

Many of the fundamental tenets of humanism were first articulated, at least in the modern era, by Rousseau. A key axiom of humanism is that persons are essentially incorrupt and free from sin. 'Man's first instincts,' wrote Rousseau, 'are always good.' (see, for example, Rousseau, 1967, p. 426). And his successors have expressed a virtually identical belief. For

Carl Rogers (1967, p. 194), 'The basic nature of the human being ... is constructive and trustworthy.'

Instincts are one thing. Whether one is willing and in a position to follow them can be quite another. Humanists are, for the most part, not unrealistically optimistic about the way people are likely to behave. Again, the line taken by Rousseau (1953, p. 405) has tended to set the general tone: 'There are no perfect beings to be found in Nature. Their examples are too remote from our world.' Maslow, who like Rogers was an American psychologist, considered that one sign of maturity was an awareness of the shortcomings of the human species.

For humanists, the environment plays a critical role in influencing our development. 'Climates,' declared Rousseau (1953, p. 381), 'seasons, sounds, colours, darkness, light, the elements, food, noise, silence, movement, repose; they all act on our machines, and consequently on our souls.'

However, our surroundings do not, in the last resort, determine either our personalities or our behaviour. It is we who ultimately have both the responsibility and the capacity to decide whether or not we wish to try and become persons worthy of respect. 'Virtue is only difficult through our own fault,' as Rousseau (1953, p. 69) declared.

What then, for humanists, is the ideal of a person? It certainly is distinct from any theological notion since, if humanism has one major defining characteristic it is that it does not accept belief in a personal God. For this faith, the purpose of existence cannot be a life lived in and for the illumination of the divine.

'The realization of the real self' and 'self-actualization' are terms which have been used to describe the humanist vision of the true ends of a person. Maslow (1954, p. 46) considered that individuals were motivated to develop their gifts to their utmost, and that they would become discontented unless they were able to be true to their own nature. 'A musician must make music, an artist must paint, and a poet must write, if he is ultimately to be at peace with himself. What a man can be, he must be.' The same, one assumes, goes for women.

Individuals who were, if not necessarily 'self-actualized', at least clearly 'self-actualizing', exhibited, according to Maslow, a number of key characteristics. These included concern for others, a sense of social responsibility and a sense of personal autonomy. Such individuals also derived inspiration, strength and even ecstasy from the everyday happenings of life. Further, they could have peak experiences, greatly valued feelings of being outside time and space. It is evident, from the work of Maslow and indeed many others, that the humanist model of a person is, in various important respects, not only moral, but also spiritual.

The humanist idea of a person is perhaps best exemplified in the work of Carl Rogers (1967, pp. 123–4). Here we see the characteristic belief in the significance of personal development and its achievement crystallizing into a clear-cut concern with questions of identity and self-fulfilment. 'Each individual,' says Rogers, 'appears to be asking himself a double question: "Who am I?" and "How may I become myself?"'. Here we also see an approach to an individual's environment which interprets it potentially, not only as a source of disturbance, but also as a source of support: 'In a favourable psychological climate a process of becoming takes place; the individual drops one after another of the defensive masks with which he has faced life ... he experiences fully the hidden aspects of himself.'

And here, finally, as the concealed features of the individual human being emerge into the light, we see the charactistics which are most highly valued. The ideal person is one who is 'a sensitive, open, realistic, inner-directed member of the human species' (Rogers, 1967, p. 181); who is 'creatively realistic, and realistically creative' (*ibid.*); who has 'an openness to and acceptance of other individuals' (p. 174); and who, perhaps above all, is someone who is 'open to all the elements of his organic experience ... who is developing a trust in his own organism as an instrument of sensitive living' (p. 124).

In essence, what is of the greatest significance to Carl Rogers, and in this he is typical of many humanists, is, as he put it in the title of his best-known work, becoming a person. Present being and future achievement are both incorporated in a dynamic view of personhood. In this, all that is truly valued is synthesized in a continuing experience of ever-present development.

The economic person

The inherited models of a person have tended to disregard economic motivations, aspirations or concerns. Partly in consequence, the idea of humans as economic beings has traditionally been ignored by schools, or, where acknowledged, seen as a regrettable reality. There has unquestionably existed throughout education what has been called a 'disdain for *homo economicus*'. Moreover, while such an attitude is less strong than it used to be, it is by no means simply a historical phenomenon. It persists. And, understandably, it has been widely attacked.

What schools require is clear enough. They need a view of a person which, while properly acknowledging attributes and motives appropriate to economic behaviour, is at the same time worthy of respect.

Schools have been inhibited from developing a positive approach to people as economic beings, at least in part, by the existence of strong cultural forces, which they have both reflected and helped to sustain.

In England the notion of economic activity has been devalued by the class system and the manner in which power has been distributed and used within it. Mathew Arnold (1964, pp. 308–9) pointed out in his report on 'Schools and universities on the continent' (originally published in 1868), that we have 'A professional class brought up ... with fine and governing qualities, but without the idea of science; while that immense business class ... is ... cut off from the aristocracy and the professions, and without any governing qualities.'

In schools, this resulted in the much-discussed phenomenon of a fault line appearing between liberal and utilitarian education, with the former looking down on the latter from what it saw as the moral, and also not entirely incidentally, the social high ground. By the early twentieth century, a point had been reached where, as Martin Wiener (1985, p. 23) has put it, 'The ethos of later Victorian Oxbridge, a fusion of aristocratic and professional values, stood self-consciously in opposition to the spirit of Victorian business and industry; it exalted a dual ideal of cultivation and service against philistine profit seeking.'

Through the twentieth century such attitudes, while challenged frequently and with a sense of increasing urgency, even despair, for the most part became further entrenched and extended. 'The ideology of liberal education, public service and gentlemanly professionalism,' says Philip Elliott (1972, p. 52), 'was elaborated in opposition to the growth of industrialism and commercialism...It incorporated such values as personal service, a dislike of competition, advertising and profit, a belief in the principle of payment in order to work rather than in working for pay and in the superiority of the motive of service.'

Today, the influences which questioned the place, purpose and worth of economic effort as a human activity are in decline. The possibility exists of moving forwards, towards an agreed ideal, and away from the dogmatic positions into which numbers of the various protagonists have dug themselves over the years.

However, there exists a wide range of possible forms of economic organisation. One can reasonably talk of a social market, a free market, a controlled market, and so on. Each of these is likely to be sustained by rather different notions of what an economic person should be.

What then are the main economic ideas of a person?

An initial problem arises because there has been relatively little detailed exploration of the nature of individuals as economic beings. Thinkers concerned with this field are, by and large, more interested in systems than in persons. Where analysis of human motivation and behaviour does occur, it is typically inferred from, or illustrative of, economic structures. One does not look to economists for depth psychology.

Having said that, if one considers first the free market idea of the economic person, one finds reasonably clear, if rather general ideas of human nature. To begin with, it is said that persons have a range of interests (not identified or explored by free-market thinkers in much detail), which they pursue more or less regardless of other people's concerns or any wider considerations. As Will Hutton (1995, p. 228) has put it, 'The economic man of free-market theory is an amoral fellow ... [he] ... exists to consume and indulge his pleasures.'

More specifically, wants are most likely to be satisfied through the acquisition of financial assets. 'An augmentation of fortune,' said Adam Smith (1986, p. 441), 'is the means by which the greater part of men propose and wish to better their condition.' There is, moreover, an intimate association between the possession of riches and personal fulfilment. Bentham (1931, p. 103) considered that 'Each portion of wealth has a corresponding portion of happiness.'

The wants of the free-market person are liable, whether taken individually or as a whole, to prove unlimited. There is a restless and insatiable desire for further gratification. A *laissez-faire* capitalist is not likely to have any notion or experience of inner serenity or a balanced lifestyle. 'There is,' wrote Adam Smith, in the same passage quoted above, 'scarce perhaps a single instant in which any man is not so perfectly and completely satisfied with his situation as to be without any wish of alteration or improvement of any kind.'

It is also worth noting, since the point recurs so frequently in subsequent debate, that Bentham (ed. Stark, 1952, vol. III, p. 430) believed a desire for happiness, and so for wealth, inevitably led to a desire for power. He put it like this: 'Human beings are the most powerful instruments of production, and therefore everyone becomes anxious to employ the services of his fellows in multiplying his comforts. Hence the intense and universal thirst for power; the equally prevalent hatred of subjection.' Such a view may seem to have lost some of its force in the electronic age. However, it still seems to be the case that the sort of person who is highly motivated to make money is also often gratified by the exercise of control over others.

Free-market persons have, of course, been widely criticized for this inherent self-interestedness and the resulting avaricious and dominance-seeking behaviour. Lord Hailsham, as Quintin Hogg (1947, pp. 51–2), referred to individuals under capitalism as being involved in, 'an ungodly and rapacious scramble for ill-gotten gains'. More recently, the judge who presided in the Guinness fraud trial attacked in a public lecture what he described as 'the power-driven, greed-fed, dishonest excesses of the 1980s' (Sir Denis Henry, 1992).

The defence of such behaviour ranges from the crude to the subtle. Ivan Boesky, one-time Wall Street financier and guru, before being jailed for fraud, used to inform cheering graduates at graduation ceremonies (film exists of one of these speeches) that 'Greed is good' – a statement which he apparently felt no need to justify, presumably on the grounds that, since it was axiomatic, it did not require vindication.

David Willetts (1992, pp. 85–7), in his book *Modern Conservatism*, took a rather different tack. He protested against the perception that free markets rest 'on a base view of human nature, according to which we are driven by greed and self-aggrandizement'. Rather, he argued that 'Modern free-market economics makes no claim to be a psychological theory of behaviour. Individual economic agents have a host of different motives.' He wrote that only one or two basic assumptions about the nature of persons are made, 'such as unmet material wants'. However, the drive to meet such wants is precisely what is meant to power the free market. Consequently, it must be of significance in the capitalist view of the nature of persons.

In the classic theory of free markets it is argued that the pursuit of economic self-interest may be justified, through no virtue of the agent, but as it were through grace, by the mysterious workings of a greater, benevolent, almost divine design. This 'invisible hand', as Adam Smith famously called it, is thought to lead individuals, through their private and selfish activities, to promote the general economic good.

The difficulties with this idea are first, that it does not offer any notion of redemption for individuals from the intrinsically mercenary egotism of their natures; and, secondly, that it hardly corresponds with observed facts. Whether in the nursery or the business place, sustained and persistent self-seeking behaviour appears more likely, in practice, to end in tears than in harmony.

Market capitalism, according for instance to Nigel Lawson (*Financial Times*, 4 September 1993), is based on freedom and liberty. It would seem reasonable to infer from this, as indeed Lawson does, and in no uncertain terms, that free-market persons are endowed with the attributes characteristic of free persons. Undoubtedly, they do, at the least, appear to have the capacity to make choices.

It is true that the capitalist economy does offer a degree of freedom, albeit greater for the winners than for the losers. Furthermore, by contrast with any fixed order of society, free enterprise can encourage social and geographical mobility. As such it helps individuals to redefine their social and economic roles. In particular, they may express their preferences as consumers, and decide in what particular persona, as producers of value, they will attempt to make their fortunes.

However, the ability of the individual, through the enjoyment of freedom, to develop as a person is, in certain respects, limited in a free-market society. People do not have any real opportunity, whether acting on their own or collectively, to attempt to develop according to their aspirations through the creation of forms of social and economic arrangement that differ significantly from market capitalism. Persons in a *laissez-faire* economy are at liberty to roam at will around the market-place, to purchase, barter or set up in trade. What they are less free to do is set up a prayer meeting on site, work for personal satisfaction rather than profit, challenge the morality of the market rules, act on a personal motivation inspired by an ideal of service rather than of profit, or move beyond the boundaries with a view to constructing a different sort of arena for human activity. The individual who does not wish to be or become free-market person is liable, where the writ of *homo economicus* runs, to be forced to be free.

Free-market persons are social beings, but only just. They have to compete in order to survive, and if possible to prosper. The ability to compete is both their *moyen* and their *raison d'être*. Such individuals have no interest, and hence negligible skills, in cooperative behaviour. Each is an atom, careering around at random, every now and again colliding with, fusing with, or destroying others.

Alternatives to the free market rest, as it does, on particular views of *homo economicus*. These views are often, explicitly or by implication, critical of the free-market model of the person.

Thus, it is argued, that persons in their economic roles ought to be seen less as isolates and more as social animals. Only where this happens, as J. Gray (1993) has written, can there be a chance of developing that rational approach to planning necessary to create the conditions in which enterprise can flourish and markets operate in an orderly fashion.

Further, it has been suggested that economic persons should be seen as having a sense of and a desire for justice. Where this is not respected, economic inefficiency, or disruption, may well result. Thus, Marc Thompson (1993), in a study for the Institute of Manpower Studies, has reported that the introduction of performance-related pay could be counter-productive where workers considered it to be unfairly structured or managed. Similarly, Robert Solow (1990) has argued that a vital key to making the labour market effective is to respect people's desire for fairness.

Economic behaviour is governed, according to Robert H. Frank (1988), as much by the emotions as by rational (but necessarily seldom fully informed) estimates of profit and loss. In particular, humans are capable of altruistic behaviour. This is not simply an optional extra, a sort of fashion accessory for the conspicuous consumer of morality, but a necessary condition of economic success. An individual who always pursues self-interest is bound to fail, argues Frank. On the other hand, he suggests that morality often conveys material benefits on those who practise it. In other words, humans can act as moral beings, and whatever the more spiritual benefits may be, this characteristic is cost-effective.

There is a long, and well-established, tradition which holds that economic individuals of their nature aspire to find work intrinsically worthwhile, look in fact for 'job satisfaction'. Thus, for Plato (1955, pp. 74–5), work is something which one cannot but do for its own sake: 'The shepherd's only care is the welfare of the flocks of which he is in charge ... the doctor brings us health, the pilot a safe voyage, and so on.'

However, it does not follow that, because one's first priority is to do the task in hand, one should not also look for payment. In fact, says Plato, it is necessary to be paid, since otherwise, apart from any other considerations, one would be unlikely to be in a position to continue practising one's particular expertise.

Plato is also clear that work which is fairly rewarded is as desirable for society as it is for the individual. Payments which are consistently too high or too low undermine any sense of the value of work, intrinsic or pecuniary, and are likely to lead to trouble. 'Wealth and poverty ... one produces luxury and idleness and a passion for novelty, the other meanness and bad workmanship' (p. 167). Furthermore, concluded Plato (p. 327), 'Love of money and adequate self-discipline in its citizens are two things that cannot co-exist in any society.'

Particularly during the Enlightenment, but also discernible earlier, there emerged a view that persons who choose, or are forced, to work only for money are likely to be at the mercy of their own motivation, or of their paymasters, or of the unpredictable forces of the market-place. This perception, sharpened by a resentment of the powers of autocratic patronage and of the emergent workings of *laissez-faire* economics, was essentially stimulated by a desire for a non-capitalist freedom: freedom of self-expression, freedom to be one's own master, freedom to explore and to express the full range of one's own abilities. 'Nothing vigorous, nothing great,' wrote Rousseau (1953, p. 375), 'can flow from an entirely venal person.'

In this tradition, work is seen as an inherent source of human well-being. As Caleb Garth put it, in George Eliot's *Middlemarch* (1994, p. 562), 'You must have a pride in your own work, and in learning to do it well.' And some modern economists are returning to this understanding, developing it, and relating it to contemporary circumstances. Robert Lane (1991) of Yale University, for instance has explored, in his book *The Market*

Experience, the role of work not as disutility, as a tedious activity justified only by the financial compensation it should bring, but as an occupation which should be individually enriching. Production and work, argues Lane, are key sources of both utility and satisfaction. It can encourage personal development, deepen skills, help bring humanity and structure into lives. In particular, it has the potential to make us more clever, and more independent.

Clearly, any educational ideal of an economic person cannot be partisan. It would be neither right nor acceptable for schools to ground their relevant teaching on any particular philosophy. Still less would they be justified in aiming to produce, for example, capitalists or socialists. It is this consideration, quite as much as any cultural antipathy to *homo economicus*, which has hindered schools from developing an agreed notion of what an economic person should look like.

Nevertheless, the outlines of what could become an acceptable ideal can now, if with some difficulty, be discerned (see, for example, Sir Ron Dearing's 1996 *Review of Qualifications for 16–19 Year Olds*).

Thus:

- Individuals have a right to gain satisfaction from what they do. Accordingly, work should be widely defined, to include occupations, paid and unpaid, from home and family care to labouring or banking. Persons should expect to work, and be able to work.
- Persons have an ability to choose, and this ought to be practised in relation to occupation. Of course, individual circumstances or the way in which the economy is organized and managed may make this difficult or virtually impossible. However, that is a consideration which suggests that society should be run along different lines. It does nothing to invalidate the view that an intrinsic attribute of persons as economic beings is the ability to make career choices.
- Persons, as beings endowed with cognitive faculties, should have a grasp of key economic concepts such as wealth creation. They should have an idea of the relationship between economy and society in different economic systems, and of the role of government and of international agencies.
- As social beings, all persons should have the opportunity to play a worthwhile economic role, whatever their intelligence, ability, social background, gender or ethnicity.
- As moral beings, persons should, in the words of a National Curriculum Council paper, *Education for Economic and Industrial Understanding* (1990b, p. 5), be capable of developing such attitudes as 'respect for alternative economic view-points and a willingness to reflect critically on their own economic views and values; sensitivity to the effect of economic choices on the environment; and concern for human rights, as these are affected by economic decisions'.
- As socially responsible beings, persons ought to be aware that a desire to make money is morally neutral, in itself neither good nor bad, right nor wrong. They need to know that people have to make up their own minds about how far a desire for wealth is justifiable in terms of

intention and outcome; and about what, in practice, is the golden mean for themselves, as individuals and as members of society, between avarice on the one hand and the sort of laziness or arid self-denial on the other, which erodes the well-being of oneself and of others. Above all, they should be prepared to accept that moral responsibility for personal economic aspirations and behaviour rests with the person and not somehow, somewhere, Beyond, immanent in the mysterious workings of the system.

The school's working model of a person

In addition to ideals of a person which are predominantly acquired or inherited from society, schools have what I refer to as a working model of a person. This does not replace but supplements education's other ideals. It is a 'working' model in the sense that it provides an educationally useful notion of what persons are capable of becoming and should become. The working model is referred to by educators in various terms, or is often implicit, or taken for granted. Nevertheless, it does and has to exist in some form or other because without it, it becomes virtually impossible to plan and practise worthwhile teaching.

The working model, inevitably, has its own perspectives and emphases. However, it also incorporates some of the main features of the ideals I have discussed. On balance, it offers a focus for consensus rather than for conflict. As such it can help professionals to work together towards shared goals. It also enables schools, insofar as they attempt the task, to discuss more easily with the outside world – parents, the local community and so on – what sort of persons they would like students to become.

The working model is dynamic. At its best, it is responsive. However, of its nature it is not a finished product. This means it can appear to lack sharp outlines, or to be somewhat disjointed. However, such inherent problems do not, for the most part, interfere seriously with its functioning.

There is room for argument about what are the more significant characteristics of the working model. The main educational concern, however, appears to be to establish a viable ideal of human nature, which takes into account the actual characteristics of young people, which students can reasonably be expected to value, and which a good education can help them to achieve.

According to the working model, individuals should become whole persons. This is taken to mean that they have spiritual, moral, social, cultural, mental and physical attributes which should be developed harmoniously, and in mutual balance, for the benefit of the individual and of society. This view was reflected in various official documents during the 1970s and 1980s, and culminated in the 1988 Education Reform Act.

Underlying much educational practice is a particular view of the person as learner. This, as one would expect, is consistent with the main findings of modern research, and in particular the findings of child psychology (see for a detailed and outstanding exploration of the relevant issues, Donaldson, 1978, 1993).

The working model sees individual learners as protean, and not readily to be interpreted in reductionist terms. This understanding derives, in part at least, from cognitive social psychology, which portrays humans as infinitely complex learning animals. H. A. Simon (1969) has reported, for example, that people engage in a huge range of indeterminate behaviour which cannot be fully explained by any constructable model, and the motives for which can be varied in the extreme.

The working model tends to perceive persons as beings who gain knowledge and understanding through experimental behaviour. Relatively little emphasis is placed on the role of pure reason, and considerably less on revelation. To put it at its simplest, learners are mostly seen as individuals who progress through making guesses which are accepted, modified or rejected in the light of experience. This, in its essentials, is the view argued by Karl Popper (see Chapter 7, p. 69).

Individuals who are capable of learning through the intelligent management of trial and error, and through reflection on the results, are bound to have a degree of freedom, choice and autonomy. They are accordingly, to some extent, responsible for their own learning.

It is assumed in exploratory learning that persons are creatures who come by knowledge in a social environment. An obvious implication of this for education is that teachers should do their best to make certain that what is to be learned is matched, at appropriate levels of difficulty, to the existing knowledge and experimental skills of the student. Much of modern education is, therefore, very concerned to ensure that this happens.

It is sometimes believed, by supporters and critics alike, that experimental learning necessitates a more or less exclusively experiential approach. However, while the emphasis is undoubtedly on activity, it does not have to be. Students can effectively accommodate new information, didactically presented, provided certain conditions are met. Students must have the necessary intellectual skills. Data or ideas must be presented in terms which make sense in terms of students' current understanding. And, finally, students must be given the opportunity to interrogate whatever material is presented; in this way, they can not only assure themselves of its internal consistency, but can compare it in their minds with their previous understanding of the matter being considered.

The working model includes ideas of persons as creative and imaginative beings. It draws such notions in part from traditional views. Thus, for instance, it is influenced by the Judaeo-Christian concept of *homo creator*, an individual made in the divine likeness of the creative God. As Richard Harries, Bishop of Oxford (1993 p. 102) puts it, 'Human beings, made in the image of God, share in the divine creativity. We also have the capacity for creative, beautiful ordering ... Artists of every kind share in the work of the divine artist by giving form to recalcitrant matter. They make music of inchoate sounds and speech of incoherent babble. They give shape to the shapeless and in doing so reflect the work of eternal wisdom.'

Also of significance in influencing the notion of persons as creative and imaginative individuals have been ideas derived ultimately from the romantic movement, with its valuing of emotion, inspiration and vision, its questioning of the hard-edged rules and rationality of classicism, its openness to the demands of the unknown, its suspicion of the preordained, and its awareness of Other. 'The primary imagination,' said Samuel Taylor Coleridge (1965, p. 167), 'I hold to be the living power of all human perception, and as a repetition in the finite mind of the eternal act of creation in the infinite I AM.'

The working model, however, although clearly influenced by traditional views, is, as one would expect, more evidently the product of contemporary thinking. It has evolved, in part, in response to an educational belief that young people have imaginative and creative faculties which need to be developed. Thus, David Holbrook (1961, chapter 4), quoting from John Stuart Mill's autobiography, argued for a 'culture of the feelings', writing that if we are to be able to make sense of our existence, we must be capable of exploring and sharing 'experience in fantasy'.

Equally influential has been the growing interest in the processes of creativity. This helps to inform understanding both of the nature of persons and of how people learn. Whether through the work of psychologists such as Jerome Bruner, or of art critics such as E. H. Gombrich, or of creative writers and thinkers such as Arthur Koestler, teachers are coming to see how students can and should be considered as imaginative and creative beings.

Accordingly the working model, in its interpretation of imagination and creativity, tends to focus on these faculties as enablers of learning and moral sensibility. An ideal emerges which may be represented along the following lines:

Persons are seen as active participants in the world of the imagination. They are thus well placed to conjure up those pictures in the mind which can suggest the sort of questions and hypotheses which lead to meaningful explorations of reality. They are also in a position, through observation of contrasts, to distinguish that which may prove to be substantial from that which could turn out to be illusory.

Individuals exercise the imagination, not only to throw light on the nature of that which is, but also to explore and exploit the considerable territory of metaphor for its own sake. It is here, not least through the language of poetry and the arts, that human beings can perhaps best come to express themselves and to understand each other. A whole person is one who is equally at home with actuality and fable, and who is in a position to see both as aspects of a greater unity.

All living things inherit a created world. Persons are also involved in its creation. As they learn to discriminate with sensibility between the subtle and overlapping shades of that which is real and that which is imagined, they are composing in their minds a reflection of, and also a reflection on, what is perceived. Thus, in his Reith lectures, the biologist J. Z. Young (1951, p. 61) said, 'The brain of each one of us does literally create his or her own world ... In some sense we literally create the world we speak about.'

In this perspective, we originate our personal reality. In so doing, we can come to discover how far that reality is shared with, and how far it is distinct from, that of others. In terms of our own understanding, we can also investigate and evaluate not only the nature of the physical world, but also the nature of the social world which has been created in the past and the interpretations of which are carried in and transmitted through the cultures of our society. Finally, we become well placed to make our own contribution to the making of the future.

Persons can express their creativity through the medium of art. In attempting to depict visual experience, the artist, as E. H. Gombrich (1960) has argued, follows a rhythm of schema and correction (or, in the parallel terminology of cognitive psychology, of construct and modification), which is similar for both perception and representation. The eventual end-product of this process is not simply a copy or record of what has been observed, but 'the faithful construction of a relational model' (p. 90). In other words the artist, even when apparently reproducing, is in fact creating.

More evidently, creation can be seen to be occurring where something clearly new is presented, something that has little similarity with any artefact, composition or notion that has previously been encountered. As Arthur Koestler (1964) has pointed out, creation of this sort is often believed to arise from a moment of given certainty, a flash of inspiration. Be that as it may, whether or not insight comes dramatically, what we are dealing with in this instance is essentially creation which arises from discovery rather than observation. Picasso said that he did not seek, he found (see Gombrich, 1956, p. 438). Here, images emerge from the inchoate, the imagination responding and giving form to the hints, suggestions, even revelations which emerge in conversing with the chosen medium. In this mode, the creator is less craftsman, more seer.

The sort of persistent thought and action which result in creation can, in the final resort, only be sustained by what is perhaps most appropriately described as moral optimism. The ability to make or find, and give form to, that which previously did not exist or was unknown, gives substance to the autonomy and freedom of persons. It helps individuals to be more than simple, passive consumers of life's goods, able at best to opt between given offerings. It enables them to envisage, and strive for, not only the given, but also that which previously was hardly imagined, or even unknown.

In creating, persons give identity and meaning to themselves, and to their world. Through what they shape and become, they reveal what it is they value. Intrinsic to acts of creation are questions of worth. Through the free play of the imagination and openness to reality individuals have the opportunity to develop a self and an environment which they believe to be worth working for.

CHAPTER 6

The personal school

How, then, should schools set about educating students to respect persons?

Thought, policy and practice need to be informed by awareness of contemporary culture's concerns about the nature of persons. If schools are ill informed they are not well placed to orientate what they do towards the perceptions of the modern world; they are liable to become detached from reality and, in the negative sense of the word, academic.

Schools must recognize what persons, of their nature, necessarily are: living human beings, female and male, embodied, having the attribute of consciousness, of varied intelligence and ethnic origin, complex, social and protean. Respect for these characteristics should be taught and learned.

Schools need to be in dialogue with students about their personal ideals. Young people can have strong ideas about what they desire to become. Some may even hold that they were born to become a certain sort of person. They may believe that they have a calling, or simply that they have certain abilities which must be developed. Their ideals for themselves, where they exist, can vary from inspired, through the socially acceptable, or the idiosyncratic, to the apparently or actually subversive. Schools need to be ready and able to discuss with young people, in their own terms, how to become worthwhile sorts of persons.

But what about the differing inherited and current ideals of a person? Christian, classical, rational, humanist and economic? And what of the contemporary educational debate, with its references to ideas of wholeness and balance, of spirituality, of the person as learner, of imagination and creativity? Schools need to have a view of how these both do influence and should influence educational aspirations and practices. Only where schools have such a perspective are they fully and securely in a position to start effectively exploring with students and teaching them how to become persons worthy of respect, and how to respect others.

In education, there is a sensitive balance to be achieved between introducing students to a clear and realistic moral vision of how they could develop and respecting their right to choose for themselves what sort of person they wish to become. Where a school succeeds in achieving such a balance, it can with justice claim, in this respect at least, to be a good school.

Aspirations

Schools may be tempted quietly to obscure or ignore any spelling out of what sort of persons they intend students to become. And some at least of their reasons for doing so may appear persuasive.

First, there is the sheer complexity of the situation. It is not as if schools are dealing with one or two straight-forward, readily described and communicated ideals. Secondly, there is the potential for dissension. Schools are naturally wary of becoming arenas of conflict. Staff, parents, students and others may, explicitly or implicitly, be committed to differing ideas of what they think a person ought to be. Once these are identified, and become of evident relevance to discussion about a school's purposes and planning, then it is quite possible for sometimes acrimonious debate and argument to arise.

However, a school leadership which, even if it is clear in its own mind about what sorts of person it wishes its students to become, fails to communicate its aspirations to others, is hardly in a position to provide education of quality.

So, headteacher and governors need to elucidate their own beliefs about what persons should become. Within the general sense of direction given by a sense of common purpose, a school should become a forum where contrasting ideals of a person are clarified, common ground discovered, and differences respected.

All this is far from being a paper exercise. Developing and sharing notions of what human beings ought to become is demanding. The process engages with questions of identity and value about which individuals frequently feel strongly, and not least where the education of young people is concerned.

Where a school does achieve a commitment to the significance of particular ideals of a person, it can develop a confidence in itself as an institution which has high and appropriate expectations of the sort of persons students can become; and it can be significantly strengthened in its efforts to create in students a sense of self-worth and of informed respect for others. On the other hand, a school leadership which attempts to achieve its aspirations without consultation, or which simply funks the challenge, is liable to find itself faced with apathy at best, disaffection at worst.

Aims, curriculum and pastoral care

Ideals of a person do not appear in decontextualized isolation, intellectual wares waiting to be chosen according to taste. They may, and of course should, be specifically identified. But they are also encountered through the rhythms and accidents of school life. The ideas they represent underpin, sustain and are reflected throughout the fabric of education.

Schools, accordingly, need to be clear not only about their own beliefs about what persons are and should become, but also should be able to identify where their aims, and curricular and pastoral care approaches, are promoting particular ideas of a person.

There should be little difficulty in discovering where schools have been influenced by the Christian idea of a person. One would look, at the least, to their general aims, to religious education and acts of collective worship, to the study of literature (English and modern foreign language), to the humanities, and to their pastoral treatment of students.

How deeply and extensively schools look to educate students in the light of Christian ideals will inevitably vary. Living as we do in a multi-cultural society, and in what has been called a post-Christian world, it would be easy to take a view that the significance of the Christian ideal of the person is being marginalized in education. However, quite apart from the fact that Christianity continues to be a lived faith for very many individuals and communities, its values and ideals continue to echo through our school system, with its church and secular schools, as well as through our educational practices and debates.

The study of the classics is disappearing from the curriculum of the vast majority of schools. Nevertheless, in education as elsewhere one still finds strong traces of the Greek notions of what a person ought to be. To this day, especially perhaps in the aims and objectives of schools, one discovers recurring reference to self-fulfilment, the achievement of excellence, the development of the whole person, the exercise of reason, and the particularly Platonic notion that the individual ought to have and develop capacities as a moral, truth-respecting individual who is above all else motivated by a search for the good.

On a less exalted note, speech days, silver cups, prizes of all sorts, team photographs, etc. all bear witness to a continuing belief in the importance of encouraging and rewarding a striving for, if not personal fame at least public recognition. Also still identifiable in some institutions, though more as a covert sub-text of the educational lexicon, are intellectual elitism, the belittling of women and fear of the emotions.

The notion of the rational person has exerted very considerable influence in education. For instance, the encouragement of autonomy remains an important objective for many schools, and while this may no longer attract the zealous support it once did, it continues to be widely seen as a worthwhile and valid goal.

The curriculum – particularly but by no means only at secondary level – is as a rule organized so as to promote all-round intellectual development. In this it now receives significant help from the National Curriculum. However, less support is usually offered for spiritual, aesthetic, physical, creative or emotional education.

Choice, a key attribute of the rational person, is frequently seen as a good in itself, as well as a necessary means to the achievement of particular ends. Guidance and advice on the selection of curricular options, exam courses, careers, higher education and post-school activity in general are built into the life of schools. Naturally enough, given the inclination to value those students who are skilled at thinking, the quality of what is available to them is often better than it is for their contemporaries.

Education, where influenced by the ideal of the rational person, has been inclined to pay relatively little attention to the significance and value of relationships. Accordingly, the needs of individuals arising from their existence as social beings has, at times, been a matter of relatively little concern. Some English schools, particularly perhaps those of a more academic nature, have, at least until recently, characteristically perceived themselves as places where various separate persons, who ought to be rational even if they are not always apparently so, meet together for the primary purpose of developing their minds.

The influence on schools of humanism, and particularly of humanist psychology, is a relatively recent phenomenon. But it is a considerable one. It has also been accompanied by some controversy.

Humanist-inspired thought and research has played a significant part in moves to child-centred education. At best, this involves a concern to understand how children learn, and to match classroom activities, together with teaching methods and materials, to students' developing needs and abilities. At worst, it leads to the pursuit of process at the expense of content, to the apotheosis of the 'how' of education at the expense of the 'what'.

The provision of pastoral care is a long-standing tradition of English education, albeit one that from time to time has been submerged or ignored. The motivation to provide it was frequently religious, as the term itself indicates. More recently, however, humanist-influenced approaches, particularly deriving from humanist psychology, have made their own significant contributions. Humanism has done this through offering its own perspectives on the nature and needs of children, and through suggesting relevant curricular and pastoral strategies. Where such approaches have remained isolated, and have not been fully integrated into overall school approaches, they have sometimes been charged with lacking effectiveness.

Humanists have been active in any consideration of the place of religious education and worship in schools. Their contributions, while certainly distinctive, have only occasionally been provocative. Indeed, humanists have frequently worked together with members of religious faiths in questioning the spiritual propriety of the notion of compulsory worship; and in seeking to secure that religious education is just that, and not simply initiation into particular dogmas, doctrines and practices.

In the debate over the extent to which schools can justifiably promote the religious idea of what a person is, humanists have claimed to speak for a fairly wide constituency. Just as there are apolitical people, so there are those who are areligious, whether lapsed, sceptical, atheist, agnostic or simply uninvolved. Addressing themselves to many of these, if concerned with education, humanists have articulated positions on the teaching and practice of religion in schools which have sought to clarify views about what schools should be attempting to achieve (see, for example, the 1995 pamphlet by the British Humanist Association, *Education for Living: A Humanist Perspective*).

Humanism brings optimism to education, and that is perhaps its greatest contribution. Believing, as it does, that all individuals are innately good and, moreover, that they each have their own unique gifts, it strongly believes that education has both the obligation and the capacity to help students develop as fulfilled and moral members of society.

Ultimately, humanism holds a democratic rather than an elitist ideal of personhood. For this it has been attacked, sometimes directly, more often indirectly. However, it is hardly surprising that such a notion of a person has come to find a place in the theory and practice of modern education.

English schools, as I have already discussed, have traditionally done very little to educate students as economic beings. However, compared with even the recent past, the scene is changing with gathering speed. School aims and objectives often talk of the economic development of students. In personal and social education, pre-vocational and other courses, in tutorial programmes, and through cross-curricular links, ways are explored, with admittedly varying success, of promoting economic knowledge and understanding. And work experience, increasingly related to the curriculum, is now usually provided for all students. Schools do now accept and, for the most part take seriously, their obligation to the individual and to society to encourage personal economic development. However, few if any would claim to have evolved all-round successful practice. Good in parts, like the curate's egg, is probably the best that can realistically be claimed.

The working model is, essentially, concerned to provide an ideal which takes full account of the actual characteristics of young people, and which reflects the broader shared values, explicit and implicit, in current approaches to education.

The notion, crucial to the working model, that students should develop as whole persons, spiritually, morally, socially, culturally, mentally and physically, now appears, in one form of wording or another, in the aims of the great majority of schools. However, sometimes, that is where the matter rests. Much can remain to be done, at least as far as the structure and management of the curriculum and pastoral care is concerned, to ensure that students may indeed have reasonable opportunities to develop as complete persons.

Perhaps the most evident influence of the working model is to be seen as a result of the emphasis it places on the person as learner. Both in primary, and increasingly in secondary schools, subject content and method, as well as assessment procedures, attempt to take into full account the nature of learning. This has, at times, led to an under-estimation of the importance of the logic and disciplines intrinsic to particular subjects. Hence there are sometimes reservations expressed about child-centred education – however, it must be said that these can arise from an instinctive rejection of the idea that young people should be anything other than passive recipients of knowledge, the wax upon which the pedagogue inscribes.

Imagination and creativity, insofar as they are implicitly or explicitly recognized as part of the learning process, nowadays usually, but by no means inevitably, find some place in the curriculum. They are most likely to be discovered in art, English and drama, but also, where the teaching is lively, may be found across a range of other subjects and courses.

Nevertheless, ingrained habits die hard. The once overwhelming influence of the rational ideal of a person still inclines many schools to envisage imagination and creativity not so much as fundamental personal attributes but rather as luxury extras, to be acquired from peripheral and often optional timetable activities, and indulged in once the really serious learning has taken place elsewhere.

School nature and ethos

The ideals of a person held by a school are significantly influenced by its nature and ethos. Thus, schools with particular religious foundations will intend to educate students as good Christians, Jews, Muslims, and so forth. Public, and some other longer established, schools are likely to nurture both Christian and classical ideals. Schools selecting on the basis of academic ability will be inclined, at least implicitly, to place a fairly high value on the belief that persons should aspire to be rational beings. Comprehensive schools frequently emphasize the importance of educating the whole person.

More generally, any school which is fee-paying, whatever its other ideals, will more probably find itself in tune with economic, and more specifically free-market, notions of a person than one which is not. On the other hand, non-fee-paying schools will tend to see the virtues of humans as social creatures, dependent on and contributing to society.

Where schools cater for students of particular social, cultural, faith or even economic backgrounds they often serve relatively homogeneous communities or groups. Under these circumstances, one might assume that it should be fairly straight-forward to define and organize education in such a way that it helps a school to fulfil particular ideals of a person. Specifically, one would expect that one or two ideals would be identified and attract general support, and that other ideals would be adopted so as to play a complementary role, or would be marginalized or rejected.

In practice, to a certain extent, this is what does often occur. Thus, for instance, in a Roman Catholic school, the Christian notion of a person will usually in reality, as always in theory, act as a unifying ideal for all who work in that community.

However, in an open society a school cannot, any more than an individual, be an island 'entire of itself'. For a start, the way it has evolved will have been influenced, not only by the character of its foundation, but also by external forces. Whatever the dominant ideal, differing notions of a person will be found to feature even in the most tightly controlled curriculum, to be alive even within the most orthodox ethos.

And this is as it should be. While there is every justification to teach in the light of certain beliefs, indeed to do so is a characteristic of all good schools, education can have nothing to do with any approaches motivated by an intention to impose or inculcate particular doctrines.

Schools, as well as making their own stance clear, need to help students to look outwards. Whatever their founding and guiding principles, schools should acknowledge the range of ideals which different people hold regarding the ends of being; and they should offer students a balanced insight into the ideas of a person that are valued by those with experiences or perspectives which may be in contrast to their own. Where this is not done, there can be little worthwhile education in respect for persons.

Perhaps the greatest opportunities, and by the same token the greatest dangers, in educating students to respect persons lie not so much with those schools which select their students, on whatever grounds, or with those which in some sense offer a special or distinctive curriculum and ethos, but with those schools which in principle and practice aim to provide for all the children, and the children of all families, in their area.

The direct influence of classical civilization, and to a lesser extent of Christian faith, on our culture and education is fading away. As this process, regretted by some, welcomed by others, gathers pace, it is gradually becoming apparent that it is through comprehensive schools that there now begins to flow the mainstream of educational traditions and present-day concerns. It is in these schools, with their commitment to a contemporary inclusiveness of culture, mind and society, that can be most fully manifested the full range of perceptions of human nature – what it is, what it is capable of becoming, and what it should be – which our civilization has inherited and which it is exploring.

At best, comprehensive schools provide that richness and variety of understanding of persons which is the foundation upon which any education of quality has to be built. From such schools can come students who are learning a real respect for themselves and for others, arising from informed understanding of how many and valuable are the ways of being to which individuals may aspire.

But, where comprehensive schools fail to realize what they can and should achieve in encouraging respect for persons, the results are often dismal. Such schools can damagingly lack belief in the importance of what they are doing and in their capacity to succeed. Here, amidst apathy and confusion, students can be counted lucky if they achieve even a blurred vision of what it means to be, and how to become, a worthwhile person.

For all schools, whatever their nature, the challenge is to create institutions and communities with the knowledge and confidence to enable students truly to learn to respect persons, self and other.

CHAPTER 7

The whole truth

'The absence of respect for truth seems to me one of the greater casualties of the modern world.' So said a recent Archbishop of Canterbury (Runcie, 1990). It would be hard to dissent from his judgement.

If the contemporary curriculum is to have a good opportunity of effectively encouraging genuine and informed respect for truth it must be put together, organized, taught and learned in the context of an informed understanding of those forces (whatever they may be) which are liable to undermine it.

The attack on truth

Attacks on truth are mounted by various forces. Amongst these, two groups are of particular significance. The first operates informally. Its members consist of those individuals who, through their actions, reveal that they have little concern for truth as a guide for behaviour. The second favours more systematic and overt tactics: from differing theoretical perspectives, the meaningfulness and value of the notion of truth are challenged.

As can happen in conflict, the effectiveness of assaults may be diminished by some apparent ambivalence amongst the assailants. Thus, those whose behaviour is consistently or profoundly deceitful may publicly subscribe to the importance of valuing truth. Conversely, those with philosophical doubts about truth may personally be models of probity. In their different ways, personal hypocrisy and private virtue may well result in a certain weakening of attacks on truth. In the long run, however, a secure belief in the importance of truth is hardly likely to survive simply because some inconsistencies may exist among those who, for whatever reasons, wish to undermine that belief.

There are cases where truth, while being respected, may be modified for the sake of what is seen, in particular circumstances, as a greater good. This is, of course, familiar territory for ethical debate. Thus, one may argue that it is justifiable to withhold from an ill child, frightened of death, the fact that she is suffering from an incurable disease. It is surely hardly reasonable to identify a temporary subordination of truth to a course of action explicable in terms of concern for the well-being of others with any sustained undermining of the notion of truth as such. There can be no sustained and effective attack where there is no hostile intent.

In detail, different aspects of truth are attacked; motives vary accordingly.

As we all know only too well, some people in both private and public life are capable of lying to get their own way, or to cover up any wrong-doing. They can also convince themselves that what they believe is true, even if there is apparently little evidence to support them. So far as private individuals are concerned, some psychologists have described such perception as 'narrative truth', i.e. that is true of their personal experience which people believe to be true, irrespective of the facts. This has been contrasted with 'historic truth', i.e. that is true of individuals' past personal experience which corresponds with what are generally accepted to be the established facts and circumstances. The way in which the value of truth can be overridden and justified by the need for the effective psychological functioning of the individual has been documented in detail by Philip Rieff (1966, 1975).

Public bodies can also seem to believe their own, what can appear to some others, idiosyncratic versions of the truth. Executives of McDonald's, for example, have apparently sincerely upheld the view that the food they sell is nutritious. They have, nevertheless, been contradicted by various experts and, in some American states, officially ordered to cease from advertising their food as nutritious. People can come to have faith in their own advertising, or even propaganda. While the line is thin between intentionally deluding others and unknowingly deluding oneself, it would nevertheless be unrealistic to deny that it can exist.

While to the detached observer self-deception may often seem inexplicable, or even bizarre, certain motives, even although in the nature of the case inevitably unconscious, can in fact make quite good sense. Thus, a sufficiently strong commitment to one's own particular version of the truth may well lead, especially if supported by a helpful arrangement of supporting evidence, to others coming to share it. Where this does happen, the rewards, whether personal or not, can be considerable. So, for example, false allegations or denials of sexual abuse may come to be credited. Or a food retailer may succeed in convincing its customers that the company has their well-being at heart, and so succeed in selling more goods.

Truth suffers where its problematic nature is over-emphasized. The motive for doing this may be to provide, by way of a smokescreen, a defence for untruthful behaviour. Thus, government officials, faced with a need to justify alleged political dishonesty, may at times resort to raising doubts about the notion of truth. 'Truth,' suggested one civil servant in a notorious remark, in 1993, to the Scott inquiry into alleged government involvement in illegal arms dealing, 'is a very difficult concept.' Commented another, when asked, during the 1985 trial of Clive Ponting on secrets charges, whether ministers had a duty to give truthful answers to MPs, 'In highly charged political matters one person's ambiguity may be another person's truth.'

Obscuring the meaning of truth may arise unintentionally, and not out of malign intent, but from apparently quite reasonable motives. For whatever reasons, there is no doubt that interpreting what is meant by truth can cause difficulty.

Thus, the philosopher J. L. Austin has written that 'A statement is said to be true when the historic state of affairs to which it is correlated by the demonstrative conventions (the one to which it 'refers') is of a type with which the sentence used in making it is correlated by the descriptive conventions' (quoted in Hamlyn, 1970, p. 133). Austin's thesis has been described by D. W. Hamlyn, a fellow philosopher, as 'easy to state'. That may well be. It may also be that it throws light upon areas hitherto seen as dark by those professionally concerned with the interpretation of language. However, the argument, at least as formulated, is unlikely to be of much use to anyone other than those seriously interested in linguistic philosophy. Unfortunately, the use of technical terminology in debates about truth may have, at least in the short term, the effect of leading lay persons towards believing that a serious concern with truth is an arcane matter, quite possibly beyond them, and one which it is perhaps pointless to worry too much about.

And so, we reach the point where we need to consider systematic and speculative questioning of the nature and value of truth.

The main theoretical assaults on truth are mounted by those thinkers and schools of thought whose arguments, whatever their differing points of departure, all tend to lead to the conclusion that truth, for whatever reason, is 'relative'.

Thinkers whose influence has been strongest in relativizing truth, have included those who have attacked the traditional Western notion of the centred person. For these philosophers and intellectuals, neither truth nor persons exist as ends in themselves; rather, they are primarily perceived as dependent variables.

The notion that truth can be defined in terms of the interests of the state is perennially convenient for individuals and groups who wield political power. Those who hold such a belief owe much to Hegel. Debts of gratitude to him have been openly acknowledged by numbers of apologists for totalitarian regimes (and more discreetly by some democratic politicians).

Hegel considered that 'The state has, in general, to make up its own mind concerning what is to be considered as objective truth.' He reached this conclusion by equating the real with the rational, the so-called 'doctrine of identity'. Reality he saw as the state: 'The state is real.' He perceived the state as a conscious organism, endowed with free will: 'To the complete state belongs, essentially, consciousness and thought. The state knows what it wills.' What is real is not only rational, but necessary. Consequently, any action taken by the state must be moral, needful and self-evidently right: 'The state is the actually existing, realized moral life.' (All quotations are from *The Philosophy of Law*, except the last, which is from *The Philosophy of History*: detailed references given in Popper, 1966, vol. 2, p. 305, n. 8.)

However, this is only a part of the picture. Even states are more or less imperfect or unreal. But each is striving to become the embodiment of reality and reason, or as Hegel also put it, 'the absolute Idea'. The state is inescapably caught up in a dialectic struggle for survival and dominance. In this permanent condition of war, potential or actual, no holds are barred, for there exists no morality other than that dictated to each state by its own interest. The state which conquers comes, by virtue of the nature of the dialectic process, closer to reality. Hence it follows that 'might is right'.

Where does all this leave truth? 'Truth,' said Hegel in *The Philosophy of History*, 'is the unity of the universal and subjective will, and the universal is to be found in the state.' Or, as he expressed it in *The Logic*, 'This unity is the absolute and all truth, the Idea which thinks itself.' (Quotations given in Russell, 1954, pp. 761, 767.)

From these highly abstract notions certain practical consequences follow. First, since the truth is the whole, nothing which is not the whole can be wholly true. Secondly, states, on account of the collective unity of their nature, and amongst states the most powerful, are closest to embodying the truth. Consequently, the state is not only best placed, but has a moral duty, to define what is and is not true.

Strictly speaking, Hegelian truth, from a philosophic point of view, is absolute. But, historically it is partial, or as Hegel himself put it 'relative', because it is conceptualized in situations which are dialectically always more or less distant from the universal. More specifically, it varies in practice because it always has to be interpreted by states. It varies not only between states, but also within individual states over time and depending on circumstances, as the interests of the state dictate. However, the more powerful a state, the closer will it be to the unity of the universal will: hence, the more truthful are its interpretations of reality likely to be.

Marx, like Hegel, dismissed the idea of objective truth as commonly understood, and redefined it in his own terms. 'The question is,' wrote Marx in 1845, in the 'Eleven theses on Feuerbach' (in McLellan, 1977, p. 156), 'whether objective truth belongs to human thinking is not a question of theory, but a practical question ... The truth, ie. the reality and power of thought, must be demonstrated in practice.' What this implies is that an idea is only true if, having prompted action, that action can be demonstrated effectively to have promoted 'reality'.

Precisely what Marx meant by reality is notoriously difficult to pin down with any degree of precision. However, it is at least not seriously misleading if one thinks of it as dialectic progress through time, driven, not as for Hegel by spirit, but in the first instance by matter, and secondarily by mankind, in its necessarily dependent relationship with matter.

From such a premise it followed, as Engels wrote in a letter of 1890 (quoted in Williams, 1962, p. 260), that 'According to the materialist concept of history the determining element is ultimately the production and reproduction in real life.' In other words, the processes and relationships involved in economic activity provide the foundations of society in all its manifestations.

On this basic economic structure rises what Marx, in the 'Preface to a critique of political economy', (in McLellan, 1977, pp. 389–90) called 'a legal and political superstructure'. This, in turn, has corresponding 'forms of social consciousness', or 'ideological forms', specifically, 'the legal, political, religious, aesthetic or philosophic'.

Thus, what we have is a two-fold system, consisting of an economic structure, and a legal and political superstructure, together with its related ideological frameworks. It is with the latter, and particularly the philosophic form, that we are concerned.

It follows from what has been said that any philosophic forms, or what Marx also called, 'habits of thought and conceptions of life', are generated by 'the several forms of property ... the social conditions of existence' (quoted in Williams, 1962, p. 259). Thus, any ideas that classes, groups or individuals may have will inevitably have initially been received through mediums, in particular 'tradition and education', totally dominated by and integrated with the economic groundwork of society. It may be that a person, or a 'unit' to use Marxist terminology, considers that his mental habits and conceptions 'constitute the true reasons and premises for his conduct'. If anyone did believe this, they would be suffering from an illusion, fantasizing, a victim of false consciousness. In the last resort, economic forces determine ideas, and hence any behaviour which is influenced by ideas.

All this suggests that, since there can be no such thing as genuinely free thought, any human initiatives resulting from beliefs, values, induction, deduction, interpretations of observed data, and so on, are likely at best to be not inconsistent with the current stage and direction of the material powers of production; at worst, they are likely to be more or less seriously, if impotently, mistaken. The former situation would be likely to arise where the thinker was a historically aware, conscious, member of a newly emerging class, say, the proletariat; the latter where the thinker was a falsely conscious member of a class threatened by a transformation of the economic foundations from which it derived its identity and power, say, the bourgeoisie.

In fact, in Marx's view, this is not entirely the case. Particularly as Marx's and Engels' thought developed, reflective reason and any resultant initiatives came to be viewed as operating within, and having the capacity to make some positive contribution to, the complex, subtle, evolving and multi-dimensional field of human activity. As Engels, in the letter already quoted above, put it, 'Political, legal, and philosophical theories, religious ideas and their further development into systems of dogma ... exercise their influence upon the course of historical struggles.' While no such notions could in the long run divert the general course of history from its inexorable progress towards socialism, they could exercise significant influence. For better, or for worse, they could facilitate or distort the onward path of history towards its preordained future.

So it comes about that truth, for Marx, is simply a practical matter. Insofar as a concept of what is true is part of any intellectual system, it must in the final analysis be defined in terms of materialist determined structures, forces and relationships. However, since beliefs, theories and ideas can lead to actions which have meaningful effects, then notions of truth can also play a part in the world of current affairs. Ideas which approximate least misleadingly to truth are those which are seen to bring closer the dawn of socialism.

Truth is, at least to some degree, an element in those ideas which promote materialist progress. Falsehood, on the other hand, is reflected in those ideas which oppose it. Marxist truth is relative in the sense that it changes in line with the requirements of given circumstances in any particular stage of the class-based dialectic of history. Truth is what those with the most scientifically accurate grasp of history say that it is at any given moment.

The Marxist perception of the nature of truth is neatly illustrated by the attitude adopted by most communist parties to publication in general, and to the press in particular. The press must be concerned with truth. Indeed, the organ of the communist party in the former Soviet Union was called *Pravda* ('Truth'). But this truth does not imply the objective reporting of facts. This is mostly opposed. Truth is interpreted as requiring the presentation of information in such a way as to further the progress of socialism; and more specifically, to serve the interests of those particular individuals or groups, either wielding or seeking power, who see themselves as best placed to ease the advance of history. Thus, it was entirely consistent with a Marxist view of the duty of a press serving the interests of truth that *Pravda* should have supported, by propaganda amongst other means, a putsch intended to overthrow the recently established liberal democracy of Russia, and to replace it with a communist government. That same liberal democracy was perhaps less true to its own beliefs when it suspended *Pravda*.

In parenthesis, it is necessary to mention the debate about sociology and values. One of Marx's most fruitful insights, and one which was revolutionary at the time it was made, proved to be his perception that the social environment was a critical factor in influencing not only behaviour, but also belief. In the wake of Marx (and also of Comte, of the ultimately less influential social Darwinism of Herbert Spencer, and of others), emerged the new discipline of sociology. The part played by institutions in the promotion and maintenance of social cohesion and unity was explored by Durkheim and his followers.

The massive body of research and controversy associated with the whole range of sociological work has sometimes been interpreted as, in the general tendency of its assumptions and findings, promoting a relativist approach to values. Certainly, numbers of sociologists have been or are Marxist or neo-Marxist in their approach. For these, and no doubt for some others, values, including the concept of truth, are relative in a materialist sense.

However, in the context of the present argument, sociological enquiry is not seen as necessarily, either on account of its premises or of its methods, leading to the conclusion that truth is relative. Of course, sociologists may investigate the effect of social structures, functions, conditions, and experience on the formation of values; and they may, following Levi-Strauss and others, enquire into how far the *mentalités* or ideologies generated by a society can develop from epiphenomena into independent, guiding, even coercive systems of thought, in their turn playing a less or more active role in influencing society and its individual members.

All this can assist us in seeing the subtlety and complexity of the way in which moral concepts, such as truth, can develop within and come to effect human behaviour and social environment. Such sociological enquiry does not, however, in any way establish as inevitable the relativity of truth. Indeed, not only is it perfectly feasible for practising sociologists to hold beliefs, whether philosophic or religious, which at the least countenance the possibility of objective truth; but the commitment of sociology as a rational, intellectual discipline to scientific methods of enquiry in itself should preclude the possibility of sociology being seen as, of its nature, subversive of that aspect of truth concerned with respect for facts.

An epigram of Nietzsche's holds that 'Truths are illusions which one has forgotten are illusions.' This challenging dictum, which would probably have found favour with both Hegel and Marx, has certainly been looked on with approval by structuralists.

For Derrida and others, language is the actuality which reveals meaning. Linguistic reality is interpreted as being a self-referential, internally related and enclosed system. The intricate patterns and movements of words, *le jeu des signifiants*, occur on a field of play entirely cut off and isolated from the ordinary world.

Language, therefore, is not understood as being owned by the people who commonly use it, as arising from the exigencies and contexts of daily life, as emerging from incarnate existence as part of a persisting effort to make sense of, and come to practical and moral terms with, the human and natural world of phenomena. Rather, language forms a separate universe in terms of which, for those who have the expertise, real meaning can be established.

In such a scheme of things facts have no primary significance or integrity. They are there to be shifted about, toyed with even, so that they may become intelligible in the light of autonomous language. In this situation it would hardly be rational to attempt to establish a correlation between observed fact and belief. Consequently, respect for evidence becomes extremely difficult, if not impossible, to defend.

Post-structuralists, in fact, show little sign of concern for truth. They are not, therefore, really bothered about attempting to define, or to redefine it. Whether or not it may be understood as relative is hardly an issue. For them it is a concept of marginal significance; it is not really worth the effort of trying to adapt its meaning to their own perception of authenticity. As deconstruction proceeds, so truth happens to become an incidental casualty, a sad relic from an era of European philosophy, religion and civilization which has had its day.

But why do some thinkers postulate essences, whether spiritual, material or linguistic, whose natures as variously manifested lead, among other things, to a questioning, a relativizing, a destabilizing of accepted notions of truth?

In the kingdom of philosophy there are Queensberry rules which lay down that, in the event of combat breaking out the contestants should confine themselves to rational argument. In particular, any form of personal attack, of *argumentum ad hominem*, is frowned on.

Nevertheless, not even philosophers are above temptation. From time to time they do indulge in doubtful practices. In particular, they are prone to question each other's motives.

It has been argued that Hegel, Marx and the post-structuralists have all, in different ways, been affected in the development of their thought by self-interest. Thus, Karl Popper (1966, vol. 2, pp. 34–5) argued with regard to Hegel, 'We have more than sufficient reason to suppose that his philosophy was influenced by the interests of the Prussian government by which he was employed.' Popper went on to interpret Hegelianism mainly 'as an apology for Prussianism'.

Marx, existing in a political wilderness far, far outside any ruling circle, was in no way subject to the enticements which lurked for Hegel. However, by the very nature of his concerns he was almost bound to be deeply interested in, even fascinated by, the exercise of civil power. Some evidence, at least, including correspondence with Engels, suggests that he was not above seeing the proletariat, whose necessarily emerging strength he himself had identified, as a vehicle for his own advancement (Schwarzschild, 1986). Whatever Marx's motivation, there is no doubt that many theoreticians who followed in his footsteps, from Lenin onwards, revealed an ability to develop political and moral theory as a springboard to personal power.

As for the post-structuralists their inclination, despite their individuality, to see themselves as part of an exclusive set has been remarked on often enough. Iris Murdoch (1992, p. 208), for instance, has suggested that initially, 'The motives, or ideals, of structuralism have as their nemesis or accompaniment the wish to establish oneself as a member of an elite.' She sees the original intellectual desire to explore the nature of reality metamorphosing into a predominantly psychological drive to secure an esoteric, perhaps almost shamanistic status; to be admired, even envied, as something like a thaumaturge for our modern times. 'Here,' says Iris Murdoch, 'the search for truth becomes a search for magic formulae and the seeker desires to become a privileged initiate of a secret cult, a sorcerer or *pharmakeus*.' This, she points out, 'is a form of a familiar and enduring style of thought, Gnosticism, knowledge as power'.

Attacks on truth of metaphysical origin may in part be discredited or their impetus diminished by querying the good faith of the assailants. However, in the final analysis, these offensives arise from perceptions of reality at odds with those which sustain conventional and traditional views of truth. When it comes to counteracting the arguments of those who question the value and meaning of truth it may be that the best form of attack is defence. Truth is liable to suffer weakness, and to get progressively weaker, unless we clearly understand and can effectively justify both what it is and the reality in which it is grounded.

Ideas of truth

Confidence in truth ultimately depends on a sound grasp of, and a commitment to, what should be understood by ideas of truth. Further, it requires an awareness of how truth may be verified, and of the nature of the reality which may underlie it. While truthfulness, i.e. faithfulness to truth, may well arise instinctively, and needs to be maintained by acts of will, it is more likely to be secure where it is informed by relevant knowledge.

The main theories of truth may be stated simply. The *correspondence theory* proposes, in Bertrand Russell's words (1946), that 'A belief is true where there is a corresponding fact, and is false where there is no corresponding fact (p. 129) ... truth consists in some form of correspondence between belief and fact' (p. 121). This is, of course, the common-sense criterion of truth. It is a bedrock definition, embedded in everyday language, and as such fundamental to ensuring a realistic, normal contact with truth. It serves most people, from children to adults, reasonably well. The cry, 'But it isn't true!' is generally accepted to mean – give or take the odd qualification – that a statement fails to correspond with fact.

The *coherence theory* concerns, in Hume's phrase, the 'relation of ideas'. In this context, ideas deal with *a priori* propositions of mathematics and logic. Here, a belief is true where propositions are mutually consistent.

The *metaphysical theory* can be variously formulated. I will deal mainly with Platonic and Christian ideas, since it is these which have been most influential in education. For a Platonist, the supreme form of the Good is ultimate reality and truth. All unembodied forms derived from the Good, together with the embodied and particular instances which are more or less flawed reflections of such forms, are true only insofar as they partake of the One form.

For a Christian, a metaphysical belief is true to the extent that it is infused with and reflects divine reality, itself both Being and Truth, the Augustinian *esse ipsum, verum ipsum* (Being itself, Truth itself).

These theories are just that. They have to be viewed in the light of a range of reservations. Thus, correspondence theory has been called, in Karl Popper's words (1983, p. 181), 'a strangely elusive idea'. As debate from Locke to Wittgenstein demonstrates, perhaps the main problem lies in defining with sufficient clarity the nature of propositions and facts, and so their interrelationships. The less well defined these matters are, the less reliable will be any correspondence claimed.

The coherence theory, it is generally agreed, is watertight if tested simply in terms of the analytic and logical relationships between propositions, or between component premises and conclusions. Where doubts do emerge they arise from a questioning of the theories of reality which sustain the propositions and associated concepts employed. So, for example, are logical and mathematical truths discovered or invented? Do they derive from a universe of Platonic ideas, or can they, in some sense, be derived from the material world? These questions, and the differing answers to which they give rise, ensure that propositional truth cannot be grounded in anything like absolute certainty. Nevertheless, for both practical and theoretical purposes, the truths of mathematics and logic work remarkably well. That is quite sufficient for all except the purest of academics.

Metaphysical theories of truth, whether Platonic or theological, have been widely dismissed, in particular by those influenced by logical positivism. It is argued that the term 'truth' can only properly be used in connection with statements of belief that are in principle either empirically verifiable (i.e. 'correspond'), or logically justifiable (i.e. 'cohere'). A proposition that fails to meet these conditions can not ever be described as true in any sense. It must, as A. J. Ayer (1936) argued in the preface to the first edition of *Language, Truth and Logic*, be metaphysical, and 'Being metaphysical, it is neither true nor false, but literally senseless.'

One can, then, place question marks against the various theories of truth. Nevertheless, we have not yet reached a point where there is a generally accepted view that they lack viability. Accordingly, we can now go on to ask how, in any particular case, we could find out whether any belief is true or false – or, in other words, to discover how to verify a given proposition.

Verification has been described as a search for certainty. This is one of those journeys where one needs to travel hopefully. The difficulties start with the nature of persons as observers and interpreters of experience, whether sensory, emotional or spiritual. Humans are fallible, and remain so, however stringent the precautions taken to save them from themselves. 'It must be admitted,' said Descartes (1968b, p. 169), 'that the life of man is very often subject to error in particular cases, and we must, in conclusion, recognize the infirmity and weakness of our nature.'

Nor can our environment, whether artificial or natural, be regarded as wholly dependable. For instance, if we rely on it to support our research, it may let us down. To take just one example, even demonstrations of logical or mathematical truth can be falsified by computer error.

Much more fundamentally, the universe is unpredictable. Of course, for practical purposes, many expectations of the future have to be, and can be, relied on. And some predictions, for example that the sun will rise or objects fall to earth, are regarded as so secure that we come to look upon them as governed by laws. Nevertheless, any scientific truth which is established in relation to a particular set of facts and circumstances will not necessarily always remain true. For the disposition of the facts, and the nature of the circumstances may, in due course, change.

Furthermore, because persons are by nature valuing and evaluating creatures they can never succeed, however hard they may try, in entirely detaching themselves from the values they hold, or which, viewed from another perspective, may be considered to hold them. Our values inescapably influence both what we choose to observe and how we observe it. 'In deciding what the initial data are, we are working with values. Value goes right down to the bottom of our cognitive situation' (Murdoch, 1992, p. 384).

And value inheres not only in ourselves, but in our world. In the first place, the wealth and infinity of its facts, in all their multiple aspects and manifestations, force choice upon any person trying to make sense of it all. The essential nature of both person and world impregnate the relationship with value, and so with partiality.

Finally, all ideas; persons; facts; circumstances; and cultural, social and economic phenomena; together with their interrelationships; are encountered and interpreted through language. The language we use is value laden; and remarkably resistant to attempts to sterilize it. Language does not create bias; but it helps to integrate us irretrievably in the universe of values.

In the light of all this, verification of truth is unlikely to enjoy much success unless carried out with the greatest possible care. And even when this is done any findings, however apparently secure, need to be scrupulously reexamined over time, and as circumstances change.

So, let us now return to correspondence theory. Here, for a start, the inductive approach is out. According to this, it was believed that conclusions could safely be drawn from unbiased observation of value-free facts. Quite apart from the now recognized social-psychological naivety of this method, its reasoning procedures are suspect. Thus, an example might be, 'All crows observed were black; therefore all crows must be black.' The difficulty here is that, unless all crows have been observed, one or more may not be black.

The various problems so far discussed, as far as correspondence theory is concerned, are taken account of in the 'falsification' theory of Karl Popper (1959; 1966, vol. 2, p. 260). He accepts that any statement of belief, or hypothesis, can be no more than a 'crystallisation of a point of view'. This point of view may be the outcome of any number of processes, singly or in combination, for instance pure thought, reflection on observed facts, intuition, imagination, inspiration, etc. If empirical tests confirm the hypothesis, then the original proposition can be provisionally accepted as true. However, it cannot be accepted as wholly true, now and forever, because it only requires one finding that fails to correspond with the hypothesis for it to be disproved. A counter-instance is always possible both because the original experiment (or experiments where there has been replication) may have been flawed, or because circumstances relevant to the test have changed over time, or because of human error.

Truth as coherence is verified, through the use of logic, by establishing consistency between propositions. Thus, it may be demonstrated that a chain of mathemetical reasoning lacks inconsistencies: proofs, including proofs by contradiction, may be constructed, and so on. Verification, as required by coherence theory, may, but does not necessarily have to, involve considering the possible truth of first principles, or other related propositions. Where no attempt is made to verify axiomatic statements they may be regarded as purely formal. Provided the terms are defined, and agreed, they may be used in any structure of propositions. Of course, where this occurs, any conclusion demonstrated will be tautological; that is to say, its meaning will be entirely dependent upon and contained within the original premises.

Metaphysical truth, like the truth of coherence theory, cannot be tested by scientific methods. For a Platonist, it is primarily verified through the philosophic use of reason. Here, what is essentially attempted is a demonstration of the logical necessity of forms. Insofar as such arguments can be shown to be self-contradictory, then metaphysical truth in this system of thought has to be regarded as not established.

Where metaphysical truth is presented in theological terms it has long been recognized that significant problems arise where any efforts of verification are made. As the seventeenth-century divine Richard Hooker (1845, p. 470) expressed it, 'That which is seen by the light of grace, though it indeed be more certain; yet it is not to us so evidently certain as that which sense or the light of nature will not suffer a man to doubt of . . . I conclude, therefore, that we have less certainty of evidence concerning things believed, than concerning sensible or naturally perceived.'

Verification of religious truth is basically undertaken by, and for, those who are, in Paul Tillich's phrase (1953, vol. 1, p. 26, and chapter 1), in 'the theological circle'. Both the formulation and the acceptance of religious truth is essentially dependent, whether directly or indirectly, on faith and spiritual experience as interpreted within a given dogmatic framework. Thus, as regards Christianity, those who do not accept its teaching in some form (whether, for instance, because they are members of other faiths, or are agnostic, or atheist), are most unlikely, in fact are not really in a position, to accept the particular arguments of Christianity for religious truth.

Nevertheless, arguments for the truth of religious propositions are addressed to those outside as well as within the theological circle, and rightly so. Within the circle, believers need to know how to approach the task of distinguishing the real from the bogus, and of providing their faith with firm foundations. Outside the circle, the agnostic and the interested will be more likely to respect theological notions of truth, or to move towards personal acceptance of it, if they encounter reasoned consideration of the grounds on which it might be accepted. Finally, religious truth is hardly likely to earn proper attention in any discussion of the overall nature of truth if the ways in which it may be verified are not made explicit.

Theological truth may, in principle, be verified through those ontological and cosmological arguments (see, for instance, Davies, 1982, chapters 1, 4, 5) which seek to establish proofs of the existence of God, in whom is truth. It may also be apprehended through what is perhaps best described as intuition, a sort of halfway point between faith and revelation. For a Christian, intuition involves the exercise of rational, moral, emotional and spiritual attributes. In considering Cardinal Newman's theology his biographer, Ian Ker (1990, p. 645), interprets intuition as follows: 'It is the cumulation of probabilities, which cannot be reduced to a syllogism, that leads to certainty in the concrete. Many certitudes depend on informal proofs, whose reasoning is more or less implicit ... Such implicit reasoning is too personal for logic. The rays of truth stream through the medium of our moral as well as our intellectual being. As we gain a perspective of a landscape, so we personally grasp a truth with a "real ratiocination and present imagination".'

Ultimately, religious truth, certainly for a Christian, is made manifest through divine revelation. Disclosure may occur to persons, in scripture and the word, through history, or through nature.

How may one confirm whether or not a claimed revelation is authentic?

Revelation may be authentic where, when received personally, it seems so to transform the nature of the person's life that it appears an 'imitation of Christ'; or, in the case of Christ himself, a reflection of Divine Being.

Revelation may be authentic where, when recorded by word or in scripture, it seems to be validated by the various techniques of textual analysis.

Revelation may be authentic where, when emerging through history or nature, given events, facts, things or objects can be shown to prepare for the final revelation. In the sense used here, 'final revelation' is taken to mean the absolute manifestation of transcendent Being in Christ. From the time of Jesus, this revelation has been potentially open to all persons.

Clearly, actual verifications of metaphysical religious propositions can be, and frequently have been, challenged. Doubts are expressed not only from outside, but from within the religious circle. However, a point sometimes overlooked is that while theological truth cannot be conclusively demonstrated, there is no universal agreement that it can be convincingly disproved. In this respect, theological truth is not so very far from scientific truth. While the latter is not wholly secure because it may at any time be disproved, the former is not wholly insecure because it may at any time be proved.

The verification of statements, whether factual, logical or metaphysical, needs to be supported and confirmed through critical debate. Accordingly, propositions ought to be publicly stated, in terms that allow them to be verified as appropriate, and in language that minimizes the likelihood of misunderstanding.

The pursuit of truth is not only a personal, but also a social, activity. Individuals explore and propose. Groups appraise, suggest and affirm. This, of course, is not to go so far as to claim that a belief can only be true when it is accepted by those deemed trustworthy judges, or more widely by society at large. What has been called 'inter-subjectivity' is essentially a verification procedure.

The question now arises: are these theories of truth, together with their related methods of verification, associated with *one* reality, however differentiated and complex, or with various and not necessarily compatible realities?

Falsification theory has no direct bearing on this issue. That a proposition, once proved, may subsequently be falsified, does not necessarily mean that it will be. 'If an assertion is true,' says Karl Popper (1966, vol. 2, p. 221), 'it is true for ever.' On the other hand, even if a proposition is true for all eternity, we do not on that account know whether it is grounded in a unitary or in a plural reality.

The belief that all knowledge ultimately reflects a whole is deeply rooted in Western ways of thinking. Reflecting and reinforcing this perception of Being as One is the traditional European view of the nature of persons. This has always seen individuals as being endowed with a capacity, even a desire and a need, to understand all phenomena as facets of a single totality. Our modern culture inherits, often subconsciously, this interpretation of human psychology. We tend to have an initial expectation that what is, is ultimately One. 'The idea of a self-contained unity or limited whole is a fundamental instinctive concept,' writes Iris Murdoch (1992, p. 1). 'We see parts of things, we intuit whole things ... The urge to prove that where we intuit unity there really is unity is a deep emotional motive to philosophy, to art, to thinking itself. Intellect is naturally one-making. To evaluate, understand, classify, place in order of merit, implies a wider, unified system.'

Nevertheless, even leaving out of account relativist and post-modernist attacks on truth as such, considerable difficulties lie in the way of accepting that truth must be associated with a unitary view of reality. Such a view typically justifies, and is justified by, a metaphysical system of thought. Whether a system is, for instance, Platonic, Christian or Hegelian there are those who are not persuaded by the axiomatic propositions, together with the dependent or supporting chains of reasoning, which are needed to sustain these or similar structures of ideas.

Further objections arise insofar as it is quite possible to discover statements which, while verified according to particular theories of truth, are nevertheless apparently incompatible. Looking back on the intellectual history of his time, Noel Annan (1990, p. 277) suggested that 'Values collide and often cannot be made to run in parallel. And not only values. Propositions too. Truth is not a unity.' In fact, from whatever angle one approaches, reason can suggest that to sustain a view of reality as a whole is more likely to be founded on an act of faith than of intellect.

On the other hand, both psychologically and intellectually, there is a price to pay where ontological unity is denied. Psychologically, we can become disorientated, even feel a sense of disenfranchisement as persons, where the existence or possibility of oneness is queried or denied. 'We fear,' says Iris Murdoch (1992, p. 1), 'plurality, diffusion, senseless accident, chaos.'

Intellectually, in the absence of a belief in the coherence of reality, there is an ever-present danger that all forms of enquiry, including the academic, will come to be characterized by narrow-mindedness, dogmatism and timidity. Specialists, unable or unwilling to look beyond the boundaries of their particular interests, will be inclined to assume that the actuality with which they are working represents the only significant essence, and that by reference to its terminology all can be interpreted, or alternatively, dismissed. 'Doctors and philosophers,' wrote Rousseau (1953, p. 245), 'only admit to be true such things as they are able to explain; they make their own understanding the measure of all possibilities.'

The pursuit of truth requires an open mind. This is encouraged where there is a belief in the unity of existence, in that no phenomenon is likely to be dismissed as detached from significance. On the other hand, acceptance of plurality, while it well may, does not necessarily predispose one to a limited focus on one entity amongst many. It can develop a regard for the value of contrast and dissonance.

We need an open mind if we are to perceive hitherto unrealized connections. It is through these, whether analytic or artistic, whether within or across disciplines, that we can achieve new insights, and go on to establish worthwhile truth. It is truths that emerge from the recognition, or creation, of relationships, which are likely to transcend the mundane, and to illuminate understanding.

'Only connect,' wrote E. M. Forster. This ability is dependent on what persons know. We can only connect where we have concepts that can be connected. We therefore need to acquire knowledge. In this respect, the more restricted our knowledge, the less likely are we to become aware of, or to discover, significant truth.

However, with the best will in the world, there are limitations on the knowledge humans can acquire. It is not simply that, even where he knows of infinity, what an Einstein knows cannot be infinite. It is also that, notoriously, the explosion of knowledge in modern times makes it impossible, except perhaps at the highest levels of generality, to gain any sort of realistic overview of the major fields of human learning. The days are long gone when Mozart's father, Leopold, writing in 1770 to his wife from northern Italy, could report that he had encountered 'two gentlemen who in all respects have the same outlook, friendliness, placidity, and a special love for, and insight into, all branches of knowledge' (Anderson, 1989, p. 122).

It is, however, one thing to accept the obvious, the finitude of what we can know. It is quite another, in face of that recognition, to retreat into intellectual dead-ends where no worthwhile connections have a chance of being made, and where the only truths one can recognize are the trite and the tedious.

The initial fascination, and indeed necessity, of truth lies in the act, and the risk, of discovery. However rewarding, and rewarded, exploration of truth demands an understanding of truth in all its complexities, and of the whole truth.

CHAPTER 8

The true curriculum

The curriculum, as a whole, should provide, in intention and practice, an explicit and balanced treatment of ideas of truth. That is to say, objectives and activities, taken together, should give due regard, as it has been expressed, to 'the forms of enquiry and justification appropriate to different kinds of knowledge and experience' (Seminar, University of Cambridge Department of Education and King Abdulaziz University, Jeddah, 1993). In particular, there should be clear identification of correspondence, coherence and transcendental ideas of truth, and of possible ways in which they may be verified.

I do not intend to imply that the curriculum should be confined to teaching related to systems of thought and knowledge, of which truth is the first virtue. It should also be concerned with promoting other virtues, and in particular justice and responsibility. Accordingly, any well-balanced timetable, in addition to activities concerned with truth, should also deal with institutions, of which justice is the first virtue, and with community, of which responsibility is the first virtue.

Likewise, there are a range of expressive and practical activities which may, or may not, be justifiable in terms of the first educational virtues. Even if they are not, valid reasons for their inclusion in the curriculum can frequently be provided on a number of other grounds.

It follows from all this that there is no question of my intending to argue that a curriculum is only properly grounded where it can be demonstrably vindicated in terms of justifiable true belief. This is a necessary, but not sufficient, basis for a curricular rationale.

What I am suggesting is that schools have no option, whether morally or educationally, but to commit themselves to the teaching and learning of truth. This must be a major curricular obligation.

The battle of the truths

An explicit and balanced curricular approach to the teaching of truth can be difficult to achieve because, as I have argued in the previous chapter, schools have to contend with a pervasive climate of thought and action which disparages the value of truth. Further, even assuming that the general importance of teaching students to learn about truth is accepted, controversy is liable to arise over the weight which should be given to different ideas of truth. Such dispute, whether overt or covert, makes its own baneful contribution to inhibiting the thriving of a true curriculum. It is this question which I now wish to explore.

Initially, conditions exist for controversy, rather than for a fair-minded and amiable exchange of views about differing perspectives, because our sense of personal identity and worth can be inextricably involved with notions of truth. Thus, if I see myself above all as a rational individual, I will be likely to differ, in the nature of my commitment to, and perhaps even understanding of, different ideas of truth, from someone who, for example, sees himself or herself as a religious person. Further, as a rational creature, at least in my own eyes, and because I value being that sort of person, I may wish to persuade others to try and become rational persons. Conversely, if efforts are made to convert me to being a religious person, then I may well feel threatened, and resist. Here are circumstances with ample potential for conflict.

Disputes over the nature of truth have loomed large, and from the beginning, in the history of Western thought. They were certainly rife in classical Greece. Plato, in particular, was a notable polemicist. For him, truth was transcendent and coherent. The idea that truth might be concerned with any sort of correspondence between belief and fact was rejected. Consequently, scientific observation was deemed irrelevant to the pursuit of truth. 'If anyone tries to learn anything about the world of sense, whether by gaping upwards or blinking downwards, I don't reckon that the result is knowledge – there is no knowledge to be had of such things' (1955, pp. 297–8).

Artistic and creative approaches to truth were also rejected. In what Plato referred to as a 'long-standing quarrel between philosophy and poetry' the latter was condemned. In particular, Homer was to be excluded from the ideal Republic. As for architecture, art, sculpture and drama, they fared little better. The inexcusable error of all these artistic activities did not essentially lie in what they were mostly trying to achieve. For the leading dramatists and artists were, like Plato himself and indeed the Greeks generally, predominantly interested not so much in mere mimesis, a copying or representation of transient ephemera, as in, to quote Maurice Bowra (1957, p. 160), seeking out 'an abiding reality behind the gifts of the senses'. No, the difficulty in Plato's view was that any artistic or creative approach to truth was hopelessly and irredeemably flawed in its methodology. Painting, for example, on account of its use of such techniques as perspective, was dismissed as 'falling little short of witchcraft'. The senses could, at best, only perceive, and so evoke, a distorted reflection of ultimate reality; thus, any exploration of truth that depended on use of the senses would be bound to go off track. Only pure thought could hope to approach truth. Art, poetry, drama, even science, might usefully illustrate and support truths propounded by philosophy; but they could not have any sort of independent role.

Plato's view of truth was, ultimately, metaphysical. He perceived the

Good (even if he was not very specific about defining it) as the source of all reality. It was to be approached by reflection, contemplation and pure thought. Plato's follower, Aristotle, albeit deeply concerned with scientific observation and classification likewise, in the final analysis, held a metaphysical notion of truth. For him, real essence was to be intuited, not approached through any sort of empirical process.

With the advent of early Christianity, and in particular of theological thought, a second strand of metaphysical understanding became established in Western thinking. Here, truth was equated with, and seen as deriving from, the one, omnipotent and universal Godhead. From Augustine to Aquinas and beyond, truth was established, ultimately and above all, through divine revelation. In the absence of revelation truth was, at best insecure, at worst non-existent.

These metaphysical approaches to truth, albeit differing, did not initially prove irreconcilable. Indeed, they came to establish a long and comfortable joint hegemony. For over a thousand years, and especially through the universities of medieval Christendom, the congruent doctrines of neo-Platonism, of Aristotle, and of the theological Summa, reigned supreme. This was a universe of truth received, not observed.

With the Renaissance, however, came a subversive and enquiring turn of mind. In particular, there were now demands to know how this material world, in its astonishing diversity of manifestations, actually worked. And further, it was being asked whether such knowledge, once acquired, could be put to practical use for the benefit of mankind.

It was very clear that even Aristotelian reasoning, let alone Platonic rationality, or Christian revelation, were little interested in addressing issues of this nature; and insofar as they were, they were signally failing to come up with satisfactory answers.

Consequently, a different notion of truth, and of approaches to verifying it, began to be considered. Francis Bacon argued that Man was the servant and interpreter of nature. 'Gaping upwards or blinking downwards' were at last back in favour. For Bacon, truth was established inductively through the disciplined observation of systematically collected and organized data. It was this type of scientific thinking which Descartes (1968a, p. 78) had in mind when, anticipating the sort of utilitarian uses to which research findings would frequently be put, he wrote:

> Instead of the speculative philosophy taught in the Schools, a practical philosophy can be found by which, knowing the power and the effects of fire, water, air, the stars, the heavens and all the other bodies which surround us ... we might ... make ourselves, as it were, masters and possessors of nature. Which aim is not only to be desired for the invention of an infinity of devices by which we might enjoy, without any effort, the fruits of the earth and all its commodities, but also principally the preservation of health.

The search of Renaissance and Enlightenment thinkers for more satisfactory and differentiated notions of truth set the scene for the emergence of characteristically modern modes of thinking. Compatible with the Platonic-inspired tradition there developed the idea of truth as coherence, that is the notion that logical and mathematical statements are true where propositions are consistent. Also surviving, but beleaguered, was belief in truth as of divine origin. That is true which exists in the mind of God. But it is the notion of correspondence which has emerged as the dominant idea. Truth is held, above all, to emerge where fact and belief can be convincingly shown to match.

These ideas of truth are not, of course, held by everyone to be necessarily mutually exclusive. Nevertheless, each has attracted its camp following of active, indeed at times pugnacious, adherents. These are not necessarily always content simply to pursue their own paths to truth. Some of them, not infrequently, are given to mounting assaults on those whom they see as rival bands of truth seekers. So, scientists, as good empiricists, may attack a passing choir of theologians. Logicians and mathematicians, on a different flank, may have a go at the same quarry. Scientists and mathematicians have the occasional skirmish over the possible existence of pure forms. And philosophers, as is their wont, are liable to sally forth, behind diversionary smokescreens of concepts, against any one who looks vulnerable.

And all this is reflected in the curriculum.

As in the wider world, so in the school, one can readily detect signs of conflict over differing ideas of truth, over the value which should be placed on them, and over the priority they should be given.

In certain respects, these curricular conflicts can be viewed simply as replays, in a minor key, of the greater controversies. But they are much more than that. For it is only too well understood that the curriculum, for better or worse, influences minds, attitudes and values. Consequently, control of the curriculum can be used to promote particular beliefs, and not least those related to truth and its nature. What is taught to young people not only reflects, but is a critical element in, the struggles over truth.

One should not expect to find, if one considers the evolution of the curriculum as exemplified by its changing subject-matter and method, that any one theory of truth succeeds in establishing its kingdom at the permanent expense of others. For, at least from the perspective of the protagonists, the various verities are eternal; accordingly, it is hardly likely that any one idea of truth will be left entirely without its apologists. At worst, one might fear to discover an apparently endless battle of attrition, with fortunes swaying, but with no ultimate victor. At best, one could hope for some sort of arbitrated or agreed armistice, where at least those involved would agree to respect each other's territory.

From the earliest moments in the recorded history of the curriculum in the Western world we can start to trace the influence upon it of the changing priorities accorded by society to the different notions of truth. At the height of Greek civilization, prior to Plato and Aristotle, schools in fifth century Athens provided a common curriculum (Castle, 1961, part 3). This was open to, and as a rule attended by, all the sons (but not the daughters) of free citizens. While a basic grasp of the three Rs was taught, the main emphasis was on poetry, drama, art, music and physical education. All Athenian citizens learned in detail and depth about their cultural heritage, and about how to perform, create and evaluate in a wide range of artistic activities. Above all, they learned that by trained and sophisticated use of the senses and the emotions it became possible to seek out and to express the nature of the underlying, true reality.

The Platonic counter-reformation eventually led to the predominance of a very different sort of curriculum. It focused on intellectual and moral capacity. While it gave, in theory, equal rights to male and female (a principle followed in practice by very few Platonist educators), it was otherwise elitist and selective. In the Republic, only the guardian caste qualified for any education worth the name, and only the brightest and best survived the full course. Classes other than the guardians were taught how to ply their more or less menial trades, and to obey the laws and other edicts of the state as laid down by the rulers.

The Platonic curriculum found no place for any empirical or investigative activity. While the term 'science' was mentioned, its function was simply to illustrate or demonstrate what had been discovered by logical thought. Similarly, the arts, literature, drama and poetry were rigorously censored, and relegated to an extremely restricted supporting role.

By contrast, the study of mathematics was given a high priority. Indeed, above the entrance to Plato's Academy were inscribed the words, 'Let no man enter who knows no geometry.' Above all, however, the curriculum was concerned to educate the intellect so that those few who proved to have the capacity might 'look straight at reality, and at the brightest of realities, which is what we call the Good' (Plato, 1955, p. 283). This, in the final analysis, was a curriculum designed to enable those who followed it to achieve, through exercise of the mind and of virtue, the intellectual contemplation of transcendental truth.

The Platonic curriculum, in some respects given a rather more civilized veneer by the Aristotelian emphasis on education as 'liberal and noble activity', became over the succeeding centuries the standard model. Following the rise of Christianity, the ecclesiastical authorities, who controlled virtually all of education up to the Renaissance, and who continued at the least to influence much of it subsequently, found little difficulty in evolving a curriculum on the basis of Platonic thinking. During the medieval period it taught 'the seven liberal arts', logic, grammar and rhetoric, together with arithmetic, geometry, astronomy and music. The latter, consisting as it did mainly of a training in the performance of divine praise, safely subordinated education of the senses to the fulfilment of spiritual purpose. The grand educational aim was to train students, according to their social position and spiritual and intellectual capacity, in contemplation of the nature of divine being as realized in the Holy Trinity of God the Father, God the Son, and God the Holy Spirit. This was a curriculum founded in a belief in metaphysical truth, both divine and rational, and designed to secure and spread that belief.

Following the Renaissance, and right up to the present day, the curriculum can be seen as a battleground where wave after wave of assaults have been mounted on the sorts of courses of study derived from the philosophies of medieval Christendom, and of classical Greece.

The major stronghold in English education of the traditional curriculum has historically been found in the public schools. Through much of the nineteenth and twentieth centuries these represented a late idiosyncratic, but nonetheless robust, flowering of neo-Platonism. What they taught was a splendid edifice of knowledge, balancing impressively if precariously on the twin pillars of respect for revealed and rational truth.

This curriculum was buttressed, not simply by the strength of the public schools as such, considerable in social and economic terms though this was, but by the nature of the education system as a whole. At the height of its influence, the public school curriculum both embodied a neo-Platonic notion of truth and was at the apex of a more or less coherent hierarchy of schools designed to educate the whole school-age population in accordance with the principles of rational and theological hierarchy, at least insofar as this was possible in late imperial Britain rather than in twilight imperial Athens, or medieval Christendom.

Thus, any attack on the public school curriculum, to have any chance of serious success, also had to be an attack on the whole system. At this point, I am only concerned with the curriculum. However, it would be unrealistic not to acknowledge that curriculum and system were linked. Each formed, philosophically and educationally, part of a single entity.

It followed from this, first that, since it was integrated into one conceptual and social whole, any changes to the public school curriculum would be very slow in coming. For it would not be simply a matter of altering courses, but of redirecting and redesigning the sum total of the national educational arrangements through which were planned to flow those streams of thought intended to irrigate the minds of the young. It also followed that when changes did eventually arrive they would be accompanied by a gradual transformation of the national organization of education.

Thus, as one approaches the contemporary scene, one increasingly finds that an emerging modern curriculum is supported by a different system of education. In place of the old hierarchy, hesitantly and with large exceptions but nevertheless perceptibly, one sees the public schools becoming academies for the brighter offspring of an ambitious plutocracy; and the former elementary, secondary modern and grammar schools coalescing, albeit in the face of substantial opposition from the old order, into comprehensives, institutions which can perhaps best be understood as aspiring to become communities of students of all classes and abilities.

Particularly as developed from the late eighteenth century onwards, the major features of the traditional curriculum which have been subject to attack have been:

- first, the absence, or at best minimal presence, of any *enquiry-based*, and more specifically *scientific*, teaching;
- secondly, the general downgrading of the *arts*;
- thirdly, the central emphasis on the *transcendental*, in particular when perceived as Christian divinity;
- and finally, the reluctance to provide for *practical*, including *technological*, subjects.

Demands that the curriculum should include *science*, and more generally *enquiry-based* activities, grew in urgency and frequency from the earliest period of the Enlightenment. In certain areas of education, these were heeded. Thus, by the time Victoria came to the throne, science was a normal part of the curriculum in most private and dissenting academies, and in many grammar schools (Wiener, 1985, p. 17).

In the socially dominant public schools, however, it was a very different story. Here, the *a priori* approach continued to dominate. Throughout the nineteenth century, and in many cases well into the twentieth century, the introduction of science on to the timetable was strenuously opposed, or at best allowed on sufferance. The much-admired headmaster of Rugby, Thomas Arnold, gave a flavour of prevailing attitudes when he wrote to a friend, 'Rather than have physical science the principal thing in my son's mind, I would gladly have him think that the sun went round the earth, and that the stars were so many spangles set in the bright blue firmament' (quoted by Strachey, 1934, p. 188).

In public schools, and indeed in the many others of all types where science was regarded with suspicion, the subject eventually became well established. But it has been a long struggle which has lasted almost, and some would argue right up to, the present time.

Opposition to teaching empirical approaches in establishing truth centred on efforts to prevent, or to marginalize, the establishment of the sciences in the timetable. But hostilities were not confined to this sector of the curriculum. In any subject where they might justifiably be introduced, the teaching of research and enquiry methods was liable to be resisted on principle. So for instance the social sciences, unlike in numbers of other European and English-speaking countries, have never established more than a toehold in the timetable (see Hargreaves *et al.*, 1988, pp. 31–2, for a succinct summary of succeeding, post-1944 attempts, and their relative failure, to establish social studies on the timetable). Further, history and geography, until the influence of innovatory Schools Council Curriculum Projects began to be felt, were frequently simply taught as received wisdom. More generally, attacks, sometimes inspired by the press or politicians, were often made on the broad target of child-centred learning. While certain abuses undoubtedly existed, the hysterical and sweeping nature of some criticisms tended to undermine the very notion that children should be expected to think for themselves, to reach valid conclusions on the basis of evidence, and to justify findings.

The *arts* have, so far at least, had an even more difficult, and considerably less successful, struggle than science to establish themselves securely in the curriculum. And the basic reason for this is clear. While the various scientific disciplines could powerfully appeal to their own idea of truth, the arts could not.

Of course, in support of their cause, advocates of arts education can, and do, call on a range of arguments not directly concerned with the truthfulness of their subjects. Thus, to refer only to recent debate, a range of reasons have been offered in support of arts education. It encourages fuller human development, in particular intelligence and creativity (Robinson, 1989). It contributes to the development of multi-cultural understanding (Owusu, 1986; Willis, 1990). It helps in the education of feeling and the emotions (Ross, 1989). It should inform students about their own artistic heritage and that of other cultures; and it should encourage mastery of technique and the ability to perform (see, for instance, the National Curriculum Orders for Art and for Music, DFE, 1995).

Why do the arts have difficulty in appealing convincingly to a notion of truth?

The problem is not so much one of countering open denial that truth matters in art. Nor is it really, any longer, a matter of fighting professional, or even public, perceptions that any artistic truth is somehow a lesser truth, a distorted reflection at best of a greater verity.

The predominant difficulty lies in a different direction. It arises from the sheer multiplicity and richness of ideas of truth which can inspire art. Thus, there is, for instance, the notion that when contemplating human beings art should attempt to reveal what Wordsworth (1936, p. 734), in the preface to the *Lyrical Ballads*, called 'the primary laws of our nature'. Even more ambitiously, there is the almost mystical belief, articulated by, amongst others, Saul Bellow, in his Nobel lecture (1994, p. 93), that 'there is another reality, the genuine one, which we lose sight of. This other reality is always sending us hints, which, without art, we can't receive.' And such a credo can be associated with the view of the artist, not simply as an almost shamanic interpreter of ultimate reality, but as, in some sense, its creator. Deeply ingrained in the consciousness of the Western mind there is, as Kenneth Clark (1956, pp. 9–11) has expressed it, 'an instinctive desire not to imitate, but to perfect'.

In contradistinction to a perception of the artist as unique, universal interpreter, or creator, of transcendent actuality, there is the perception that art is to do with making sense, through disciplined observation, honest attention, scrupulous interpretation of the phenomena of existence. In Karl Gombrich's words, 'language does not give name to pre-existing things or concepts, so much as it articulates the world of our experience. The images of art, we suspect, do the same' (1960, p. 90).

Thus the very variety and dissimilarity of interpretations of artistic truth create problems for education. There is no sustained and systematic tradition that deals with the notion of artistic truth; or, more precisely, with the idea or ideas of truth that art may explore or exemplify.

All this substantially helps to explain why the arts have not been well placed to make a coherent and clearly focused case for their presence in the curriculum on the grounds of their truthfulness. Nor has there been much help in this regard from elsewhere. With few exceptions, neither philosophers, nor theologians, nor anyone else very much, have directed significant attention to art in their investigations and definitions of truth.

So, in the battle of the truths, the arts suffer. There have been some apparent advances; for instance, a widely welcomed government report (Department of National Heritage, 1996) recently advocated strategies for promoting the arts in schools. Nevertheless, the curricular case for the arts remains handicapped by the lack of its systematic and explicit attention to notions of truth.

A belief that truth is *transcendent* and *divine* is represented and explored in the curriculum predominantly through religious education. Characteristically, religious education is also concerned with related subject-matter, covering such issues as the religious beliefs, practices and lifestyles of Christianity and other major world faiths.

However, in the absence of any belief in, or at least acceptance of the possibility of, divine truth, it could be argued that the study of religion deals with little more than a curious, and possibly dangerous or delusory, cultural phenomenon (see, for example, an article by Richard Dawkins in the *Spectator*, August 1994).

And indeed, in a multi-cultural society such as ours, there are those who, since they cannot accept any notion of truth as emanating from God, at the least question the right of religious education to a place in the curriculum.

Although modern questioning of the validity of transcendental religious truth had its roots in the Enlightenment, and indeed in even earlier periods, the teaching of religion in the great majority of schools remained secure so long as religious bodies remained substantially in control of education.

However, as the state first became directly involved in the provision of education there began a questioning of the content and purpose of religious instruction (as it was then called); in due course, this developed into overt attempts, by some, to undermine the subject.

At the time of the first national legislation dealing with schools, the Education Acts of 1870 and 1902, it was taken for granted, with only rare exceptions, that all students should learn about religion. Compulsion was unnecessary, and so was not legislated for (see Murphy, 1971). The only real arguments, which admittedly could be ferocious, were over whether teaching in publicly provided schools should, or should not, be denominational. It was originally decided, by the so-called Cowper-Temple clause of the 1870 Act, that, in the newly created Board Schools, 'no religious catechism or religious formulary which is distinctive of any particular denomination shall be taught in the school'. This is a principle which, although initially frequently challenged, has, for county schools, and for grant-maintained schools which were formerly county schools, remained intact up to the present day.

However, circumstances had changed considerably by the time of the next great piece of national legislation concerned with education, the 1944 Act. Various subsidiary, but nevertheless important, issues had arisen. For example, there was anxiety about what should be the nature of religious education to be taught in those church schools which catered for all students in a particular district. The main issue, though, was not so much about what should be taught, although that still retained some of its former power to divide, but about what place, if any, the teaching of religion should be accorded in the curriculum.

Various diverse, and not necessarily mutually supportive forces, threatened the traditionally secure place of religious instruction.

First, there was the growing disaffection from organized religion, so characteristic of the twentieth as compared with the nineteenth century.

This might, but did not necessarily, involve a rejection of the spiritual values religion claimed to stand for. It did, however, incline many to view with distaste any denominational squabbling over the content of religious instruction.

Secondly, however, there was increasingly vocal, if not necessarily very widespread, hostility to religion on grounds of principle. This was usually, but not necessarily, stated in humanist or rationalist terms, (as, for example, in Bertrand Russell's *Why I Am Not A Christian*, 1957).

Finally, there was the long-standing liberal belief, originally articulated by John Stuart Mill, that all schools should have control over their own curricula, and that any state intervention should be resisted on the grounds that it would be likely to interfere with individual freedom. As the social consensus which had secured the place of religious instruction in schools began to disintegrate, the principle that schools should be free to chose what they taught clearly evoked the possibility that, institution by institution, religious instruction might fade from the timetable.

While R. A. Butler's education bill was being debated, there was considerable concern, and not only among Anglicans, Roman Catholics and Nonconformists, over the negative impact all this might have on the place in schools of the teaching of religion. It was one thing for adults to give up regular, or even all, religious observance. It was quite another to be faced with the prospect of present and future generations of children being educated in ignorance of the beliefs, practices and lifestyles of Christianity. 'There is, I think,' said Chuter Ede, the parliamentary secretary to the Board of Education, in the parliamentary debate on the education bill, 'a general recognition that even if parents themselves have ... encountered difficulties that have led them into doubts and hesitations, they do desire that their children shall have a grounding in the principles of the Christian faith as it ought to be practised in this country' (*Hansard*, 10 March 1944, vol. 397, no. 45, col. 2425).

There was much discussion. One favoured action was to make religious instruction compulsory. Of course, there were those who opposed this (see Dent, 1966, p. 25). However, the mood of the time was against them. Parliament duly voted for compulsory religious instruction.

For the teaching of religion, the new legislation represented a watershed. Not only was this, as Dent (p. 25), put it, 'a new departure in educational legislation'; it also gave religious instruction unique status as the only subject which had to be taught by law.

However, the 1944 settlement was rooted in a paradox. On the one hand, compulsion was deemed necessary because Christianity, once so powerful in society that schools unquestioningly taught it, now, as A. J. P. Taylor expressed it (1965, p. 568), 'had to be propped up by legislative action', because 'the Christian devotion of teachers, or of parents, could no longer be relied on'. But, on the other hand, there was the widespread, even if by no means universal, public desire to ensure that the subject continue to be taught.

The effects of the paradox were to exert strong, if almost inevitably contradictory, influences on the teaching of religious education over the long period leading up to the Education Reform Act of 1988. There were those, particularly in the schools themselves, who came to resent legislative ukase. The subject generally acquired, if it did not already possess, low status. It was often regarded with condescension, if not outright hostility, by heads and by the generality of teachers; while students frequently resented having to take it. Indeed, the legal requirements were widely ignored, whether blatantly or deviously.

But support in the country for religious education as it at last began to be called, while only often little more than half-hearted and anaemic, nevertheless stubbornly refused to die away. One influential survey, for instance, even found that parents considered the subject more important for their children to learn than science, modern languages or history (Schools Council, 1968).

Any underlying support for the teaching of religion was reinforced by a number of factors. Organized religion, for instance, continued to be able to exert, even if only intermittently, effective political and public pressure. Religious educators themselves began to take a range of initiatives (for example through the Schools Council Religious Education Curriculum Projects) to reform and bring up to date their subject.

More intriguingly, there now appeared some participants in the field who previously had hardly existed, and where they had, had intentionally kept a low profile, or had simply been largely ignored or sidelined. Many members of world faiths other than Christianity, mainly but by no means exclusively from new immigrant communities, began to express an active interest in what schools were doing. Jews, who had had their own aided schools since 1944, Muslims, Hindus and others essentially believed strongly in the importance of religious education, or at least religious instruction. However, they often queried the nature of what was happening in state schools. In particular, questions were raised about the preeminent status of Christianity in the curriculum.

As in 1944, so in 1988, the introduction of a comprehensive and reforming education act proved to have significant implications for religious education (for a detailed analysis of government policy and religious education 1985–1995, see Robson, 1996). The government's initial proposals, laid out in *The National Curriculum 5–16* (DES, Welsh Office, 1987), revealed an indifference, if not actual hostility, from ministers and their officials towards religious education: understandably, this came as a shock to many advocates of the subject. However, in some respects, the attitude should perhaps have been expected. Ministers in the Thatcher administrations, and not least at the Department of Education and Science, had frequently been antagonistic to the interests of ethnic minorities, and these interests certainly included religious education. As for civil servants, they, in their tidy-minded, rationalist, Confucian way, have nearly always tended to feel uneasy with the numinous, through whatever set of beliefs it may be expressed. Given this official climate of opinion, it was perhaps hardly surprising that a low priority was given to finding a place in the curriculum for religious education.

What was bizarre, however, although perhaps just explicable given the nature of the administration, was the neglect and apparent ignorance of the lessons history had to offer. Those responsible for framing the bill appeared to have overlooked entirely the potential which the issue of religion in schools had always had to provoke national controversy.

And mayhem duly erupted. Many voices were to be heard, but it was predominantly bishops and lords who articulated in Parliament the various anxieties. Two major issues came to the fore. First, it was felt that a guaranteed place for religious education in the common curriculum was at risk. This anxiety remained even when ministers explained that religion's place was still guaranteed by the relevant sections of the 1944 Act, which would remain in force. Eventually, with great reluctance and after much prevarication, the government legislated to include religious education as part of the 'basic curriculum', thus reaffirming its position on the timetable.

However, the solution to one concern uncovered the other concern. If religious education was safe, what about the place within it of Christianity? Traditionally, of course, it had been generally assumed that the teaching of religion and of Christianity were to all intents and purposes synonymous. But, as we have seen, that situation was changing. As in 1944 the apparently growing secularization of society made it necessary to afford religious instruction legal protection, so now in 1988 the increasingly multi-faith nature of the country meant that the status of Christianity in religious education needed similar statutory help. Having failed to bury this issue, along with religious education itself, the government moved with some alacrity to deal with it. Subject to various safeguards, it was enacted (Education Reform Act 1988, 8(3)) that the teaching of religion should 'reflect the fact that the religious traditions in Great Britain are in the main Christian whilst taking account of the teaching and practices of the other principal religions represented in Great Britain'.

Following the passage of the Act, controversy over the place of religious education, and by implication or explicitly of the significance for teaching and learning about transcendental truth, continued virtually undiminished. On the one hand it was argued, for example by Richard Dawkins, in a whole range of articles, that religious education syllabuses were inadequate in their view of life and the universe in that they failed to deal with the questions raised, and the answers proposed, by scientific enquiry. On the other hand, in defence of religious education, the chief executive of the Schools Curriculum and Assessment Authority (SCAA) (Tate, 1995) criticized educational and social attitudes which dismissed 'anything to do with religion as relics from the infancy of mankind', and which saw virtue only in 'a narrow, utilitarian view of the curriculum'.

On a more practical level, there were certainly continuing reasons for anxiety over the place and effectiveness of religious education. Various sources of evidence, not least inspection reports (e.g. OFSTED, 1995), suggested that both timetable coverage and students' knowledge of the subject were often less than satisfactory.

Nevertheless, there were grounds for considering that the place of the subject might be becoming more rather than less secure. The reinforced statutory requirements, new inspection arrangements and guidance from SCAA, such as the model syllabuses issued in 1994, all combined to encourage many schools to take their responsibilities more seriously.

Further, the revision of the National Curriculum undertaken by Ron Dearing led to both history and geography becoming optional for 14- to 16-year-olds. As a result, religious education became the only compulsory humanities subject at Key Stage 4. Finally, greater flexibility in public examination requirements allowed short course GCSEs to be awarded. All in all it was arguable that the status of religious education was slowly being raised, and was on a rising trend for the first time in many years.

Practical education became a matter for debate and concern in the United Kingdom from, at least, the late nineteenth century onwards. In 1887, for example, the National Association for the Promotion of Technical Education was established. In part, without doubt, the interest in practical education was inspired the successful German system of technical education, and spurred on by anxiety about the technological advances of Germany.

However, those who fought to see practical education introduced as a significant element of the school curriculum, and indeed of the school system, faced, at least in the first place, particularly intransigent opposition. The main problem was that supporters of the traditional curriculum saw it, and persuaded many others to see it, as occupying, to the virtual exclusion of any other possible arrangement of courses, the moral high ground.

In effect, the argument ran thus. The aim of the curriculum is ultimately moral. The substance of the curriculum, its content and procedures, are mainly concerned with knowledge. The first virtue of knowledge is truth, and particularly *a priori* truth. Practical education has little or nothing to do with truth, however understood. Therefore, practical education can be no more than a peripheral and inferior curricular concern.

There were, historically, various unhappy consequences of this dismissive view of practical education. Prior to, and even to some extent following, the introduction of comprehensive education, it meant that, reinforced by the hierarchic implications of Platonic philosophy, an élite would follow a curriculum predominantly concerned to promote reflective ability and the powers of abstract reasoning; while the lower on the educational scale one found oneself, the more likely one was to follow a course restricted to the three Rs, religious instruction (or education) and a number of practical subjects. This was liable to be the case whether students found themselves in the lower classes of particular schools, or in a school near the base of the educational pyramid.

Paradoxically, however, the denial to the élite of skills relevant to the world of work in no way impaired their employment prospects – far from it. As one Thomas Gainsford remarked in the nineteenth century, 'Greek not only elevates above the vulgar herd, but leads often to positions of considerable emolument' (quoted in Healey, 1989, p. 13). This has meant that one of the reasons parents have battled to get their children into 'top' schools has been, not so much to equip them to contemplate the nature of the Good, but to get them off to a flying start in their careers.

Perhaps the most unfortunate effect of the Platonic-inspired hostility to practical education was the dynamic of arrogance and resentment which it helped to build into the educational system. Originally, this could be powerful indeed. Those educated in public schools seldom had much regard for those who attended lesser institutions. In memoirs published just after the First World War, a chief inspector of schools (Holmes, 1920, p. 64) wrote of the pupils whom he had seen that 'as they all belonged to the "lower orders", and as (according to the belief in which I had been allowed to grow up) the lower orders were congenitally inferior to the "upper classes", I took little or no interest in ...[them] ... either as individuals or as human beings.' Hardly surprisingly, elementary education was widely perceived to be 'training in followership' (Eaglesham, 1967, p. 53).

Two strands, in particular, can be distinguished in the arguments of those who supported practical education. First, it was said that numbers of students would come to be better motivated if what they were learning was related to the real world, and if its ultimate purpose could be seen to be of direct relevance to life after school. This line of thinking can be traced from Cobbett, who attacked 'book learning abstraction', through the Hadow Report of 1926, *The Education of the Adolescent*, to the Newsom Report of 1963, *Half Our Future*, and right up to the present time. However, this sort of argument has tended to lose credibility, although not necessarily cogency, through its tendency to direct itself at the needs of students of lower ability and social class.

The second major strand of argument put forward in favour of practical education has in recent times perhaps come to receive the greater attention. It is concerned less with the needs of the student and more with those of society. It proposes that schools have significantly failed to prepare young people to make an adequate contribution to the world of work, and thereby have been a significant cause of national economic underperformance. As a publication of the Social Affairs Unit (1984, p. 12) expressed it, 'Our school pupils have not been adequately educated for employment and enterprise; this is responsible for high unemployment, for Britain's economic decline over the last half-century, and her failure to keep pace with other nations.'

The proper response to such an analysis was seen as being greater emphasis on the practical aspects of education. 'The nation's prosperity,' declaimed a National Curriculum Council report (1990b, p. 1), 'depends more than ever on the knowledge, understanding and skills of young people. To meet this challenge pupils need to understand enterprise and wealth creation and develop entrepreneurial skills.'

In principle, this argument was directed at the curriculum of all students. In practice, a continuing emphasis on the importance of academic achievement, especially through GCSEs and A levels, and the published success in these public exams of the selective schools, whether in the private or state sectors, had the actual effect, yet again, of relating proposals for curricular reform predominantly to the schools and the curricula for the less advantaged, and the less able.

Various means were advocated, and some implemented, even if frequently only as experiments, of achieving a wider introduction of practical education. Success was often limited, and where secured, usually hard won. Perhaps the clearest progress was made with teaching method, where it has become generally accepted that one significant criterion of good teaching is that it should be practical in the sense that it relates to the real world and to students' actual experience. Some success (though perhaps not as great as was sometimes claimed) was also achieved through giving a reasonable priority to subjects with evident practical aspects, as the National Curriculum did with technology and science; through supplementing the curriculum with vocational and pre-vocational courses; and through cross-curricular initiatives.

More problematic were attempts to reinterpret, or even redesign, the curriculum as a whole so as to give it a more practical spin. A 1981 Schools Council working paper, 'The practical curriculum,' proved too general to exert any significant influence. The suggestion by a professor of education (Skilbeck, 1982; *Times Educational Supplement*, 23 February 1982), that English, maths, science and modern languages might be made optional, and that a core curriculum of practical pursuits, identified as health, physical education, creative arts and interpersonal relationships might exist, was praised as original or dismissed as dotty depending on one's point of view. Either way, it hardly seemed realistic. The Education Reform Act of 1988 required, in principle, that the curriculum should have a practical aspect, stating that it should prepare pupils for 'the opportunities, responsibilities and experience of adult life'. However, apart from the emphasis on science and technology already mentioned, the Education Reform Act actually did little directly to enable the effective introduction of a practically orientated curriculum.

Finally, and most ambitiously, changes in the system both of education and even of government were introduced. A new category of school, the City Technology College, was established. And in 1995 the Department for Education was amalgamated with the Department for Employment. However, the extent and influence of the City Technology College initiative proved less than was hoped for by ministers; and it remains to be seen whether governmental reorganization, not generally a very successful means of changing ingrained national practices, habits and cultures, proves effective in helping to establish practical education more firmly in school curricula.

Lack of official will (despite all the fine words), together with considerable continuing academic opposition, have both made their contribution in rendering pretty ineffective the plethora of attempts to raise the status and worth of practical education.

However, perhaps the bedrock of opposition has come, over the years and right up to the present, from significant numbers of parents and students (as exemplified by the critical attitudes to the General National Vocational Qualification revealed in a 1995 Gallup survey, as reported in the *Times Educational Supplement*, 18 August 1995). They have continued to believe, despite any official protestations to the contrary, that practical education, particularly when it comes in the form of vocational or pre-vocational courses, are likely to cater for the less able, to lead to restricted post-school opportunities, and to suffer from teaching and content of a lower quality than courses leading to academic qualifications. They choose courses, and indeed schools, accordingly.

And so we come to the heart of the matter. The fact is that practical education has not successfully challenged for a place on the moral high ground of the curriculum. Until it does so it is unlikely to find itself with a secure, valued and significant curricular presence.

How can it realistically hope to mount an effective challenge? The apparently obvious move, at the level of principle rather than practice, would be to develop a rationale for practical education which demonstrated that it, too, was concerned with enquiry into and verification of truth.

There is no doubt that much could be done in this direction. Whatever else practical education should concern itself with, it should certainly aim to develop in students an informed and realistic, i.e. true, understanding of adult occupations, of the nature and expectations of the work-place, and so on. Equally, it ought to teach accuracy in a range of practical skills. Here, a respect for truth is required insofar as it is necessary to the achievement of a close correspondence between the plan of what is required and the actuality of what is produced. Products of accurately used skills will be true to the extent that they match a particular model or pattern, or effectively meet a perceived and real need, social, occupational, industrial, etc.

However, practical education can and should be justified not only in terms of truth, but also in terms of responsibility. The argument runs like this. Practical education helps prepare for life in the community, particularly, but not only, in its economic aspects. The first virtue in relation to community is responsibility. Learning the nature of responsibility, and how to exercise it, both helps students to achieve practical learning and ought itself to be an aim of practical learning.

Practical education has, in fact, a moral justification which rests securely on its intrinsic need to promote the virtues of truth and responsibility, both as means and ends of its activities. Accordingly, it is entitled to quite as secure a place on the commanding curricular heights as any discipline which is grounded in the same or other first virtues of education. That practical education continues, by and large, to scrabble around in the curricular foothills, is arguably due to the fact that it has largely accepted, or at least not seriously attempted to challenge, the Platonic-inspired view of its modest place in the moral and educational scheme of things.

The whole curriculum

It should, I have argued, be an evident purpose of the curriculum, as a whole, to provide explicit and balanced coverage of ideas of truth and their verification.

To what extent is this the case in schools today?

Initially, one needs to have an idea of what is happening in individual subjects.

Nationally, the National Curriculum subject orders have no common structure of aims, and no individual subjects have specific statements of purpose. Accordingly they are poorly placed to say anything about any overall intentions to take account of truth in teaching. Religious

Education, while not featuring in the National Curriculum, does have non-statutory model syllabuses, issued by the SCAA in 1994. They, at least, provide clear aims. While these do not specifically refer to the concept of truth, they do make statements which implicitly, and in general terms, encourage it to be taken into account. The suggested content in the various subjects, as identified in the National Curriculum programmes of study and the Religious Education model syllabuses, make a range of references to ideas of truth, and to their verification. These mainly arise, however, incidentally and unsystematically. This one might well expect, given the absence of relevant identified aims.

Within schools, subject schemes of work and other relevant material provide little evidence of any systematic or sharp focus on truth as an end or means of achieving knowledge. In the first place, this almost inevitably arises from the lack of helpful national guidance. But there are other, powerful, reasons which also contribute to this situation.

Thus, there is for some subjects the absence of any overall, differentiated theoretical framework which can readily enable educational practice to take account of questions of truth. As I have already argued, this is particularly true of the arts, and of practical fields.

For other subjects there can be a disorientation, a lack of intellectual security and confidence, which may arise as a result of an academic questioning in their disciplines of the worth or applicability of notions of truth.

So, amongst historians (see, for example, Appleby *et al.*, 1994; Davies, 1996, pp. 2–6), there may be worries about the way 'general impressions' of historians may be not only influenced, but also possibly inevitably distorted, by time, place, gender, ethnicity, culture, and so on. There may, further, be deep anxieties over the extent to which evidence may be rendered suspect by the possible powers of *mentalités* to determine social life, and of language to construct its own realities. While Appleby *et al.*, like many other historians, believe that, whatever the difficulties, 'qualified objectivity' remains feasible as well as desirable, it would hardly be surprising if such debate made some teachers of history a little circumspect in identifying the role of truth in their subject.

Similar difficulties can arise in English. Here it has traditionally been considered that the curriculum should provide opportunities for students to consider whether 'life', or existence, is such of its nature that it would be reasonable for a writer to try and distinguish between universal and contingent elements of character and circumstance. In literature, at least until relatively recently, it has been more or less taken for granted that it was a proper undertaking to explore what was immutable. So for example, Turgenev (1898) in his short story, 'A Lear of the Steppes', writes of 'Shakespeare and his types', and of 'how profoundly and truly they were taken from the very heart of humanity'. A group of friends 'admired particularly their truth to life and their actuality; each of us spoke of the Hamlets, Othellos ... whom he had happened to come across'. Here, the notion of truth being considered refers to the correspondence between what is observed and depicted, and an idea of nature or being as unchanging and eternal in its essence. Current critical argument, and not least in Shakespearean studies, rages around the question of universality. Its possibility may be denied outright, as for instance by cultural materialists (Hawkes, 1992); or it may be subtly modified but in practice defended by, for example, accepting some commonality of experience through time, if not universality in the full meaning of the word (various modern followers of the Victorian critic A. C. Bradley). This, then, is the drift of much of the argument in contemporary literary criticism. In view of all this, it would readily understandable if, like some history teachers, a number of English teachers, at least the more aware and up to date, were somewhat wary of exploring their subject in the language of truth, however interpreted.

All this may serve to undermine the effectiveness and confidence with which various subjects relate their activities to truth. It does little, however, to lessen the mostly subterranean struggle to establish the supremacy of particular truths in the curriculum. Scientific truth persistently works to secure its preeminence through physics, biology and chemistry; logical truth does its best maintain its place, particularly through mathematics; transcendent truth timidly defends its modest corner in religious education. And all, to a greater or lesser extent, assert their claims across the curriculum.

From all this, two conclusions emerge with some clarity:

First, the different subject areas, individually, are in urgent need of developing an explicit and systematic approach which relates their teaching to notions of truth and to procedures for verifying it.

Secondly, schools need to develop curricular policies which enable them to establish a balanced approach to the teaching of truth.

For both of these objectives to have a reasonable chance of being achieved, schools have to be able to think and plan in terms of the curriculum as a whole.

So, the question arises. To what extent do thinking and policy at national level encourage, and enable, schools individually to operate in terms of a whole curriculum?

The current position is that the vocabulary of education does indeed include in its terminology the notion of 'the whole curriculum'. Moreover, its defining characteristics are legally identified. It must be broad, balanced and relevant (DES, 1989, 2.2). Further, a quite detailed 'description' has been offered by the National Curriculum Council (1990a, p. 1).

This, however, although necessary, is by no means sufficient. The whole curriculum also requires a structure of aims, and a coherent form. In the absence of these it is liable, as we have seen, to degenerate into an inert mass, lacking intelligible and purposive relationships between its constituent, and very possibly mutually antagonistic, elements. In such circumstances, the quest for truth can neither be properly identified as an overall purpose of teaching nor planned in an explicit and balanced way.

So, does the curriculum as a whole, nationally and locally, have a structure of aims? Until quite recently, it certainly used to. Indeed, during the 1980s considerable effort at every level, from government to individual school, was devoted to developing objectives for the overall curriculum (DES, 1981a; DES, 1981b, DES, 1983; DES, 1985a; DES, 1986). More generally, the Education (No. 2) Act of 1986 (sections 17 and 18) required that local education authorities (LEAs) 'make and keep up-to-date, written statements of curricular policy' and that governors of maintained schools consider the LEA policy, and 'the aims of the secular curriculum', and produce their own policy. Even before the introduction of the legal requirement, all the government-initiated activity was beginning to achieve significant success. Her Majesty's Inspectorate (HMI) were able to report that aims proposed by the government 'command widespread support and they are reflected in the aims drawn up by many local education authorities and individual schools' (DES, 1985b).

However, with the introduction of the Education Reform Act came a change of direction. The original bill included no reference to any requirements for the curriculum as a whole; these were only added (section 1.2) in the face of government reluctance, during parliamentary debate. In effect, from 1988 onwards, the government showed little interest in promoting whole curriculum aims at national level.

At local level, however, schools and LEAs continued to be exhorted to develop statements of curricular purpose. The National Curriculum Council proposed (1990a, p. 8) that schools should, in carrying out a curricular review, ask themselves whether they have 'a whole curriculum policy'. And in a discussion paper on primary schools the so-called 'three wise men' (Alexander *et al.*, 1992, p. 47) argued that 'effective headteachers have a vision of what their schools should become ... The vision will have at its heart a clearly articulated view of what constitutes the school curriculum ... and of how planning, teaching and evaluation will be undertaken in order to ensure that the aims and objectives of the curriculum are translated into pupil learning.'

Splendid rhetoric. But it is asking a good deal to expect individual schools to develop whole curriculum aims when, at national level, that very task is being evaded, and by implication devalued, by the government and its educational agencies. The real message schools have been given is that they should pose no serious questions for their curricula to answer, but should concentrate on administering an imposed system.

So, if aims of the curriculum as a whole are neglected, is the position regarding coherence any better? Some uncertainty can exist about what precisely is meant by coherence. David Hargreaves (1991, pp. 33–34) has clarified this question, and I intend to follow his definitions. Coherence, he proposes, exists where 'the various parts of the curriculum have a clear and explicit relationship with one another'. There is 'content' coherence, which is 'about the relationships between knowledge and skills', and this applies both within and between subjects. There is also 'experiential coherence, or coherence as it is experienced in the routine world of the classroom by both teachers and pupils'.

If there is to be any possibility of coherence being consistently experienced, it must first be intended.

Is there any evidence to suggest that those responsible for national policy have been interested in promoting the coherence of the curriculum as a whole?

The professional world of education, including those responsible for advising the government, has consistently advocated coherence in the whole curriculum. However, Conservative governments, at least from the early 1980s, opposed it. Thus, on the one hand, early in the Thatcher administration, HMI (DES 1980a, p. 15) argued for coherence. On the other hand, the government White Paper, *Better Schools* (DES 1985a), while listing various 'fundamental principles' of the curriculum, omitted coherence. Following the Education Reform Act, the National Curriculum was developed in line with government-dictated procedures which effectively denied the possibility of curricular coherence being promoted. In contrast to initiatives taken both in Northern Ireland and in Wales (Northern Ireland Curriculum Council, 1990; Curriculum Council for Wales, 1991), in England no working party was established with responsibility for producing a whole curriculum framework. Further, curriculum working parties were set up, not simultaneously, but in sequence, thus effectively removing the possibility of any more or less informal joint planning.

Despite all this, the professionals did not, at least immediately, entirely surrender their position. The National Curriculum Council (1989, p. 1), in early guidance, stated firmly, 'above all, schools need to give the curriculum structure and coherence'. Second thoughts, however, showed a greater awareness of political realities. The paper on *The Whole Curriculum* (1990a) made only incidental reference to coherence. Meanwhile, the National Foundation for Educational Research (Weston *et al.*, 1992) was carrying out a survey, *The Quest for Coherence*, into how schools managed the whole curriculum. The research illustrated how substantially government policy, in practice, restricted schools' ability to develop coherent approaches to the whole curriculum. The report concluded, nevertheless, that coherence remained educationally desirable, and that the best chance of achieving it lay, despite the impediment of government policies, with schools themselves. In the circumstances, this looked suspiciously like putting the best possible gloss on what was interpreted as a bad situation.

Why was government apparently so opposed to the development of strategies which could support effective development of whole curriculum policies in schools?

To begin with: why, at national level, did government discourage the articulation of aims for the curriculum as a whole, including the national curriculum? The key point here is that, at least in the existing educational context, the process and achievement of identifying aims would have been likely to encourage reflection and discussion, and quite possibly to encourage yet further calls for curricular change. While many interested parties might have been expected to contribute, one of the most active groups would certainly have been teachers and educationists generally.

But, it has become almost a cliché of political discourse that educationists, largely left to their own devices as they mostly were for generations, have failed to secure sufficiently high student achievement across the school population as a whole. Where exactly the blame lies for this state of affairs is open to discussion. That it exists is, however, well documented.

Accordingly, it seemed to many, and not least to those in government, that educators were as much a part of the problem as a solution. Consequently, there was much to be said for keeping them quiet and telling them what to do, rather than encouraging them to give tongue. And what better way of doing this than by laying down a National Curriculum, and by omitting to state its specific aims, thus minimizing any opportunity for discussion of curricular nature and purpose? (The autobiography of Kenneth Baker, 1993, particularly chapters 8 and 9, makes very clear both the ministerial suspicion of educational professionals – 'the educational establishment' – and governmental determination to establish its own highly pragmatic, and confined, view of the curriculum and its objectives.)

The next issue is this: why did the government set its face against the development of coherence for the curriculum as a whole?

In a specifically educational context, the answer is because it became wedded to the idea of a curriculum of subjects.

This, however, in turn raises the questions, first, of why the government wished to understand the curriculum predominantly in terms of its discrete components; and secondly, of why this led to hostility towards considering the overall form and interrelationships of the subjects considered collectively.

The government supported a subject-based approach, at least in part, because at the point when the introduction of the National Curriculum was being considered, no other alternative presented itself which it found convincing. Thus, educational philosophers and some others had for a considerable time been discussing proposals aimed, for instance through demonstrable analysis of particular conceptual frameworks and tests of truth, to justify particular higher order categories of knowledge and meaning (Phenix, 1964; Lawton, 1973; White, 1973, 1982; Hirst, 1974; Bailey, 1984). These, however, tightly argued though they were, proved to be open to criticism. They were also more or less discrete, thus inhibiting the emergence of any consensual view. Finally, although the theoretical structures were worked out in terms of curricular requirements, the various proposals were sometimes considered to lack educational realism. In particular, they were not seen by either politicians or their officials and their advisers as offering a pragmatic basis for legislation.

It might have seemed, and indeed this has been suggested, that the thinking of HMI could have provided a framework for the development of the curriculum. The inspectors, through a series of exercises, had tried out and developed areas of 'learning and experience'. These, however, specifically disclaimed any ambition to serve as fields of knowledge which could be taught as such. Their purpose was quite different. They were to 'constitute a planning and analytic tool' (DES, 1985b, p. 16). In other words, these areas were to be employed in relation to an existing curriculum, not as a substitute for it.

Finally, if one looked at schools to see what happened where the subject approach was dispensed with, the evidence was varied. Nevertheless, where integrated approaches were adopted whether for instance in primary topic work or in GCSE humanities, there did at times appear to be a lack of rigour and clarity. Even critics of a subject-based approach, aware of its capacity for encouraging a narrow, compartmentalized, inward-looking pedagogy, could hardly claim with confidence that school experience of non-subject-based work indicated a proven and viable alternative approach.

So, a National Curriculum of subjects it was. And of course subjects were tried, tested, of proven durability and known strengths (Ribbins, 1993).

But a curriculum of subjects does not necessarily have to result in a state of maximum possible curricular incoherence. There have been in the past, after all, and indeed are today, societies, cultures and socio-economic classes which, in their different ways, have evolved education systems where curricula have been perceived as coherent, albeit categorized into areas that we would have little difficulty in recognizing as subjects.

So, for instance, what Maurice Bowra has called the desire of the ancient Greeks 'to find an abiding reality behind the gifts of the senses' (1957, p. 160) was the inspiration for the coherent curriculum which emerged under Athenian democracy. Here, supported by the social unity of the *polis*, a curriculum was constructed whose internal consistency derived immediately from the priority accorded to the arts, and in particular to poetry, drama and music.

The same search for ultimate being, transformed by Plato and Aristotle into a philosophic quest, came to coexist with Christian theology, and eventually to provide a framework for the English public school curriculum of the nineteenth and twentieth centuries. Here, classics and religion ruled, and other subjects enjoyed more or less status depending on the extent to which they demanded the exercise of powers of reflection and abstract reasoning.

And, in communities of faith, knowledge and understanding are characteristically seen as fundamentally unitary. 'All that exists as contemplated by the human mind,' wrote J. H. Newman (1982, p. 33), 'forms one large system or complex fact, and this of course resolves itself into an indefinite number of particular facts ... knowledge is the apprehension of these facts, whether in themselves or in their mutual positions ... all possess a correlative character one with another, from the internal mysteries of the divine essence down to our own sensations and consciousness.' Seen against this background, subjects are simply 'various partial views or abstractions by means of which the mind looks out upon its object'. And, naturally, a hierarchy of subjects follows, those concerned with ultimate, religious truth, and the whole, being at the apex.

There are, then, identifiable professional and political reasons why England, nationally and locally, lacks coherent and unified,curricula. But, why is it that our particular society has had such difficulty in generating a community of shared knowledge, where the parts are related to the whole through one underlying philosophy, or, more generally, a common view of existence?

We inhabit, or so it seems, a world characterized by diversity, multi-culturalism, and even, from time to time and place to place, anomie. Perhaps we should start to look here for any deeper explanations of the fragmented curriculum. Our cultural environment is at once product and cause of social, economic and intellectual dispersion. Coherence in modern society is only likely to be found within particular communities, whether of faith, interest or social group, which are ready to stand firm against the undertow of history. And in education, it is, quite possibly, only schools belonging to such communities that are likely to have any ready success in securing a coherent curriculum.

To exacerbate matters further, society in England has generated an academic culture the currently dominant forces within which both reflect and reinforce atomization. Thus, if we consider universities, we find a milieu often described as characterized by anxiety, antagonism and absence of mutual concerns. Here we have disciplines, as Harold Perkin (1989, pp. 395–6) has expressed it, 'using strategies of closure to segregate themselves from the laity and from one another'; and who, not content simply to exist in self-sufficient and self-regarding isolation, struggle for supremacy. Perkin refers to the study of English literature as a good example of academic Darwinism. This discipline, which as he points out only became a university subject in the early twentieth century, 'has since tried to become *the* humane discipline, the modern substitute for theology and philosophy'. In fact, with its inevitable backwash into the theory and practice of the curriculum in schools, what we have is what Peter Scott, in his study of *The Crisis of the University* (1984) has referred to as an unravelling of political, intellectual and moral fabric.

There is perhaps no better way of summarizing the position than by referring to the analysis of T. S. Eliot (1939, p. 41). He talked of 'a negative liberal society', i.e. a place where individual rights and freedoms reign over any sense of tradition, continuity, social obligation, or even respect for others. Intellectually, the result is predictable. 'You have,' writes Eliot, 'no agreement as to there being any body of knowledge which any educated person should have acquired at any particular stage: the idea of wisdom disappears and you get sporadic and unrelated experimentation.'

Such a multi-form, disjointed, atomized academic cosmos is not inconsistent with that individualistic, libertarian philosophy, predominantly originating with thinkers of the early nineteenth century, and resurrected by the apologists of Thatcherism. It was therefore perhaps to be expected that the conservative government which introduced and implemented the curriculum reforms of the 1988 Education Act should have been hostile to the notion of shared purposes, and of coherence. And that those who attempted to promote such approaches should have found the task, whether politically, philosophically or practicably, hard-going.

So, we have come full circle. An explicit, balanced approach to teaching concerned with truth requires the development of a whole curriculum, directed by relevant aims, and coherent in form. However, while the idea of a whole curriculum exists as a working concept, it is seriously underdeveloped, at national and at local level, both intellectually and in its practical applications. The reasons for this are to be found immediately in the prevailing climate in which government policy-making and educational thinking occur; and more fundamentally in the nature of modern society.

The outcome in schools is that the whole curriculum is seldom, if ever, conceived, presented or practised in ways which enable the question of truth to be systematically addressed. What we have is a static curriculum, lacking in detailed, declared and debated intentions, and consisting of fragments which might once arguably have been understood to belong to a greater whole, but which now are widely seen to be isolated pieces having minimal mutual relationships. Insofar as it is possible to analyse and interpret what is actually taking place in classrooms it seems reasonable to conclude that truth is taught, or indeed sought, in a way that is insufficiently purposive, explicit, informed, systematic or balanced.

Given the weakness of practice in relation to truth, the fundamental virtue of knowledge, it is hardly surprising, although there may also be other reasons for it, that criticism is ever more loudly voiced, and not least from higher education, that school students' knowledge is inadequately informed by a sound grasp of the principles and practices of particular subjects. It could also be added that, insofar as they are not educated about the nature of truth as a whole, young people are not afforded their rightful opportunity to develop fully as whole persons.

The way forward

Where do we go from here? One thing is transparently clear. The clock cannot be turned back. We have to start from where we are, not from where we might like to be. There is no option but to work on the curricular foundations laid by the Education Reform Act, and to join in the discourses of the culture which generated, and are being furthered by, that curriculum.

Another fact should also be evident, although unfortunately it may be necessary to spell it out. We should root all our curricular approaches in those political, philosophic and theological systems of thought which value truth, respect for self and others, justice and responsibility; and which, accordingly, encourage us to understand teaching and learning as a process by which individuals may be educated to take their place in, and contribute positively to, a world with the potential for meaning, coherence and mutuality.

Given these principles, there is action that we should support.

First, building on the Education Reform Act, we should articulate and develop through dialogue national aims for the whole curriculum. These should, mutually and taken together, give moral purpose and direction to the teaching and learning of schools. They should give priority to respect for truth. They should also make clear that the curriculum should contribute to developing respect for self and others, and a sense of responsibility and fairness. (See National Forum for Values in Education, 1996, which also identifies these values as being of key importance for schools.)

Secondly, we should try to ensure that the profession of education is fully enfranchised to make its proper contribution to any consideration of the purposes of the curriculum within the national education system.

Thirdly, we should make certain that the curriculum is so planned, organized and monitored that in its parts, and as a whole, it enables students to learn through a balanced and coherent experience what is meant by the first virtues of education, and in particular, by truth.

Finally, in gaining knowledge and experience, students should be educated to practise particular truthful attitudes, skills and behaviour:

- Young people need to learn to pay attention, to discriminate, and to reflect upon their experience so as to be able to get things right factually.
- They should discover that, in order to find out for themselves whether or not something is true, they must be able to think creatively, to pose relevant questions, to suggest hypotheses, to make, construct and compose that which may reflect or establish truth.
- They should learn to reason logically, whether in concrete or abstract terms.
- They should begin to explore the manifold implications of the possibility that in the depths and heights of existence there is to be found an ultimate presence which is, and manifests itself as, transcendent truth, that which is.
- They should be helped to realize that truth, in all its manifold complexity and diversity, gives meaning to all forms of imaginative undertaking. Whether in making or in evaluating, the student of the arts must be encouraged to speak the language of truth. For the artist, as Iris Murdoch puts it, using the word in its broader meaning to include all expressive arts, 'truth is always a proper touchstone ... and a training in art is a training in how to use the touchstone'. And as for the critic, 'a study of any good art enlarges and refines our understanding of truth, our methods of verification ... Critical terminology imputes falsehood to an artist by using such terms as fantastic, sentimental, self-indulgent, banal, grotesque, tendentious, unclarified, wilfully obscure, and so on' (Murdoch, 1992, p. 86).
- Students should learn that the pursuit of truth requires sustained application, courage, and the sort of humility which is prepared to admit that, in the light of the evidence, one is in error.
- And as students advance in their understanding of what is meant by truth, they will need to recognize that there are limits to the extent that truth can be explored, by whatever means, by those who are personally careless of truth. Sustained, informed and genuine respect for truth requires both intellectual clarity and individual integrity.
- In every classroom, and throughout school-life, students should be enabled to learn how to be truthful as persons, how to be true persons.

CHAPTER 9

Justice and responsibility

Each school is bound to do its best to ensure that students learn, in theory and practice, about justice and responsibility.

Justice and responsibility are social virtues. They acquire contingency and depth in the context of institutions and communities and in the context of their related forms of control. This holds true at local and national level, on a small and on a large scale.

Different societies give expression to differing notions of what is understood by justice and responsibility.

Schools are themselves institutions and communities. They are also situated within larger societies. If they are to understand how they themselves do, and should, function as moral societies, they must have an initial idea of their location in the networks of values, expectations and beliefs, inherited and contemporary, which influence both the way they do operate and the views of how they should function to promote the social virtues.

To begin with, therefore, I need to deal, albeit only in outline, with certain key questions. First, what are the major ideas of society (and also of government), which have, over time, exerted a significant influence on educational thought and practice? Next, how, within such notions of society, are ideas of justice and responsibility understood? And finally, how does our own culture perceive justice and responsibility?

In the light of discussion of these questions, one becomes better placed to consider what should be the approach of schools to justice and responsibility.

Societies and government

Certain central traditions of political philosophy have exerted particular influence on education, whether beneficially, or otherwise.

Thus, there are individualistic authoritarian ideas of society. Here, the world is viewed as little more than a savage terrain, where humans, lacking all grace and love, bleakly struggle to survive and dominate. They may fight as individuals, or as groups. Thus, for Hobbes, persons, governed by self-interest, and by 'passions' such as ambition, covetousness and anger, exist in a condition of perpetual dissension and fear.

In a society of individuals dominated by human aggression and egotism an autocratic state may be established simply by the strongest, and ruled predominantly or exclusively in their own interests. Alternatively, as Hobbes advocates, such a society might be ruled, equally autocratically, by a monarch. However, such a monarch would not have seized power, but have had it given to him by the people so that he could, in the interest of all, establish the rule of law. A Hobbesian veneer of legitimacy may have its significance in justifying an autocratic regime. However, from the point of view of the ruled, the distinction is likely to be largely immaterial.

Authoritarian societies may be identified, not as individualistic, but as organic. Here, the emphasis shifts from the more or less desperate and benighted condition of the individuals who form society, to the idea of society as such. Society is characteristically envisaged as one single whole. However, it may, as in Marxism, be seen as being made up of constituent parts, or classes, each of which in its own terms, functions as a whole, and which is locked into the rest of society in a struggle, through the mechanisms of the materialist dialectic of preordained historical process, for control of the totality.

An organic society is, in essence, an association of persons where, as Aristotle succinctly expressed, 'The whole is naturally superior to the part' (quoted in Jowett, 1905, p. 143, at 1288a). Two features are particularly characteristic of organic societies. First, they may be perceived as specific living entities. As Tom Weldon (1946, p. 45), amongst others, has put it, 'The fundamental principle of the organic theory is that society or the state is actually and not metaphorically an individual person; and that, as such, it has the same unqualified control over its subordinate members as is sometimes allowed to reside in a biological organism.' The second feature is that all 'subordinate members' must serve the interests of the whole, and not vice versa. Thus, in the words of the Protestant theologian Dietrich Bonhoeffer (1964, p. 150), hanged by the Nazis, 'the individual is understood only in terms of his utilizable value for the whole ... the collectivity is the God to whom individual and social life are sacrificed ...'

The government in organic societies may take various forms. Power may rest with a philosopher king, as in Plato's Republic, or with a hereditary monarchy, as in the nineteenth-century Prussia of Hegel, or with a fascist tyranny, as in Nazi Germany, or with the dictatorship of one class over others, as in Marxist states, etc. In every instance, however, government would claim to be carried out in the interest of society as a whole, irrespective of the particular claims or alleged rights of individuals.

In authoritarian societies of whatever sort, individuals may find a degree of security and some sense of belonging. But not only do they pay the price of a drastically restricted personal freedom; such protection as they do enjoy, and indeed such identity as they may be granted, may always be diminished, or even removed, if the interest of the ruler, or the greater good of the whole, requires it. And this is true not only of those remote from power, but also of those in authority. The paradox of societies which often justify their authoritarian nature by appeal to the order which they can appear to provide is that, ultimately, no one is safe from the apparatus of government. As Mussolini put it, 'The individual exists only insofar as he is subordinated to the interests of the state' (quoted in Mack Smith, 1983, p. 162).

Hardly surprisingly, humans generally aspire to higher goods, including not least personal freedom, than are generally on offer from authoritarianism. In more recent times, people have mainly turned to democracy in their efforts to create a better world. And, in this country, influenced religiously by Protestantism, philosophically by the Enlightenment and economically by notions of the free market, it is especially the idea of liberal democracy which has dominated.

All democracies, including liberal democracies, are founded, morally, in respect for individuals. 'The democratic hypothesis depends upon a moral or religious faith in the absolute value of men' (Weldon, 1946, p. 126).

So, in the first place, the effective existence of any full democracy relies upon its unconditional recognition of, and respect for, what persons, in their essential nature, are. That is, complex, protean, individual, embodied, men, women and children, of whatever racial or ethnic origin, who have their being in a social and cultural environment, who are capable of rationality, but who enjoy the status of persons irrespective of their degree of intelligence.

Thus, the struggles to establish democracy, and liberal democracy in particular, can largely be interpreted as attempts to build societies which gives full membership not only to already dominant individuals, classes and groups, but to all persons, including those who historically have been underprivileged, whether on grounds of gender, race, religion or economic status.

However, when it comes to considering what persons should be, as contrasted with what they necessarily are, members of liberal democratic societies hold, not one, but a range of ideas. It follows from this that different persons in a liberal democracy hold varying, indeed virtually contradictory ideas, about the sort of democracy which they value and would like to see develop. For each, as a rule, desires to live in and promote the sort of community where the ideal of a person to which he or she aspires is likely to be favoured.

The ideas of a person which inform, and can lead to conflict over, the nature of liberal democracy are, for the most part, those which have animated the main traditions of Western thinking and debate over the nature of persons. They are consequently, and hardly surprisingly, substantially the same notions which, to a greater or lesser degree, sustain educational understanding of ideals of a person.

So, now we need to look again at those key ideals of a person which I have already considered. The question now is: what do those who subscribe to these ideals expect a democracy to offer?

The key ideals can be broadly divided into two categories. First, there are the two major European notions of a person which significantly preceded the rise of liberal democracy. These are the Christian and classical ideas. Then there are those notions which immediately inspired and substantially influenced the rise of liberal democracy. These are the rational, humanist and economic ideas.

Those who wish to see liberal democracy predominantly informed by Christian or classical ideas of a person are at a disadvantage. First, it was not their beliefs which originally led to the strongest calls for, and subsequently most directly to the evolution of, liberal democracy. Secondly, Christian and classical ideals of a person can exhibit various features which, at best do not fit comfortably into any rationally justifiable models of liberal democracy, and at worst are incompatible with them.

So, whenever contests arise over the influence which particular notions of a person should exert on the nature of liberal democracy, it becomes apparent that one group enjoys an advantage. The high ground is occupied by liberal persons, the rational, the humanist and the economic. The others, whether rightly or wrongly, can have difficulty in establishing themselves securely alongside those who enjoy the rights of original possession.

We come, first, to the Christian idea of a person. In the Augustinian and Thomist view persons have the potential, through the use of reason, to comprehend or formulate the basic precepts of the divine law. They also have a capacity, through the exercise of free will, to choose to follow divine law, and to put that choice into practice. The Christian person also, of course, whether through destructive passion, or through evil habit, or through a pervasive natural tendency to do wrong, may be inclined to choose to disobey the commandments of God.

It is in this respect that Christian persons are particularly dependent upon institutions and community. It is highly desirable, though not essential, that they live in a just society. Where they do so, they may be guided and helped to develop as persons who strive to live the Christian life, and fulfil the Christian goals of existence.

A society which is supportive of a Christian way of life will be one where the laws, institutions and customs are consistent with the will of God. Such a state may be organized on authoritarian, or democratic lines. What matters, is not so much its particular form, but rather whether its arrangements and practices can be theologically justified.

Nevertheless, at least in the contemporary Western world, very many Christians see democracy as the form of society best suited to promote, or at least not to undermine, the way of life they advocate. From this perspective, democracy should sustain a system of government which is capable both of controlling the harmful impulses of a congenitally flawed human nature and of liberating and training the more noble qualities of that same nature. 'It is,' said the American Protestant theologian Reinhold Niebuhr, 'the evil in man that makes democracy necessary, and man's belief in justice that makes democracy possible' (quoted by Tony Benn, in Mortimer, 1983, p. 35).

Such a view of democracy requires the existence; first, of some constitutional arrangements, for example of checks, balances and rules, together with laws and powers, designed to ensure that democracy is not subverted by any immoral pursuit of self-interest or power; and, secondly, of genuine and continuing opportunities for all citizens, through mechanisms and cultures of active participation, to discuss, consider and contribute to the just promotion of compatible private and public goods. Above all, however, these goods must be consistent with the beliefs and teachings of Christianity.

The classical, and particularly the Athenian idea, of a person, has exerted an ambiguous influence on attitudes towards, and the practice of, democracy. On the one hand, the individual, striving, competitive, passionate, creative, autonomous, was regarded by the Greeks with fascination and, acknowledged defects not withstanding, was highly valued. But, on the other hand, not all classes of individual were regarded as complete persons. Neither women nor slaves were accepted as citizens. Further, all individuals were seen as members of the city state, and as such to a considerable extent dependent for their sense of identity on that membership. Accordingly, sitting uneasily alongside respect for the individual was to be found a tendency for persons to be seen as parts of an organic social and political unity. Finally, this holistic propensity was allied at times with a class-driven desire for aristocratic rule. In the light of all this, it becomes evident that Athenian notions of persons, and of their possible social and political roles, were liable to provide a somewhat fragile inspiration for democracy.

The arrangements of Athenian democracy emphasized two objectives in particular. First, they were concerned to ensure the observation of contractual obligations entered into by individuals with citizens and state. Secondly, they tried to secure the full consent and participation by all citizens in managing the business of democracy. In gaining active involvement they had some much-trumpeted success, particularly insofar as they succeeded both in ensuring that citizens took on a range of roles and responsibilities and in preventing bureaucrats and specialists from getting any sort of firm grip on power. Ultimately, however, there were spectacular failures in achieving respect for contract and assent, resulting most devastatingly in civil war. The political legacy of the Athenian idea of persons to democracy includes both the statement and exemplification in practice of certain basic democratic principles, together with a deep suspicion of the viability of those same principles.

For contemporary ideas of democracy, the notion of persons as rational beings is pivotal. More particularly, it is a modern mantra that it is through the, exercise of choice that the rational person can best fulfil the rights and obligations of citizenship. Accordingly, for the rationalist, the salient characteristic of liberal democracy becomes the possibility of changing government through elections conducted according to whatever procedures may be locally acceptable. At its most basic, to today's commentator, a society where it is possible to alter national leadership through elections is democratic, while all others are not.

Humanist and economic ideals of a person, like the rationalist, place a high value on a human capacity to make choices. However, while influenced by the traditions of rationalist thought, the humanist and economic ideals have evolved certain features which have particular implications for the theory and practice of democracy.

The humanist notion of persons sees them as moral beings, concerned certainly with achieving their own ends, but also with securing the public good in the interests of all. Those who hold this rather generous view of persons have, from John Stuart Mill onwards, tended to believe in social progress, driven by the enlightened self-interest and social conscience of individuals, and assisted by active and beneficent government. Since the time of John Dewey, early in the twentieth century, they have also put increasing faith in the potential of social science, combined with open and informed public debate, to contribute effectively to the formulation and implementation of policy at national and local level.

On the other hand, the economic ideal of the person has very different implications for democracy. These have been analysed in detail by C. B. Macpherson (1977). The free-market individual, as pictured by Jeremy Bentham and James Mill, is a self-interested, amoral, materially acquisitive being. He is, in C. B. Macpherson's phrase, 'a possessive individualist'. As such, one might consider he could only be controlled by an authoritarian regime. And indeed, any state founded on this utilitarian view of persons is more than likely to have absolutist tendencies. However, economic persons, while being quite capable of anti-social and aggressive behaviour, are above all concerned to achieve their own personal pleasure and satisfaction. It is, accordingly possible, if only just, to envisage them as members of a democracy, albeit one of a particular and limited nature.

A democracy for creatures of this sort must first, as best it may, create the optimum conditions for the pursuit of private gain. Next, it must protect them from each other, and from those whom they appoint to rule in their name. Once these two aims have been met, democracy has effectively done its job. In C. B. Macpherson's words:

> In this founding model of democracy for a modern industrial society there is no enthusiasm for democracy, no idea that it could be a morally transformative force; it is nothing but a logical requirement for the governance of inherently self-interested, conflicting individuals who are assumed to be infinitely desirous of their own private benefits... Responsible government, even to the extent of responsibility to a democratic electorate, was needed for the protection of individuals and the promotion of gross national product, and for nothing more. (1977, p. 43)

Recently, of course, new life has been breathed into this model of democracy, and into the idea of persons which sustains it. Neo-conservatives have emphatically reaffirmed faith in the active existence of *homo economicus*. They have also updated the description of democracy so as to bring it into line with, indeed virtually to assimilate it into, current schema of the workings of a capitalist society. Thus, to quote C. B. Macpherson again, the purpose of democracy now becomes 'to register the desires of people as they are... democracy is simply a market mechanism. The voters are the consumers; the politicians are the entrepreneurs... political man, like economic man, is essentially a consumer and appropriator' (1977, pp. 78–80).

So, in the struggle to establish a liberal democracy fit for a particular ideal of person, which ideas have, at least so far, proved the most successful?

To begin with, one thing is certainly evident. The Christian and classical notions have never really succeeded in overcoming their various handicaps. They, and particularly the latter, remain marginally influential.

Rational persons were, in effect, the founding members of liberal democracy. As such, they continue to enjoy some preeminence and respect, if perhaps nowadays of a rather ritual nature.

The ideal of the humanist person, while it has enjoyed substantial support, has also eventually proved incapable of playing a dominant role. Positive individualism has been shown to be too optimistic in its expectations of human behaviour. In consequence, it has at times overestimated the likelihood of a motivation to perform altruistic political actions. It has also tended, when such actions have been attempted, to underestimate the capacity of malign opposition, and of the sheer intractability of facts to impede, deflect or destroy planned progress.

The ideal of the economic person has appeared at times, particularly for much of the nineteenth and for a decade or two in the late twentieth century, to emerge as the strongest influence on the arrangements and conduct of liberal democracy. However, as in the Victorian era, so again now, it is becoming apparent that negative individualism contains the seeds of its own destruction, at least as a political force.

If a society is selfishly individualistic, its collective neglect of the good of the whole permits the flourishing of those social evils which in due course are likely to make it difficult or even impossible for individuals freely to pursue their own purposes. Thus, as the Elder Zossima explains in Dostoyevsky's *Brothers Karamazov* (1958, pp. 356–7), 'today everyone is still striving to keep his individuality as far apart as possible, everyone still wishes to experience the fullness of life in himself alone, and yet instead of achieving the fullness of life, all his efforts merely lead to the fullness of self-destruction, for instead of full self-realisation they relapse into complete isolation ... everywhere today the mind of man has ceased, ironically, to understand that true security of the individual does not lie in isolated personal efforts, but in general human solidarity.'

And, in the economic sphere, much the same results follow. Possessive individualism, the promotion of sectional interests at the expense of common interests inhibits, as David Marquand (1988, p. 212), amongst others has argued, the development of those nationally shared and generated policies which alone, in the modern world, can sustain effective economic growth.

So, if the key European ideals of a person have proved, for whatever reason, inadequate effectively to sustain it, where does liberal democracy go from here?

What many now appear to be seeking is a notion of what one might call, 'persons in community', to reinvigorate, reshape and give a renewed moral authority to the theory and practice of democracy. This quest, in principle, is as ancient as civilization. It was Lao-Tzu in the *Tao Teh King* (1922, p. 67), who wrote in the sixth century BC, 'Do not desire to be isolated as a single gem, nor to be lost as pebbles on the beach.'

In essence, what modern thinkers are attempting to do is to relate Lao-Tzu's advice to contemporary circumstances. Their endeavour can perhaps best be understood as a complex, even dangerous, attempt to balance the emphasis placed, in holistic societies, on the social aspects of human being, with the absolute value placed on the individual by liberalism.

To establish and develop the concept of persons in community various traditions are being explored. Theologians and Christian thinkers have certainly entered the debate. Responding to an address by Mrs Thatcher in 1989 to the Church of Scotland's General Assembly, its moderator took her to task for her almost exclusive emphasis on the individual. Speaking as a theologian, he stressed the religious importance of 'our sense of community, our sense of belonging ... I am not just an individual. I am a person who belongs to a community' (*Guardian*, 18 February 1989).

Political philosophies, not least, are likewise involved in this dialogue. Democratic socialists, drawing on labour movement traditions of syndicalism, friendly societies, the cooperative movement and unionism, have looked to roots of fraternity, justice and egalitarianism. Conservatives have been more inclined to seek out the traditional Toryism of Edmund Burke (1901, vol. 6, p. 147) with its emphasis on society and nation not so much as an 'individual momentary aggregation', but rather as 'an idea of continuity, which extends in time as well as in numbers and space ... a deliberate election of the ages and of generations'. Within such a community traditional customs, classes, hierarchies, laws and constitution are all valued and preserved, and should not be at risk from any self-seeking, envious, disrespectful, anarchic or rebellious individuals.

Insofar as the idea of persons in the community can reasonably look to individualism for support, it is to the traditions of humanism that it generally turns. This system of thought, with its optimistic belief in the possibility of social improvement through government or collective action, provides a natural foundation for a philosophy favourable to persons in the community.

There is also a further, if subdued, feature of individualism which, it has been argued, is of relevance. This is to do with rights and duties. Always implicitly, and sometimes explicitly, most famously by Jefferson in drafting the Constitution of the United States of America, individualist thinkers have talked of the rights of the person. Less frequently, and even then mostly only by inference, thinkers in the individualist mould have also referred to the duties of the person. Some modern thinkers have recently sought to build on this strand of thought. John Tomlinson (1992, p. 50), referring to Kant and John Stuart Mill, discusses a 'republican individualism [which] puts duties alongside or before rights ... [and] ... is the kind of individualism which is no threat to moral or civic duty'. And David Selbourne (1994), in greater detail, also develops within an individualistic framework of reference, what he calls 'the principle of duty'. In such interpretations of individualism, persons are seen not just as single entities, but also as persons having social needs, and so as being necessarily involved in and committed to reciprocal and, in certain respects, moral relationships, both in the personal and civic spheres.

And, finally, all these ideas in one form or another tend to have influenced the synthetic view of persons in community presented as communitarianism. Amitai Etzioni (1995, p. 247) describes communit-arianism as 'a social movement aimed at shoring up the moral, social and political environment. Part change of heart, part renewal of social bonds, part reform of public life.' Etzioni sees this movement as needing to operate through family, schools, the social webs of neighbourhood, work, and ethnic clubs and associations, and the national society. He believes it must be sustained by commitment to democratic process and respect for one another.

Notions of the individual in the community, as the debate over communitarianism in particular is demonstrating, have certain weaknesses and internal contradictions. Nevertheless, they do offer a number of increasingly influential ideas about the practice of democracy in modern society. The sort of suggestions starting to emerge generally propose that a democracy supportive of persons in community would, at the least, identify and protect individual rights; promote the practice of correspond-ing duties; encourage active citizen participation in society at local and national level, through both informal and formal arrangements; and strive for the articulation of a sense of shared national purpose. In principle, democracy would be open and equitable. The means and conditions necessary for the implementation in practice of democratic values would be legally articulated and enforceable.

The attack on justice and responsibility

Non-democratic regimes sign up for interpretations of justice and responsibility' which are, or at least should be, more or less alien and unacceptable to those who claim to subscribe to democratic values.

To begin with justice. Where individualistic, arbitrary, regimes hold sway, ideas of fairness are defined by those in control in their own interest. As it was succinctly expressed by representatives of imperial Athens to a *polis* with which it was in conflict, 'justice depends on the equality of power to compel and that in fact the strong do what they have the power to do and the weak accept what they have to accept' (Thucydides, 1972, p. 402).

In a Hobbesian type of society the situation, for most practical purposes, is little different. 'Justice in a commonwealth,' as R. S. Peters (1956, pp. 232–3) in his book on Hobbes explains, would be 'simply what was commanded by the law of the land.' The sovereign makes and enforces the law. It is true that, in contrast to a dictatorship or to any other state where power can be employed arbitrarily, there are in theory checks on capricious acts by the sovereign. The commandments of the civil law are required to reflect the theorems of natural law. Any decree which fails to do so is inequitable. However, 'The sovereign was the sole judge of equity.' In practice, only where a sovereign is honourable, wise and conscientious is justice likely to reflect natural law, and to appear to the citizen as something other than the absolute, coercive use of power finding its only justification in the will of the supreme authority.

In organic societies, the emphasis is very different. Here, the state is regarded as a coherent whole, rather than as a dangerously disparate, potentially explosive collection of mutually antipathetic components. In such a polity justice is that which, as Karl Popper (1966, vol. 1, chapter 6), has demonstrated in discussing Plato's Republic, promotes the interests of the state as a whole.

As for individuals, they have roles, or belong to classes and institutions which have a particular part to play in maintaining or furthering the good of the state. Depending upon which organic society or philosophy one has in mind, persons may or may not have the right to social mobility. What is critical, however, is that what is just, or unjust, treatment is defined in terms of socio-economic status. Thus, there will be one set of rules and laws for government officials, another for the military, another for the workers, another for employers, industrialists, etc., and so on. Alternatively, where there are universal decrees, they will be applied differently according to the occupations of those concerned. Each group in society has a hierarchically ordered social good, or goods, which it is its duty to aim to achieve as its contribution to the welfare of the whole, to the smooth running of society and state.

For individuals in these circumstances, 'The laws,' in Hegel's words, 'presuppose unequal conditions' (Popper, 1966, vol. 2, p. 45). Or, to put it from the point of view of those on the receiving end, 'Justice is keeping what belongs to one and doing one's own job' (Plato, 1955, p. 182). What all this means is that justice is defined according to merit and desert. That is, one is protected, punished, or compensated according to one's station in life, and according to one's success or failure in contributing to the common good.

In society as understood by Marx, the sovereign is the class which, at any given moment in the materialist dialectic of historical progress, is in effective control of economic and political power. The ruling class defines justice as that which defends and promotes its interests.

Various critical issues are highlighted by a Marxist approach to justice. The first is that ideas of justice may be relative, both within and between societies. The second, is that ideas of what is just are predicated by social and economic circumstance, and are ultimately the product of historical processes of development. Thus, in a Marxist view, however strongly individuals may be fired by a personal belief in justice, and whatever the immediate benefits of any action they may take, in the last analysis they are doing no more than giving history a helping hand. The final issue is rather different. It is that, for the oppressed, the notion of justice is revolutionary. History may be on their side. But the downtrodden can be disinclined to patience. Faced with the dominant vocabularies and institutions of exploitation, they may turn to insurrection.

The notion of responsibility, like that of justice, takes on its own peculiar meanings in authoritarian societies.

The responsibility of the individual under individualistic arbitrary, or Hobbesian, regimes is reduced to little more than an obligation to look out for the interests of one's self, probably of one's immediate family, and just possibly of any close neighbours and associates. The notion of responsibility is inevitably weak because it is not at all clear to whom one is responsible. To the state? One simply fears that. To other individuals or groups? They are mostly objects of suspicion rather than secure and established sources of moral authority. To self? A fearful entity, virtually devoid of scruple or conscience.

In an organic regime, the position is different. Here, it is abundantly evident to whom one is responsible, and for what. Each person is answerable to society as a whole. And it is the duty of everyone, from the highest to the lowest, so to think and act that they at all times promote the interests of all and of the totality. Society, to whom persons are accountable, esteems as responsible those who put the prosperity of the collective, as one and in its manifold manifestations, before those of themselves and of their immediate intimates, if such there be. In the last resort, organic society and state require that all the virtues of personal life, trust, faithfulness, love, must be overridden by the demands of collective responsibility.

For Marxism, a substantially identical understanding of responsibility holds. With one crucial exception. Responsibility operates within the organism of the class, not of society as a whole. Except, of course, where a classless society has been achieved.

Justice and responsibility in a democracy

Those who live in a liberal democracy can have difficulty in reaching agreement over what they understand by justice and responsibility.

In the first place, this is simply because they live in a society which is open, and which has evolved from past societies of a non-democratic nature. It follows that citizens of a democracy have available to them interpretations of justice and responsibility which have their origins in authoritarian philosophies and practices. So, for example, justice can be understood, in a fundamentally inegalitarian view of what is fair, as a distribution of benefits and harms in relation to the moral deserts and social roles of individuals. Or, responsibility may be understood as an overriding obligation to act according to the perceived best interests of a particular class, society, institution, or of any given significant social group or organization.

Secondly, agreement about justice and responsibility can be difficult to achieve because, as I have suggested, a liberal democracy is an arena where those with varying ideals of a person vie to shape society in such a way that it will mirror their own values. Thus, there is a more or less intermittent struggle to make democracy a place fit for Christians, or classicists, or, for rational, or humanist, or free-market persons, etc. More generally, democracy may be perceived as a field for conflict between those who are committed to individualist notions of society and those who believe in an approach which places greater emphasis on community. Those who hold these differing ideals of democracy are liable to have differing interpretations of justice and responsibility.

In these circumstances, what is self-evidently required is a rationally justifiable, universal, objective standard to which appeal can be made to decide, amongst other things, what should be meant by justice and responsibility. If this existed, we would have secure and logical grounds for rejecting non-democratic notions of justice and responsibility, and for deciding among those rival views which are more or less compatible with democracy.

However, it is a defining intellectual and social condition of liberalism that it is not able to agree on any such ultimate standard. As Alasdair MacIntyre (1988, p. 334) has argued, post-Enlightenment philosophy has constantly failed, from Kant onwards, to establish 'a neutral set of criteria by means of which the claims of rival and contending traditions could be adjudicated'. Thus, we 'inhabit a culture ... [with] ... an inability to arrive at agreed rationally justifiable conclusions on the nature of justice and practical rationality' (pp. 5–6).

So, given that secure consensus has, so far at least, proved difficult to achieve, there is, at least initially, little alternative but to identify the main differing democratic concepts of justice and responsibility.

Ideas of justice are often related to rights, to notions of social contract, and to standards of utility. Ideas of justice which rely upon the concept of rights tend to appeal to advocates of the rationalist and humanist ideals; various versions of social contract, particularly where these imply duties as well as rights, can be of particular interest to communitarians; and standards of utility are liable to be quoted by those who favour free-market theory.

The varying concepts of justice have differing practical implications. Thus, notions of justice which refer to rights will be likely to require clear and enforceable statements of what those rights are; while notions which refer to contract will probably need to look to society to make explicit those webs of informal relationships, rules and laws which are necessary for the effective support of mutual rights and obligations.

The implications of utilitarian notions of justice are likely to be of particular interest where the influence of free-market thinking is strong. According to the utilitarian view, as John Rawles (1972, p. 22) has expressed it, 'society is rightly ordered, and therefore just, when its major institutions are arranged so as to achieve the greatest net balance of satisfaction summed over all the individuals belonging to it'.

From this definition, two significant points follow. First, it does not particularly matter how the overall sum of satisfaction is distributed. So, some individuals or groups may be very well endowed with the goods they desire, and others may be relatively impoverished. However, as long as society as a whole is providing its members collectively with the best possible means for fulfilment of individual desires, it does not much matter who exactly gets what. So, it is just, in principle, for very considerable social and economic inequalities to exist.

And this leads to the second point. Precepts of justice, agreed by many to be necessary for the maintenance of liberal democracy, e.g. the protection of individual liberty, appear, in the final analysis, to be of secondary importance. In practice, it is assumed that it will virtually always be needful to obey these precepts as a means of ensuring the maximization and satisfaction of society's desires. However, in principle, one has to recognize that there may be occasions where personal liberty and so on may need to be sacrificed to secure the utilitarian good of all. Where this is so it is fair to set aside, suspend or ignore any decrees which may protect the person at the expense of pursuit of the best possible overall equilibrium of fulfilment (see Rawles, 1972, p. 26). What all this means, of course, is that justice and a sense of what is fair are weak, and of marginal significance, in a free-market society. Indeed, Friedrich Hayek (1978, p. 57) has gone so far as to claim that in a 'society of free men' the phrase 'social justice ... has no meaning whatsoever'.

Given all this, one might expect liberal democracies to be riven with internal, internecine disputes resulting from lack of consensus about what is just, and a consequent inability to build, maintain and administer anything remotely approaching what its inhabitants could agree to call a fair society.

But, on the whole, this does not appear to be the case. Liberal democracies, for the most part, have seemed able, anyway so far, to maintain at least the semblance of societies which respect and abide by shared rules and laws. Of course, there are always stresses and strains, and sometimes prolonged periods of turbulence. But descent into conditions of endemic anarchy is historically rare.

How is this achieved? In the first place, there is an acceptance, indeed even an endorsement, of the realities of the situation. Namely, that members of liberal democracies, while holding, and often doing battle for, their own view of what is just, have to concede that there is no shared, universal understanding of what is fair for either the individual or for society (see Walzer, 1985).

From this it follows that, if society is to have any chance of cohering, it must have, in all the various spheres of its multitudinous activities, accepted procedures for reaching agreement.

As concerns justice, this means there must be rules which provide persons with the opportunity to secure consensus. These rules must ensure that everyone, whoever they are and however otherwise disadvantaged they may be, are: first, not excluded from the chance to participate in the decision-making processes of democracy; secondly, able, at least in principle and within limitations shared by all, to articulate and realize their perception of what is good; and, thirdly, able to appeal to, or against, society's laws, which ultimately should derive from decision-making in which all citizens can be involved. To put this in other words, in a liberal democracy, justice, whatever the practical limitations, must in principle be egalitarian insofar at least as it seeks to ensure that persons have full opportunity to be equal as members of the electorate, before the law, and as consumers or achievers of their personally identified good.

Of course, all this begs a crucial question. How on earth, given the competing views of justice, can consensus be achieved even over the identity of those procedures to be followed in pursuit of assent over what is to be called fair? The short answer is that assent arises out of continuing debate. This is not a debate which is widely expected to reach any final or substantive conclusion, although every now and then it may. Rather, it is a complex argument which as occasion demands usually, but by no means always, defines an interim position which can temporarily be accepted by all for working purposes, subject to continuing review and the possibility, indeed probability, of future emendation. Thus, in a liberal democracy, people are usually in practice prepared to accept as just those decisions, rules, etc., which result from following procedures agreed in an on-going public debate whose shared purpose is to enable a fair society, however that may be seen, to evolve (for a more detailed exploration of these matters, see MacIntyre, 1988, chapter 17).

And now, what about the conflicting conceptions of responsibility to be found in liberal democracy?

Certain of those ideals of a person which inform liberal democracy see it as a vital aspect of being human that one is responsible, in the sense that one has the capacity to accept moral accountability for what one thinks and does.

For Christianity, and indeed for other major world faiths, humans are spiritual and moral beings answerable before God, or to a transcendant reality, for the conduct of life.

For rationalism, persons may be seen as answerable to an absolute law of nature or reason. More prosaically, rationalism is liable, in practice, to see persons as responsible to themselves and others, as rational individuals, for willed actions.

The humanist is predominantly concerned with self-fulfilment, and with the individual achievement of a range of goals which she or he identifies as desirable. This allows for the idea of responsibility to self and others, insofar as personal objectives are moral. However, it can also be important to experience private felicity. Where this is a priority, any notion of responsibility, in the sense of being answerable for one's actions, is liable for some if by no means all persons to lack real vigour.

For apologists of the free-market ideal of a person, the idea of responsibility as moral accountability can have little real meaning. This is inevitably so, since the philosophy of *laissez-faire* economics recognizes no need for any moral authority, whether personal, societal or divine: the magic ghost in the free-market machine arranges everything for the best, in the best of all possible worlds. Strictly speaking, the free-market person is morally unaccountable, and therefore not constrained to act responsibly. Of course, from time to time, those who do believe in moral accountability may try to call free-marketeers to answer for their actions. Such economic persons really cannot cope with demands of this nature. Characteristically, they respond by blaming others for whatever is wrong, or even by behaviour which to the detached observer can appear more psychotic than normal.

For what are persons in a liberal democracy prepared to accept responsibility?

Individualist persons, for whatever reason, are usually ready to accept responsibility for those in their immediate circle, particularly family.

However, they may well be less inclined to pay any great attention to the notion of responsibility to community and society. The best that rationalism or humanism can usually say is that, given a suitable education, it is possible to achieve quite a broadly encompassing sense of social responsibility. 'Genuine private affections,' says J. S. Mill in *Utilitarianism* (1979b, p. 265), 'and a sincere interest in the public good, are possible, though in unequal degrees, to every rightly brought up human being.'

But, of course, for economic individualism, the notion of responsibility for whole communities or societies is rubbish. And for a very simple reason. As Mrs Thatcher famously informed readers of *Woman's Own* in 1987, 'You know, there is no such thing as society. There are individual men and women, and there are families.'

Despite the dominant influence of individualism, the belief that the idea of responsibility should include caring attitudes and behaviour towards wider communities has survived in liberal democracy. This has occurred, however, often only within the context of fading, fragmented, threatened or minority social, moral and religious cultures.

The ideals of person and society which do provide a rationale for the notion of social responsibility broadly interpreted derive from contrasting, indeed antagonistic, sources. In the first place, there is an egalitarian-inspired ideal, perhaps most frequently expressed by radical Christianity and by democratic socialism. This interprets social responsibility as needing to be exercised within and towards national or local communities of equals. Such a notion sees the practice of responsibility both as a moral end in itself and as a means of achieving agreed greater goods for all. Another way of putting this is to say that through socially responsible behaviour it becomes possible to create social capital. By social capital is meant those arrangements of coordination and cooperation which result in mutual benefit (see Commission on Social Justice, 1994, chapter 7).

Those who hold a more hierarchical view of society see social responsibility rather differently. They tend to emphasize the importance of social coherence rather than of equality. It is usually not long before Edmund Burke is quoted reverentially and extensively. The virtue of membership of 'little platoons' and of other groups, such as Church, party and nation, is characteristically invoked (see Douglas Hurd, *New Statesman*, 22 April 1988). What is usually implicit, but less often explicit, is the assumption that these platoons, and so forth, are part of larger forces, all of which are organized in interconnecting pyramids of authority. Within these hierarchies, social responsibility involves obedience and deference from those at the base, foot soldiers etc., to those in command, together with leadership and care for the well-being of underlings on the part of the higher ranking. It is the final, reluctant surrendering of active life by this pre-democratic, organic order which is now so profoundly missed by many. It is not so much that people wish to bring back a world of static, immutable privilege as that they desire to see again the practice of social responsibility which they imagine it guaranteed. But, of course, that is an impossible dream. As Joseph Schumpeter (1976) long ago pointed out, capitalism devours historical inheritance.

Finally, if one turns to consider the influence of the liberal democratic state on the understanding and practice of responsibility, one finds that its structures, procedures and actions compound the difficulties generated by the jostling of the competing ideologies to which it affords living space.

Where, as is usual, individualism predominates, it influences the state, through the development of its systems, as well as through the nature and implementation of its decisions, to create a society of winners and losers. The latter tend to feel little or no allegiance to platoons, class, country, state or anything else very much, other perhaps than to organizations antagonistic to establishment values and organizations. The practical results, all too well documented, are a persistent aversion to exercising democratic rights, a pervasive sense of alienation, and exacerbated criminal activity.

In fact, if an individualistic ethos is dominant in a state, it is likely to result, as J. K. Galbraith (1992) has argued, in a contented majority voting to ignore the needs of the underprivileged minority, who thereby are effectively disenfranchised. In such a scenario the wretched are irresponsible insofar as they refuse to involve themselves in what they see as pointless participation in society, and insofar as they may well act so as to subvert, overtly or covertly, the rules of the community. But, equally, and more culpably, the fortunate are also irresponsible. While frequently blaming the rejected, they themselves are reluctant to take any steps to ensure a more equitable society. Not only are the poor always present in an individualist state; the system operates, and is operated, to ensure that they always will be.

But, when the liberal democratic state has attempted to structure itself, and to legislate, so as to reflect and promote values and practices of social coherence, a different set of systemic difficulties has emerged. Whatever the benefits of the welfare state, it is now difficult to deny that it has created a sense of dependency as well as of security. The achievement of equal social rights of citizenship, which as T. H. Marshall (1950, p. 56), pointed out was both inspirational aim and effective outcome of the creation of a society which accepted communal responsibility for common need, was not in the event balanced by an exercise of corresponding duty. While the individualist state created selfish winners and irresponsible losers, social democracy resulted in a society where too many expected simply to get, and too few to give: here, responsibility to others degenerated too easily into an anaemic virtue.

For a society to encourage, to good effect, a balanced exercise of personal and social responsibility between equals there has to be faith in its procedures, shared commitment to common values, and clear, agreed purpose. To the extent that these conditions do not exist, the citizens of a liberal democracy will not only have disparate views of what responsibility means, but collectively will have an enfeebled sense of the importance of responsible behaviour, at least as concerns their own actions. Of course, a belief that they themselves need not behave responsibly will not necessarily hinder them from calling for responsibility from others. As things currently stand, where responsibility is successfully practised, it is achieved despite confusion, and against the grain of the values which are actually dominant.

Justice and responsibility in schools

Against this background, what approaches are open to schools to take, and which should they try to pursue?

There are essentially two paths which schools can follow in teaching students about the social virtues of justice and responsibility.

First, they can teach about them as an academic topic. That is to say, they can offer a curriculum which provides for the consideration of the major different meanings, of whatever origin, democratic or non-democratic, which can be attributed to the notions of justice and responsibility; and which explores the implications for society of attempting to implement particular interpretations.

The academic approach can be promoted through general studies or appropriate specialist courses. However, much of the subject-matter is necessarily complex, detailed and abstract. The whole curriculum cannot realistically be expected to give a high priority to this particular issue.

Schools can, however, also adopt a more overtly moral approach. And this is what society, and in particular those who appoint themselves or who are appointed to speak for it, mostly favour. That is to say, they can teach about justice and responsibility as virtues to be valued and desired. This, as in moral education generally, may be done through rational, justifiable precept and through practice. The two are mutually dependent.

Teaching the theory underlying justice and responsibility can be a relatively straight-forward matter for schools established to educate students according to particular sets of beliefs, theological, philosophic, cultural, social, and so on. Here, the notions of justice and responsibility can be interpreted by reference to the given systematic doctrines and credos.

Most schools, however, are committed, in principle, to accepting students of whatever background. For them, matters are less straight-forward.

One major difficulty arises because schools, whether they like it or not, are inescapably members of a pluralist democracy. Contemporary society, as has already been argued, has no explicit, unambiguous, coherent interpretation for either justice or responsibility. It can only offer a range of overlapping, and in places mutually inconsistent and competing, meanings.

Faced with this situation, schools apparently have a number of options. They can, in theory, choose one set of meanings in preference to another. However, for most schools this is unlikely to prove a realistic strategy. It would, no doubt, in due course alienate those groups connected with a school who did not sign up for the particular approach being adopted. If there is one thing schools are understandably very anxious to avoid it is causing conflict over values with the communities they serve.

On the other hand schools could, at least hypothetically, try to make explicit the various democratic understandings of justice and respons-ibility, and do their best to teach all these, through explanation, example, procedure and ethos.

However, one has only to spell out this possibility to see its impracticability. To function effectively, whether as a learning or a moral community, schools have to have a reasonable degree of coherence in their purposes and general arrangements. Any attempt to implement educational policy in the light of the spectrum of democratic notions of justice and responsibility would in all probability condemn a school to interior inconsistency and operational disfunction.

So, *faute de mieux*, schools, at least in the maintained sector, mostly in practise implement what is, in effect, a pick'n'mix policy. They choose, more or less instinctively, the approaches which they think will best suit them in their particular circumstances. This seldom leads to disaster, and at least usually enables schools to struggle along in a fashion generally seen as acceptable. However, as has been widely noticed, it does not always produce students with a highly developed and articulate understanding of and commitment to justice and responsibility.

Thus, this is hardly an ideal option. It does not, and cannot, offer any clear connection between a sustaining system of ideas and the moral notions and behaviour being advocated. Consequently, a fundamental duty of any education is not fulfilled. There can be no cogent explication of the nature and justification of particular notions being presented as morally desirable, in this case justice and responsibility, nor of the sort of attitudes and behaviour to which they are expected to lead.

Many schools, then, simply because they belong to a liberal democratic society, have considerable difficulties to overcome if they are to teach justice and responsibility in a justifiable and effective way. But that is not the only factor which can cause problems.

Some schools have also been hindered predominantly, but not necessarily exclusively, by historic circumstance from developing a democratic approach to educating students as fair and responsible persons. This consideration obtained more in the past than nowadays, although arguably it still may exert a certain influence on institutions, and not least, perhaps, those with a special regard for past traditions.

The problem here is that particular schools may look to a significant extent to earlier, inherited, non-democratic traditions of thought and practice to define their understanding of justice and responsibility.

Schools may, in particular, exhibit individualistic authoritarian, or organic tendencies.

In a school with individualistic authoritarian characteristics, justice primarily originates in the arbitrary will of the ruler, that is the Head. Heads may be shamelessly, indeed even proudly, despotic. More probably, however, they will claim that edicts promulgated in their name, are justifiable by reference to divine, or even natural, law. Nevertheless, even where this is so, as in a Hobbesian state, the Head is usually both the interpreter of the law and the arbiter of its application. Accordingly, for all practical purposes, what the Head says is just defines what is fair. Acting fairly involves no more, and no less, than carrying out the will of the Head, as enunciated in the rules, codes, edicts, utterances, emanating from that all-but-sacerdotal source.

In school polities where justice flows from an autocratic source of power, it is inclined to be administered coercively. Characteristically, it frequently relies for its effective implementation upon threat, retribution and punishment, until recently often physical.

This approach both arises from and provokes an absence of consent amongst the governed. In schools of this sort a counter-culture is liable to arise. While some students, as a result of official pressure or natural inclination, will probably identify themselves with the ruling adult or adults, most, in a way which Marxists would well understand, will perceive themselves as underprivileged and exploited. As such, they develop their own primitive critique of their society, together with its specialist vocabulary and concepts. The language of the oppressed will define its own understanding of justice, which will be more or less antithetical to that deriving from the Head. In an authoritarian school there are two justices, and two views of what is just. One is official, and that of the establishment. The other is covert, and potentially or actually subversive of the former.

As for responsibility, unadulterated authoritarianism, in whatever sort of social organization, blights any sense of social obligation. In schools, it encourages students to emerge as persons who are self-centred and bullying, or cowed and resentful. Either way, any feeling of social duty is likely to be restricted to immediate associates, and just possibly to family.

Schools with organic characteristics reveal a strongly hierarchical nature. Power flows pyramidically, down from the Head, a most appropriate title for the commander of a corporate body, via a duly stratified staff, through to ever inferior layers of students, from head boys and girls, through prefects, monitors, and captains of various cohorts, to students who as they get younger and younger, or less and less brainy, are seen to have less and less value or significance.

Such an institution is rule ridden. There are rules for everything. The rules provide a framework which helps to define students' roles. Obviously, there are different rules for different groups, together with a complex range of related sanctions. The main concern in the administration of justice is to ensure that all students, whatever their functions within the body of the school, make their required contributions. Needs of individual students are not a high priority.

Within schools of an organic nature, there is a very significant emphasis on responsibility. There are, at least in principle, acknowledged mutual responsibilities between those who hold differing roles. Equally, and often in practice more importantly, each member is expected to demonstrate a sense of responsibility in regard to the good of the whole; or, as it is usually expressed, to be loyal to the school. As a result, at best, regard for the good of the school as a whole commands a real commitment from both present and past students to furthering its educational goals specifically, and its reputation more generally. At worst, however, the practice of loyalty takes precedence over the fulfilment of individual talents and ideals, especially where these differ from the culture of the school: a sense of loyalty may also may be appealed to and exploited to enable abuses within the school, or by those connected with it, to be covered up: and it can be used to further the immediate interests of the school at the expense of the greater social good.

Organic schools tend to consider that there are particular roles, with associated responsibilities, which their students should be expected to fulfil in the adult world. What they believe these roles to be is influenced by the perceptions which they and others hold of their position in the rank ordering of society.

Schools at, or aspiring to be at, the apex of the social hierarchy emphasize leadership, and an obligation to show active concern for the poor and the underprivileged. Hence, for example, at the turn of the century, there was the establishment by many major public schools of clubs for working-class boys in deprived areas. Hence, also, there was the development of what used to be called the Officer Training Corps, with its concern to teach, amongst other things, a responsibility to look after those in the other ranks.

As one descended the scale of schools, through minor public schools, through grammar schools, to elementary, and later to secondary modern schools, so values changed. An ethos which, at least in principle, favoured an ethic of duty to the less favoured, was gradually, if at times disjointedly, replaced by a social morality of submission. Students from schools intended for the least able, the least well-off, or the least socially privileged were, as a rule, expected to learn a responsibility to follow, to obey, to conform, to play their particular economic or social part, however humble, in contributing to the greater good of the integrated community. For these, deference was the outward and visible sign of socially responsible behaviour.

Of course, non-democratic educational interpretations of justice and responsibility are open, in principle, to attack and rejection on democratic grounds. Indeed, it is largely as a result of such criticism that these more long-standing, inherited ideals attract much less support than used to be the case.

Nevertheless, tradition in education can attract fierce devotion. And there are those who still value these particular ancient verities. Particular arguments have been evolved to support the non-democratic stance.

It can be pleaded that schools are in a special situation, and so more or less exempt from any obligation generally to organize themselves along democratic lines, and specifically to follow democratic notions of justice and responsibility.

In certain limited, but ultimately unimportant, respects, it is true that schools are not fully democratic.

Thus, if one considers the overall arrangements for the management and provision of education in schools, it is the case that while, at least in maintained schools, some governors are elected, no one with teaching or other professional responsibility is. On the other hand, it is not common practice for formal organizations in a liberal democracy to use the vote as a means of selecting people for particular jobs. More importantly, however, all schools are, to a greater or lesser extent, dependent on democratically provided funds. And all are answerable to its laws.

Schools are also not fully democratic in another limited sense. Most students are not of an age to exercise the full democratic rights and duties of citizenship. Nor, in any case, are they sufficiently mature or experienced to behave in a fully democratic way in school. But then, they are not in a position to act as full members of any sort of adult society, democratic or otherwise. They are at school to learn. And one of the most important things they have to learn is how to act as democrats. This they can hardly do by being inducted into non-democratic modes of thought and behaviour.

The crucial point is to do with educational aims. However the polity of a school is ordered in detail, it must in general be so structured as to enable its ethos and educational programme to further democratic values. Specifically, this means that it must be actively committed to promoting democratically inspired notions of justice and responsibility. It cannot legitimately encourage interpretations of justice and responsibility which ultimately derive their meaning from non-democratic philosophies and practices.

So, what ought to be done?

Schools should have, and in some cases are already developing, specific and explicit understandings of justice and responsibility which make sense in the educational context.

These understandings need to meet various criteria.

They must be democratic. Students should both learn about the social virtues which society believes to be desirable, and should acquire a secure standpoint from which non-democratic interpretations may be evaluated.

They must be as inclusive as possible. Of course, for the reasons already discussed, they will not be able to cover all possible interpretations acceptable within a liberal democracy. But, as far as is reasonably possible, they should not obviously exclude particular definitions.

Finally, they should be readily capable of being applied in educational activities.

Thus, one needs to establish definitions. In principle, it would be possible to suggest all-embracing, comprehensive definitions for both justice and responsibility. However, any such attempt would more than likely be self-defeating. Ultimately, it would almost certainly turn out that one had done no more than add further, and equally debatable definitions to those which already exist.

So, there is actually no serious alternative to basing any viable educational definitions of justice and responsibility on already existing approaches. It is a matter of adopting definitions which are most likely to prove generally acceptable and educationally useful.

How, then, can schools most appropriately define justice?

As a framework for an interpretation of justice I shall refer to the principles of justice as fairness proposed by John Rawles (1972).

Rawles (p. 60) formulates two main principles of justice as fairness.

- First: each person is to have an equal right to the most extensive basic liberty compatible with a similar liberty for others.
- Second: social and economic inequalities are to be arranged so that they are both:
  (a) reasonably expected to be to everyone's advantage, and:
  (b) attached to positions and offices open to all.

Where these principles are put into practice, a society or institution can reasonably be described as just.

I use Rawles's approach: first, because it is almost certainly the most comprehensive and influential contemporary account of what is meant by justice; and, secondly, because it is intended to apply not only to society in general, but also to particular institutions within society. This means that, where any reference is made to institutions, it can reasonably be assumed that it includes schools.

Of course, Rawles's theory has not only been widely discussed, but also criticized. That is inevitable, given the variety of approaches to justice necessarily characteristic of a liberal democratic society. However, the major thrust of the critical points raised is not seriously damaging to the view I wish to adopt.

One common complaint is that Rawles's theory, despite the careful procedures adopted to ensure impartiality, are in fact rooted in and reflect the values of liberal individualism (MacIntyre, 1988, p. 4). However, for my purposes, that is not a very significant issue. Rawles's principles are sufficiently broadly conceived not to exclude consideration of the key personal and social ideals with which schools ought to be concerned. And, in any case, it is appropriate for schools, in a liberal democracy, to use as a framework of reference principles of justice consistent with the values of liberal democracy.

A second sort of reservation is that the principles do not take sufficient account of the particular concerns of certain interest groups to be found in a liberal democracy. Thus, David Willetts (1992, pp. 63–4), from the point of view of the free-market philosophy, considers the principle of justice should place greater emphasis on the need for economic inequality. However, this issue is really only a matter of degree. For Rawles's principles do not posit full economic equality as a criterion of justice.

The principles of justice refer to two key concepts: *right* and *equality*. Both of these must be central to the vocabulary and practice of schools if they are to work as just institutions.

The *right to liberty*, as defined, requires, in general, that each person is able to decide his or her own good.

This, of course, includes the educationally vital right to decide what sort of person one desires to become.

More particularly, the right to liberty requires that a person has full access to certain goods which it can reasonably be assumed are desired by most, if not all, individuals. These, called by Rawles (p. 92) 'primary goods', are 'rights and liberties, opportunities and powers, income and wealth'. Some, or even all, of these social goods can be important as ends in themselves. To a greater extent, however, they are likely to be helpful in achieving the good one desires for oneself.

For a student at school, these social goods are likely to be understood in terms of freedom to chose certain courses, realistic opportunity to gain necessary educational experience and qualifications, and absence of financial, social or other constraints to the achievement of personal educational goals.

What, more specifically, are the basic rights of students?

The most important of these have been spelled out in the United Nations Convention on the Rights of the Child (see Newell, 1991), and were in 1992 ratified by the government of the United Kingdom. They include the rights of students:

- to an education which should be directed to the development of the child's personality and talents, preparing the child for active life as an adult, fostering respect for human rights and developing respect for the child's own cultural and national values and those of others (Article 29);
- to freedom from discrimination (Article 2);
- to express an opinion and to have it taken into account (Article 12);
- of thought, conscience and religion (Article 14);
- of association and peaceful assembly (Article 15);
- to benefit from an adequate standard of living (Article 27).
- to protection of privacy (Article 16), and from abuse and neglect (Article 19).

The second concept which plays a key part in formulating the principles of justice is *equality*. Rawles spells out the place of equality in some detail under what he calls a general conception' of the principles: 'liberty and opportunity, income and wealth, and the bases of self-respect – are to be distributed equally, unless an unequal distribution of any or all of these goods is to the advantage of the least favoured' (p. 303).

The question which now arises is this: in schools, are there circumstances in which an unequal distribution of goods can be to the advantage of all students, including the least favoured, and so promote justice?

To begin with, there is a semantic difficulty to be clarified. The word 'equality' means 'the condition of being equal in dignity, privileges, power etc. with others: fairness, impartiality, equity' (*Oxford English Dictionary*). The opposite of equality' is 'inequality': that is to say, superiority or inferiority to others in dignity, etc.

'Equality' can be confused, whether deliberately or not, with 'sameness', which is in fact an entirely different concept.

'Sameness' means 'the quality of being the same. Uniformity, monotony' (OED). Its opposite is 'difference', meaning 'the condition, quality or fact of being different, or not the same; dissimilarity, distinction, diversity' (OED).

It can happen that difference is identified as the opposite of equality. And, similarly, inequality can be identified as the opposite of sameness.

Where this occurs one result is simply unhelpful confusion. But another is more malign. It is that, since the idea of difference is generally valued, the idea of equality, where assumed to be its opposite, is by implication denigrated. Likewise, since sameness is not generally valued, inequality where assumed to be its opposite is esteemed.

It is clearly important that all these four terms are given their correct meaning if any discussion of equality is not to be distorted (see box).

EQUALITY	is the opposite of	INEQUALITY
SAMENESS	is the opposite of	DIFFERENCE
EQUALITY	is not the opposite of	DIFFERENCE
EQUALITY	is compatible with	DIFFERENCE

Everyone should have equal basic rights. In schools, this means that all students, whatever their needs, social or ethnic origin, gender or personal attributes, should have those rights identified by the United Nations (see p. 121).

Persons should share an *equality of regard*. All individuals, in schools as elsewhere, should see everyone, including themselves, as having what Raymond Williams has called 'equality of being' (1962, p. 305). Such equality is, in Simone Weil's words (1952, p. 15), 'a vital need of the soul'. To quote her again, 'it consists in a recognition, at once public, general, effective and genuinely expressed in institutions and customs, that the same amount of respect and consideration is due to every human being because this respect is due to the human being as such and is not a matter of degree'. That is to say, it is both a psychological need and a moral imperative that, whatever an individual's character or circumstances, he or she should regard self and others as ends not means, as ultimately significant, as sacred. At birth, in death, throughout life, all are of unquantifiable, unquestionable and equal value.

Next, there is *equality of opportunity*. As a phrase, equality of opportunity does not specify for whom the equality should be provided. Nor is there universal agreement about this. I shall take it to refer to all individuals and groups in a school.

For equality of opportunity to be wholly realized three criteria have to be met.

First, in any particular school, full and equal opportunity should exist for each student, and all groups of students, to participate in all courses of study, personal and social education provision, and extra-curricular activity.

Secondly, in all schools, a broad, balanced, coherent and efficacious range of educational experiences, taking account of society's expectations, should be offered so that students have the chance both to acquire the core knowledge and skills seen as necessary by society and to develop fully their particular abilities, potential and interests.

Thirdly, support and guidance must be given to ensure, as far as humanly possible, that students are able to take up and benefit from opportunities offered.

Equality of opportunity should lead to increasingly different and differentiated learning experiences for students. As essential, common knowledge, skills and attitudes are mastered, and as students develop as individuals, so increasingly they require a curriculum which meets their particular needs. Equality of opportunity enables students to progress from a common to a differentiated curriculum.

All persons must have full *equality as citizens* (equal right to vote, be eligible for public office, freedom of speech, assembly, thought, conscience, etc., see Rawles, 1972, p. 61). One could argue that this does not apply to students insofar as they have not acquired all rights of citizenship until they are 18. However, all should have equal status as future citizens. This means that they must all be fully educated in the nature and practice of democratic citizenship.

Finally, there is the question of *economic and social equality*. Students can come to particular schools from widely contrasting backgrounds. There is great potential benefit in this. Students gain the opportunity to get to know, become friendly with, put up with, understand, and so on, those from different class, cultural, faith and financial background from their own. They can come to see the unfamiliar, not as stereotypes, but as persons whom, whether they like them or not, have their own strengths, weaknesses and idiosyncrasies. It is in such experiences that a realistic sense of community can be rooted.

Of course, teaching students to appreciate and cope with difference is one thing. Ensuring equality is another. It is all too well established that the social and economic status of students can be of educational benefit to the privileged, and a handicap to the underprivileged. Within schools there is no moral justification whatsoever for the education offered to particular individuals or groups to be influenced positively or adversely by what can be afforded on their behalf. Any discrimination, on grounds of ability to pay, is bound to result in a denial of educational rights.

To return to the original question under discussion. Are there any circumstances in which an unequal distribution of goods can be to the advantage of all students, including the least favoured, and so promote justice? The answer must be that it is hard to find any circumstances in which any form of inequality can be of advantage to all students. Indeed, it seems likely that the reverse is true. That is to say, education of quality for each and every student is more likely to result where equality of rights, regard, opportunity, citizenship and economic treatment are observed and promoted. Consequently, a just school is one where equality, in its various manifestations, is valued and practised. Of course, it does not necessarily follow that a just system of national education might not, in certain respects, lack equality. But that matter is considered in the final chapter.

And so now, having considered justice, what about responsibility?

● In a liberal democracy, responsible persons are those who acknowledge certain legal and moral obligations, and who do their best, through their actions, to perform the duties required of them by their obligations.

This interpretation of responsibility raises two questions. First, to whom is one responsible? The short answer is that one is responsible to other rational, moral beings, or Being. Religious persons will see themselves as being accountable, above all, to divine Being, and then to other humans, especially those who, however they gain that status, appear to speak for deity. Rationalists, those strongly influenced by rationalism, and humanists, will see themselves as preeminently accountable to other rational, moral persons.

The second question is: for what is one responsible? In a democracy, a person is responsible for carrying out those duties which they incur as a result of a need to ensure that mutually held rights are respected and can be practised.

A hierarchy of duties exists, in principle, in all democratic institutions, including schools.

- First, there is a general duty to uphold the principles of justice.
- Secondly, there is a duty to cooperate with others to ensure there is a fair implementation and effective review of the principles of justice.
- Thirdly, there are duties which individuals incur as a result of the rights they should automatically acquire, simply by virtue of membership of particular types of institution. Thus, as members of a school, students have a right to a good education. Assuming this is provided, they have a duty to work and to learn to the best of their ability.
- Fourthly, there are duties which individuals should fulfil arising from any general advantage they may enjoy in an institution. Advantage for students can arise from a range of attributes, such as intelligence, age, physical development, ethnic background, and so on. They may also benefit, at least indirectly, if they come from relatively privileged economic or social backgrounds. Whatever the source of advantage, there is an obligation to use it, not only for the satisfaction of personal goals, but also for mutual benefit.
- Fifthly, individuals have duties arising from specific roles they hold in society or institutions. So, in schools, any students who have rule-making, administrative or other responsibilities have an obligation to carry them out openly and fairly.
- Finally, there is a common duty to observe, maintain and promote, in the interests of justice, specific laws and rules, provided they are fair.

All types of duty may be justified by reference to a range of moral or religious beliefs. However, insofar as they are associated with principles of justice, they can equally be justified by prudential considerations. It is in the interest of all to live in just institutions. Consequently, it is in everyone's interests to fulfil the duties which are essential to the maintenance and development of such institutions. And of course, the greater the benefit individuals obtain from belonging to a just institution, for example through personal, social, occupational or economic status, the greater will be their interest in fulfilling the duties which accompany privilege. For those who enjoy privilege without carrying out the corresponding duties are creating an unjust society. And sooner or later unjust institutions, and not least schools, together with those who benefit from them, are at risk of self-destructing, or of being destroyed.

In conculsion, as well as having specific duties which arise from membership of institutions, persons also have responsibilities for a wider community. And it is imperative that schools teach students about those responsibilities.

One must be responsible, as taught in the major religions and moral philosophies, for all other human creatures. This responsibility cannot be artificially restricted to nearest and dearest only. There is a great, but not an exclusive, responsibility for them.

However, there is more to it than this. There are wider circles of responsibility. Traditionally, Western thought has seen persons as being predominantly, albeit not always exclusively, responsible for other persons: some thinkers, such as Hume, have also emphasized responsibility for property. This is a human-centred world of responsibility.

It is now very evident that this is not enough. Both on moral and practical grounds, notions of responsibility which focus on persons are necessary, but not sufficient. Humans also have to acknowledge a responsibility for that which is created, for nature, for the animate and inanimate world. Inescapably, as human power and control over the environment increase, so must responsibility for human action taken towards it. The universe functions according to its own laws, its phenomena have their own value, and their own imperatives. There is a human responsibility for that cosmos of which we are a part, upon which we depend, but in which we have our own distinct and privileged existence.

CHAPTER 10

The school: institution and community

As an institution, the school provides an organizational and administrative framework, whose first virtue is justice.

As a community, the school provides a network of social relationships, whose first virtue is responsibility.

In schools, institution and community are interdependent. Accordingly, I shall not attempt to deal with them separately. I shall consider them together, in their mutuality.

As institutions, schools must strive to be just.

They must do this, in the first place, so as to enable students to learn, through study, observation and practice, about the meaning of fairness. Students should gain an increasingly secure grasp of what is meant by justice, both in the school and in the wider society.

Schools must also strive to be just so as to enable them to function effectively and efficiently. Where a school operates as an unjust institution, that is to say, where particular individuals and groups are favoured at the expense of others, or where rules are irrational, or are applied selectively, or are broken with impunity, then many members of that school will be discontented, resentful, alienated and underperforming. The school, to a greater or lesser extent, will be failing. Justice as fairness in education is not simply an essential virtue for students to learn and practise. It is also a necessary condition for successful education.

As communities, schools must strive to be responsible.

They must do this, in the first place, so as to enable young people to gain knowledge of the moral requirements of being good members: as students, of the school community; and as future citizens, of the wider democratic society.

Schools must also strive to be responsible for the sake of the school, here and now. Where a school fails to encourage, condones, or even actively connives at irresponsible attitudes and behaviour, by whomsoever, then such valid educational objectives and procedures as it may have, including any concern with democracy and citizenship, will be liable to be distorted, neglected, derided. Schools, like the larger society, have little chance of success, or even ultimately of survival, if its members fail to recognize and practise the responsibilities which come with belonging to a community.

How does one set about developing schools as just institutions, and responsible communities? The answer is: through leadership, structure and management. Leaders have been defined as those who 'by word and/or personal example, markedly influence the behaviours, thoughts and/or feelings of a significant number of their fellow human beings' (Gardner, 1996, pp. 8–9). The critical questions are by whom, with what purposes, and how, is leadership to be exercised?

The immediate, day-to-day leadership of a school is formally vested in the headteacher. Of course, others have a contribution to make. For example, the chair of the governing body and the governors have a contribution to make to the overall leadership of the school. Deputy heads and heads or coordinators of particular subjects and courses have a contribution to make to the leadership of particular elements of the school. But the headteacher should be the guiding light.

The overriding concern of the headteacher must be with the definition and implementation of school aims (see G. Holmes, 1993). In maintained schools, this is a legal responsibility, shared with the governing body. Schools need a range of moral and utilitarian aims. Moral aims, with which we are mainly concerned, should refer to the teaching of respect for persons; of truth through the curriculum; of justice in the school as an institution; and of responsibility in the school community.

Headteachers need to ensure that school aims identify justice and responsibility in terms which are unambiguous and pragmatic. More specifically, they should ensure that the relevant aims are supported by particular objectives, which are in turn sustained by explicit, written policies, and that these together provide realistic, substantial and comprehensive guidance on achieving the overall aims.

Objectives and policies whose purposes include the promotion of just and responsible schools should deal with rights, equalities, duties and obligations.

I have dealt with the major educational rights in the previous chapter. In general terms, they are mostly covered, if often only indirectly, in legislation. Schools, accordingly, have to take account of them. Their overall aims should make absolutely clear their commitment to recognizing all students' major educational rights.

Schools need to articulate an intention to promote the educational aspects of equality.

Equality of regard should be discussed in the context of moral and social development, and of ethos.

Equality of citizenship, and the means for ensuring that students learn about this, should be set out in what is said about the promotion of social development.

Equality of opportunity for ethnic minorities, for girls and boys, for those with special educational needs, and for potentially high achieving students, should be, and increasingly are, spelled out in detailed objectives and policies.

Schools also require coherent strategies to ensure that socially or economically disadvantaged students have full and effective access to curricular and extra-curricular activities.

The duties predicated by the experience of receiving equal treatment should be as firmly identified as the equalities themselves.

It ought to be spelled out that equality of regard is a two-way business, a question of giving as well as of receiving. Those who are treated with respect as equal beings have an obligation to treat others similarly, to look after their welfare, and certainly to refrain from abuse and bullying – racial, social or personal.

Likewise, objectives and policies dealing with behaviour, discipline and responsibilities need to articulate that students have an overriding duty to observe and promote just rules, to listen to and consider with an open mind the opinions of others, and to act with concern for others, taking reasonable account of their needs and interests.

Finally, it should be made clear that students being provided with equality of opportunity are under a double obligation: first, to use any advantages they may receive for the benefit of others as well as of themselves; and, secondly, not to diminish opportunity for others, for example through disruptive behaviour.

So, assuming relevant objectives and policies are intended or in place, what structures are required to enable students to understand and practise justice and responsibility?

The National Curriculum and religious education provide, in principle, the foundations for a curriculum which is just in the sense that all students have full and equal access to it.

Nevertheless, all is not necessarily flourishing in the curricular garden. In particular, when it comes to content as opposed to access, there is no statutory requirement, as there most certainly should be, for the curriculum systematically to cover notions of justice, right, equality, responsibility and duty. Nor, equally shamefully, do students have to learn about the rights and duties of citizens in relation to law; work, employment and leisure; public services; family and the wider community; and, more generally, local and national democratic arrangements.

There are, it is true, independent initiatives to help schools that wish to deal with such issues, for instance, 'The Law in Education Project', 1988–9, published by Edward Arnold. The National Curriculum Council has issued guidance on the teaching of cross-curricular themes, which covers some of the relevant matters (National Curriculum Council, 1990a). And, more recently, the National Forum for Values in Education (1996), set up by the Schools Curriculum and Assessment Authority, has strongly advocated model syllabuses concerned with the promotion of spiritual, moral, social and cultural values. However, despite a promise in the 1997 government White Paper *Excellence in Schools* to set up a consultative committee on citizenship education, there continues to be little indication of a serious official intention to provide statutory backing for the area.

Many schools, of course, do their best, despite the absence of legal support. But, inevitably, it is seldom enough. Other schools do little. And at the dead centre of bad schools are to be found curricula which care little for justice, rights, equalities, responsibility, duties, democracy and citizenship.

The school should be so constituted that it enables students to learn about the nature of justice and responsibility through experience, reflection on theory and practice, and discussion. Curricular and social provision should be complementary, providing students with the opportunity to gain the knowledge and the understanding, the skills, the attitudes and the insights which together contribute to the development of a just and responsible person, committed to upholding a fair and decent society.

Councils, or similar bodies, should enable students to consider a range of issues. In relation to justice and responsibility, matters such as school rules, codes of behaviour, student contracts of duties, and charters of rights, bullying, equal opportunities and racism should all qualify to be on the agenda. Equally importantly, the democratic procedures themselves, the processes by which students may or may not raise particular matters, and make recommendations or decisions, should be open for consideration. This is essential if students are to learn how citizens of a liberal democracy can debate and reach consensus about what may, and what may not, be accepted as just and responsible.

Democratic responsibilities may be learned through electing representatives, for example in councils, or through contributing to the choice of particular officials, e.g. head girls and boys, prefects, monitors, etc. In councils, and less formal groups, students should be able to learn to put their own views clearly, to pay serious attention to views which differ from their own, whether minority or not, and to accept and abide by majority decisions.

Responsibility for the observation and maintenance of rules should be learned through helping to administer rules by performing specific roles (membership of sixth form, prefects, etc.); through contributing to dealing with rule-breaking (e.g. through informal pastoral discussions, or more formally through arrangements such as school courts); and through keeping rules as members of the school community.

While a general ability to take responsibility for one's work should come through study, a more specific understanding of the nature and responsibilities of the adult world of work, employment and leisure should arise from interrelated work observation and experience, and classroom activities. Similarly, through the curriculum, outside visits or other involvement, students should have the opportunity to see how vigorous public services are dependent upon and contribute to the exercise of responsible citizenship. Finally, through a range of initiatives and activities, including, as happens in many schools, fund-raising, students can learn the social and moral responsibilities they have, whether as individuals, or as members of families, and local and international communities, towards their fellow humans, other living creatures, and the environment.

A majority of secondary schools, and a substantial minority of all schools, probably now support some form of organized democratic activity, particularly though councils of one sort or another (ACE, 1993). However, traditionally English education has been fully as reluctant to promote an experiential approach as it has been to promote a curricular approach to democratic education. Of course, there can be difficulties. The remit of councils may not be made sufficiently clear; there may be uncertainty over whether, or to what extent, there are delegated powers, an advisory, consultative or executive role; some staff may be openly or covertly hostile; many may, at least initially, lack the necessary professional abilities effectively to teach students democratic skills and attitudes. Ultimately, however, a failure in school, for whatever reason, to educate in the practice of democracy represents a failure to educate for a just and responsible society.

Bearing in mind, particularly, the need to practise and promote justice and responsibility, how should a school be managed?

The answer in general is: so as best to ensure that its structures and procedures enable it to pursue its aims, including its moral aims.

Those who manage are the staff of a school. It is misleading to suggest that there are some teachers who manage ('the management') and the rest who do not. All manage. But different individuals and groups will have different tasks.

The headteacher, deputy or deputies, and sometimes one or two others ('the senior management') have to ensure that all teachers are as well placed as possible to manage successfully.

The senior management need to make certain that a concern for justice and responsibility informs all planning. Thus, when objectives and policies are being formulated, or when particular strategies or actions are proposed, the question should always be asked: is this particular suggestion, if implemented, likely to help in building the school as a just and responsible society? If the answer is yes, then, subject to practical considerations, the suggestion should be accepted. If no, then whatever other favourable arguments there may be, the suggestion must be rejected.

Good management encourages teachers always to interpret and implement objectives in the light of the overall sense of direction provided by the relevant aims, and not least, the moral aims. The purpose of objectives is to identify the targets which have to be achieved in particular fields. This means that objectives, while clear, should be seen as being flexible, as being capable of being changed and altered, as the need arises, so as to ensure that they can provide the best possible signposts, in specific circumstances, to progressing towards reaching the ultimate goal.

Objectives ought never be permitted to become a substitute for aims. Where objectives become ends, rather than means, they are liable to become ossified into axioms.

One likely outcome is administrative inefficiency. Objectives tend to be taken for granted, and left unexamined and unchanged. Or, if changed, altered without reference to any overall rationale. Consequently, they show an increasing tendency to be incoherent, to lack consistency, and to be formulated in terms which are irrelevant to the overall circumstances of a school. Planning based predominantly or exclusively on objectives, which neglects or entirely ignores overall moral and utilitarian aims, almost inevitably becomes increasingly piecemeal, short term, perfunctory and meaningless.

Even worse, management by objectives alone encourages an authoritarian style of leadership. Where objectives are taken as given, it is usually senior management who give, or, to call a spade a spade, impose. Top-down leadership discourages professional participation and discussion of purpose. It is fundamentally anti-democratic, and, as such, in opposition to the essential moral purposes of education in a democracy. It results in, at best, passive obedience amongst teachers, at worst unreliable compliance, or outright antagonism. Where the leadership of a school manages in such a way that a sense of shared purpose is discouraged, any sense of justice and responsibility is diminished.

It follows that senior management needs to make sure that all teachers have appropriate opportunities to contribute to the development of objectives and policies. Overall, the intention should be create a reasonable professional community where all can feel included in the debate about ideas, listened to seriously, and able to exert influence as suitable. More generally, all should be in a position to comprehend, from their particular perspectives, the way the thinking of the school is developing.

If teachers are to be in a position to implement objectives and policies as intended, then the senior management has to ensure that they receive systematic and carefully considered support. This comes through fair arrangements for distribution of resources, training which meets identified need, assistance as necessary over pastoral and disciplinary issues, access to personal counselling if required, and sensible deployment of staff. It is also notoriously difficult to teach effectively in inadequate accommodation, or without proper funding. However, the capitalization and income of a school are matters which are only marginally, if at all, within senior management's control, however much most of them wish it was otherwise.

Teachers who are isolated or ill informed about what is happening or is intended in a school are poorly placed to perform as well as they could. Senior management has to ensure that there are good systems of communication, whose purposes are clear and relevant, and which function smoothly. Equally important, however, is informal communication. The school needs, as an educational community, to encourage an open atmosphere, which encourages easy exchange of views, information and support, and where informal networks readily reinforce and supplement formal arrangements.

Where staff are involved in planning, and supported in performance, the result should be that they feel committed to the aims, objectives and policies of the school, experience trust in leadership and colleagues, and gain satisfaction and motivation from performing professional tasks. Above all, they should be in a position to gain a sense of self-worth from doing, and being seen to do, a good job of work.

A number of issues arise, however.

First, there is a responsibility on teachers to respond in good faith to any opportunities offered. All need to see themselves as involved in a joint, collaborative management venture with the school leadership. Some will themselves have particular management responsibilities, as subject coordinators, heads of department, heads of year, and so forth. Others will simply have those responsibilities which come with being a subject or class teacher, or a tutor. All, however, should be ready to respond, to contribute, to initiate.

Whatever the opportunities provided by senior or middle management, however relevant their expectations, the school community can hardly be fairly, responsibly and successfully managed unless teachers respond constructively and creatively. Management is a two-way process. Just as committed teachers virtually always experience frustration when faced with poor leadership, so good senior and middle management are unlikely to do as well as they would like where they encounter defensive, inward-looking teachers, indifferent or even hostile to the notion of the school as a just institution or a responsible community.

The second issue is this: parents, governors, students and not least teachers themselves need to know how effectively and efficiently a school is promoting justice and responsibility.

Relevant and reliable information is only likely to emerge from a continuing process of evaluation.

Who should carry out the evaluating? Primarily, teachers should, and with rare exceptions virtually always do, evaluate their own performance and students' achievement. They observe what gives results, and what works less well, and they modify their approaches accordingly. Teachers should also carry out joint evaluation activities with colleagues. From such collaboration they can gain a broader perspective on their professional strengths and weaknesses. Self-evaluation can also gain from more formal assessment, whether from line-managers or outside observers, such as advisers or inspectors. However, this is only likely to be worthwhile if it is seen by all concerned not so much as an externally imposed judgement but more as a contribution to a shared dialogue about the effectiveness of what a teacher is doing. Evaluation of teacher performance is an art, not a science. It gains credibility where it illuminates and contributes to constructive debate, or consensus, about the quality and effectiveness of teaching. It loses it where it is presented as an authoritative truth. For such it can never be.

The key issue, however, is not so much who evaluates, important though this is. It is by what criteria are judgements made?

The school is developing as a just institution and a responsible community to the extent that related objectives are being met; that students are achieving particular targets; and that teachers know their subjects and their students well, prepare work thoroughly and can make good use of a range of teaching strategies and pastoral skills. More generally, the school is succeeding morally where it enables all students to progress, and teachers to perform, to the best of their abilities.

Students are showing satisfactory levels of attainment in the understanding of justice and responsibility where, at the least, they know the basic language of justice, rights, equality, responsibility, duties and obligations; where they have a sound grasp of national and local democratic legal and democratic systems; where they are able to call on personal experience to illustrate how an institution can try to ensure justice, and a community, responsibility; where they demonstrate an ability to respect the rights of others, and to undertake effectively particular social duties; where they can show, in practice, a reasonable grasp of the basic skills required of a responsible citizen in a democracy; and where they exhibit at least a minimal commitment to the school as an institution through observation of rules, and to the school as a community through good behaviour and attendance.

The evidence by which judgements are supported should come from a range of sources: observation, documents, discussion with staff and parents, etc. However, since justice and responsibility are, above all, virtues demonstrated and experienced in a social context, it is crucial that the views of students be taken into account. Do they consider that they are treated fairly and responsibly? That they are encouraged to treat others fairly and responsibly? That they are able to make their views known to teachers, and, if so, that what they say is taken seriously, and leads to action if necessary? That they have opportunities to practise worthwhile responsibilities? That the curriculum, and the school generally, offer genuine equality of opportunity? And, how do they consider that they respond to what the school offers?

Finally, one needs to have an idea of why particular teachers perform well, badly or acceptably. Of course, a teacher's possession, or not, of particular knowledge and abilities will provide much of the evidence required to make a considered judgement. However, it won't provide all the necessary information. A potentially strong teacher may, for example, be undermined by students hostile to school, and by lack of proper support. Alternatively, a teacher with weak skills may appear successful by certain criteria because, for example, students are able, highly motivated, and receiving extra help from elsewhere.

So, where there appear to be particular teaching weaknesses or strengths, the proper response is, to ask. What is it that inhibits, or destroys, teaching? Or, what is it that helps teaching to flourish, or at least get by? Is it inappropriate, or appropriate, objectives? Is it hopelessly vague, or properly balanced and detailed, policies? Is it inadequate, or adequate, support? Is it ineffective, or effective, management? Is it poorly, or highly motivated, students? It would be unjust, and irresponsible, to make judgements on teachers' performance without taking full account of the circumstances in which they have to work.

In a nutshell, a just and responsible school is a thinking, creative, reflective, self-aware society.

CHAPTER 11

Justice and the government of education

Government can be perceived as an institution.

The first virtue of institutions is justice. Accordingly, it is the exercise of fairness which should provide the main moral means by which government attempts to achieve its goals.

The educational good which a government desires should be the same as that which should be sought by schools.

It is schools, individually, which have the main responsibility for ensuring that the major goals of education are achieved, and that the first virtues are properly taught, learned and developed.

A particular responsibility, however, rests with government. Government alone can provide the conditions necessary for all schools, nationally, to have a reasonable opportunity of achieving the major aims of education. Government should exercise justice, and so provides support for schools to pursue the major goals of education, through implementing policies designed to develop and maintain a fair education system.

If government is to be well placed to create and administer just educational policies, it should have, in the first place, an informed view on two key questions. First, to what extent is the education system just? Secondly, what are the major interests, together with their actual or likely effects, which a fair system should take into account?

Justice and the national system of education

In considering to what extent the national system of education can be considered just, the central issue is this: in the terminology of John Rawles (see above, Chapter 9, p. 119), are economic and social inequalities in education so arranged that they can reasonably be expected to be to everyone's advantage?

If the answer is mainly affirmative, then it becomes possible to argue that, at least in a limited sense, the education system as a whole is just. If on the other hand the answer is mainly negative, then evidently our national arrangements for education cannot be considered as fair.

Initially, one needs to have some idea of the degree of inequality in society as a whole. The Rowntree Foundation (Joseph Rowntree Inquiry Group, 1995) has calculated that, before housing costs, the actual net income in 1990/1 at April 1993 prices for a couple with two children aged 5 and 10 in the bottom fifth of national income distribution was up to £181 per week. For an equivalent family in the top fifth of income distribution, income was at least £492 per week. For a similar couple in the top tenth, income was at least £629. Overall, wealth is far more unequally distributed than income. Since 1979, income inequality in the United Kingdom has grown rapidly. It has now reached its highest level in the last half century. In contrast with the rest of the post-war period, the poorest 20–30 per cent, unlike those with higher incomes, have not benefited from economic growth, and so have fallen behind in relative terms. Some groups, including ethnic minorities, and some areas, have suffered particularly. As for children, the Commission on Social Justice (1994) has calculated that 9.2 million, or 73 per cent, are in households earning below the average.

In the face of such evidence, it would be virtually impossible to argue that economic and social inequalities in our society can be expected to be to everyone's advantage. The better off certainly appear to benefit. Indeed, in defiance of the laws of natural justice, there seems to be a trickle up effect. However, the bottom 20–30 per cent, at best, gain no advantage. By even the weak definition of justice being used, what is being described is inescapably an unfair society.

In education, it is theoretically possible, at least for a limited time, to have a just school system within an unjust society. Indeed, it has often been argued that education should be used as an engine to drive society towards greater equality.

However, as in society, so in education, there are substantial inequalities. Within the state system there can be significant variations of funding between LEAS, types of school, and individual schools. Much greater, however, are the differences between state and private education. For example, average annual fees for a student attending a private secondary day school are approximately two and a half times the cost of providing for a place at an LEA-maintained school; while comparable costs for a private secondary boarding school are approaching five times those for an LEA-maintained secondary school. Comparable statistics for capital (buildings, land, investments, trusts, equipment, etc.) are not available. However, as in society generally, it is extremely likely that in many cases there are great disparities of wealth between the more and the less privileged institutions.

Could it credibly be argued that these inequalities are so arranged that they are to everyone's advantage?

To answer this one needs to look, initially, at the achievement of students. Despite some difficulties over interpretation of statistics, there does seem to be some agreement about certain fundamental issues. Thus, nationally, for the last twenty years at least, performance of school leavers in GCE O level, and later in GCSE, indicates a modest trend of improving achievement.

However, this overall picture obscures underperformance by two particular, and numerous, groups of students. The first of these is the less able in maintained schools, and the second is formed by the very many students from socially and economically deprived backgrounds. For the latter group, the situation is particularly unfortunate. As the Chief Inspector of Schools put it in his Annual Report (OFSTED, 1995, p. 7), 'Standards of achievement remain depressed.'

One example may illustrate the general situation. A report in the *Financial Times* (21 November 1992) looked at schooling in the London borough of Southwark. In three private secondary schools, which included Dulwich College, at least 92 per cent of 15- to 16-year-old students passed GCSE with five or more grades A to C. In no LEA-maintained school did more than 34 per cent of students gain similar good grades. The report commented, 'There lie the two nations. Attending schools often a stone's throw apart, their career paths will never meet and their salary and lifestyle are at polar extremes. It is the same in most other English cities.'

The factors which contribute to this state of affairs are various. The less able throughout the maintained system are the victims of a regrettable cultural and historical legacy. This has led our society to value, and to support accordingly, children of intellectual ability, and those from affluent families, to the detriment of the remainder. In particular, this has resulted in a public examination system which, whatever particular innovation is currently being touted to solve the problem, remains obstinately and consistently unable to provide appropriate, motivating, and publicly accepted qualifications for those students unwilling or unable to follow the GCSE and A level routes.

For young people attending schools in deprived areas, the reasons for low achievement are cumulative. High staff turnover, difficult working conditions, low morale and inadequate expertise, alone or severally, mean, in the words of an OFSTED report (1994, p. 43), that many students 'have only a slim chance of receiving sufficiently challenging and rewarding teaching throughout their school career'. Poorly planned, inadequately maintained and inappropriate accommodation, together with limited areas for games and recreation, often exacerbate classroom problems.

But, above all, a situation is now being reached where funding, in some schools, is simply inadequate to provide for a decent education. In private schools, and in maintained schools in affluent areas, parental and other sources can, as a rule, readily be called on to supplement a school's basic income, whether this comes from fees or the state. This is seldom, if ever, so for maintained schools in deprived neighbourhoods. Duncan Graham (Graham and Tytler, 1993, p. 132), chief executive and chairman of the National Curriculum Council from 1988 to 1991, has explained the position succinctly: 'As parental contributions towards the costs of essentials have risen, so have the inequalities between the "have" and "have-not" areas. Self-evidently, schools in relatively well-to-do areas are better equipped than those in run-down districts, often thanks to parents' fund-raising activities or direct contributions. The contrasts, always disturbing to the visitor, are now painful to witness.'

Nor has government, at least so far, seriously attempted to make up the shortfall. Teresa Smith and Michael Noble (1995) found that central funding programmes for disadvantaged areas and schools had been cut back, and that expenditure on social needs had not been allocated on the basis of relevant evidence. Further, the educational market, developed by government policy initiatives, financially penalizes schools with low numbers on roll. Of course, parental choice, where it effectively exists, can be a real incentive for schools to improve and take reasonable parental expectations into account. However, there comes a point where, with the best will, leadership and expertise in the world, it becomes virtually impossible for an undercapitalized school, with low income, to provide the conditions for a decent education. That point has long been passed in many inner city schools.

So inequality in the education system contributes to underachievement by the less able and those living in deprived areas. This helps to ensure that overall results produced by schools nationally are less satisfactory, and improve more slowly than is possible or desirable.

Such a situation is very evidently not to everyone's advantage. Great numbers of individual students have both educational development and career prospects blighted. And the country as a whole suffers economically and socially from an undereducated workforce and citizenry.

We have, therefore, an unjust educational system. It systematically fails to operate so as to enable all concerned to give of their best. It endemically malfunctions. This costly, ramshackle contrivance has deficient moral steering arrangements. And in any case those in charge have had, at least in recent years, an unreliable sense of moral direction.

Interests and the national system of education

In planning for a just national system of education, whose interests should the government take into account? What are they? What are their more significant effects? And are they legitimate or illegitimate?

In the first place, then, who are those who should be regarded as having significant interests? As Maurice Kogan (1975) has shown, there are a great range, and very substantial numbers, of groups who can claim an interest in education. More recently, Philippa Cordingley and Tim Harrington (1996) found that perceptions about the identity of stake-holders can vary according to community circumstances, and to whether a point of view is local or national.

Those with substantial and continuing interests in education divide essentially into users and providers of the educational service. The key users, self-evidently, are students and parents. The key providers necessarily include teachers. Of other providers, in a centralized national education system civil servants have increasingly come to exercise significant responsibilities. There will also, always, be those who contribute the thinking which helps give life to the content, practice, structure and management of education. These certainly include academics, and increasingly individual journalists, politicians, and so on: in addition, political ideologues have always had some interest in education, and in recent years this has become one of their dominant concerns. I shall consider the interests of students, teachers, parents, civil servants and political ideologues.

To begin with students. They have a stake in the system which can be understood in abstract terms, and which can be formulated in the vocabulary of rights and duties, as discussed above. From their own point of view, what students want (see, for example, Wendy Keys and Cres Fernandes, 1993) generally includes high expectations, clear explanations and regular feedback from teachers, together with good classroom discipline and fair, comprehensible and systematically applied school rules. They also expect, within reason, lessons to be relevant and interesting. They certainly believe that they should be able to leave school properly prepared and qualified for their next steps in life. In general, they like schools to be sociable places, where they can make friends and enjoy what they are doing.

Students' illegitimate interests (avoiding work, bullying, vandalism of school property, etc.) are extraordinarily well understood by schools. And they need to be. Students pursuing illegitimate interests can cause very serious educational damage. Even in the best run of institutions they are present. They always need to be dealt with effectively, in the best interests of themselves and of everyone else involved in teaching and learning.

But what happens if students consider their legitimate interests are not being met?

To put it bluntly, they use, or threaten to use, their power. And this power, despite their dependent position, can be considerably greater than many adults care to admit.

Wherein lies their power? In the first instance, it derives, paradoxically, from the extent of liberty enjoyed by the individual student. A certain element of freedom is essential to education, and exists in all but the very harshest of institutions. Legitimate dissatisfactions undoubtedly can and do coexist with the varying degrees of autonomy which schools allow students. That autonomy enables the expression of dissent.

However, student power derives predominantly, and quite simply, from strength of numbers. Whether in the classroom, or in the school as a whole, students will virtually always outnumber, and by a very considerable ratio, those in charge of them. As any strategist, from the chess-board to the battlefield knows, to have the greater numbers is potentially to be at an advantage. To be in the great majority offers the possibility of successful confrontation.

The fundamental condition of membership as a school student increases the possibility that such power as students have will be used. Young people aged 5 to 16 have to go to school. They cannot opt out (except for the tiny minority for whom other legally acceptable arrangements for education are made). Accordingly, the population of any. school is, at the least, likely to contain some unwilling recruits. Other things being equal, conscripts are more likely to feel dissatisfaction, and to try and do something about it, than volunteers.

If they are dissatisfied, how can students use their power?

Their situation is analogous in many respects to that of citizens who belong to authoritarian states. They find themselves in circumstances they have not chosen, and allocated an imposed role which is conditioned, circumscribed and controlled by complex social, moral and legal networks of rules and obligations. Ultimately, they can do no more than hope to influence the society for which they have been signed up. Certainly they cannot, at least in any formal or sustained way, control that society.

To begin with, they can complain, gently or vociferously, constructively or otherwise. It may be, it certainly should be, that school or the wider society is prepared to listen and to make reasonable changes.

But suppose school and society are not responsive? Like the citizen, the student, assuming he or she rejects the idea of submission, effectively has the choice of opting out or rebelling. Both of these are essentially negative gestures.

The individual student's main means of opting out is through the various forms of truanting.

Truanting is a threat to the reputation, if not necessarily to the smooth running, of schools. So, schools either tend to try and cover up its extent (until recently it was extraordinarily difficult to get hold of accurate truancy figures on a school, let alone on an LEA or national basis). Or they argue that its causes lie predominantly outside their control. In fact, as O'Keefe (1993) has demonstrated, truanting takes place largely for good reason. Truancy has close links with general school and lesson dissatisfaction. Truants, suggests O'Keefe, are mainly voting as consumers in the only way open to them, with their feet.

Where education is experienced by students collectively as seriously bad, and where quite possibly schools are so authoritarian, or possibly so inchoate, that the voicing of legitimate concerns is not a significant possibility, then as a last resort students may turn to rebellion. The history of English education is, in fact, marked by episodes of revolt, from the riots in late-eighteenth-century schools, of which those at Eton are probably best known, through to the national school strike of 1911, and on to the endemic anarchy in some secondary moderns following the Second World War.

Students who rebel seldom gain anything for themselves. Indeed, they have often been savagely dealt with, and their actions ruthlessly misrepresented. However, in the longer perspective things can look rather different. Where the governed withdraw consent, substantial change often follows after a discrete lapse of time. The public schools were reformed in the nineteenth century, state education was transformed by the 1944 Act, and tripartitism was replaced by the comprehensive system. While complex and multiple causes led to all these changes, it is not unusual for the most obvious cause, the unwillingness of substantial numbers of students to cooperate, to be given little attention. But where students are opposed to what is on offer, then something has to give. The educational population can be a powerful force for progress, and ultimately for justice.

Now for the interests of parents. A parent's interest in education is, quite simply, to obtain the best possible schooling for her or his child.

Recent national policies, and not only in this country, have emphasized choice of school as a means by which parents can achieve a good education for their children. Of course, other approaches are also open to parents. The interest which they take in their children's school activities, and the nature of the support they give them is crucial, whatever the quality of any particular school. Further, they may be able to influence what the school does through contact with teachers, through involvement in school activities, and through participation in policy-making, for example as governors and, in LEA schools, through local democracy.

In practice, choice does not seem to be a major issue for many parents. Mike Feintuck (1994) has pointed out that most children attend their local school. And since opinion polls show that roughly eight in ten parents are happy with the state schools providing for their children (see, for example MORI for the National Consumer Council, 2 August 1995), it seems reasonable to conclude that active exercise of choice is not seen by most parents (although, of course, it is by some), as essential, as far as they themselves are concerned, in achieving a good education.

However, as many studies now show, any system claiming to offer educational choice is bound to be deeply flawed. For many, access to choice is, in practice, a privilege, determined by income and neighbourhood. For parents in the state sector, when real choice appears to be on offer it can turn out to be no more than the right to express a preference. And, as Sandra Jowett (1995) has shown, where preference is denied, raised hopes are more than likely to turn to frustration and disappointment.

Where effective choice does operate, it can lead in the direction of social and racial segregation. Further, market mechanics inevitably put pressure on schools to compete for motivated students who will produce good exam results and who will be likely to sustain a positive ethos. All too often the result is that more successful schools attract larger numbers and increased funding, and reject students with extensive learning difficulties. In this scenario, the fortunate can choose, and have; the unfortunate cannot choose, and have not.

There is little to suggest that choice delivers what are usually claimed as its main educational objectives. In a report from the Organisation for Economic Cooperation and Development, Donald Hirsch (1994) points out there is no direct evidence that competition improves school performance. Furthermore, choice, far from promoting diversity, has a strong tendency to encourage uniformity: schools in the market-place, like politicians, fight for the centre ground – because that is the area occupied by most consumers (see Ron Glatter *et al.*, 1996).

Overall, where parental choice becomes a significant force it can lead schools, in the interests of self-preservation, to overemphasize the arts of public relations and image-making. And it can result in successful schools, not parents, doing the real choosing. Neither eventuality is likely to promote an education to everyone's advantage.

And yet. And yet. Parental choice remains a vital issue. Why?

For parents, the possibility of choice, however limited in practice, can bring a sense of empowerment. Moreover, it encourages them to think specifically about what they want for their children, and to check out the local schools.

Parents who are interested in choice, or simply, initially, in making sure that the local school is satisfactory, can have difficulty both in making sense of published evidence about schools and in knowing what specifically to look for when visiting schools. However, the issues which generally matter to them are becoming clearer (Hughes *et al.*, 1994; West, 1993). What they are mostly looking for includes schools with good reputations, closeness to home, sound academic results, a supportive atmosphere, good behaviour, and an emphasis on all-round education. Numbers of parents also want either single-sex education, particularly for girls, or alternatively, mixed education. Some of those parents whose children have a particular interest or ability may well want a school which can offer relevant specialist expertise.

For schools, having to think about what parents require can bring its own benefits, whatever the limitations of choice. Hirsch (1994) points out that competing for students can enhance the quality of leadership. It can also make schools more responsive to parental views, and so lead them to improve the quality of their communication, formal and informal, with their local community.

Parental choice, on purely pragmatic grounds, would always be likely, and rightly, to be a matter of some significance. It is, however, potent moral and social forces which have been mainly responsible for propelling parental choice towards the top of the educational agenda.

In the first place, choice must be a question of principle. We live in a liberal democratic society, where the act of choice, procedurally and morally, is of central significance. Further, our education is sustained by inherited ideals of the person, all of which share the belief that humans should be responsible and choice-making beings. To deny parents the possibility of choice would be to undermine a core value of both our society and of the curriculum and ethos of schools.

Secondly, in a pluralist society such as ours, different groups of parents hold differing sets of values. Some hold their values so strongly that they desire their children to be educated in schools which explicitly set out to educate students according to their beliefs. In a liberal democracy, the wishes of such parents have to be recognized.

So what are the sets of values parents may hold? And what, in consequence, are the types of schooling they may desire for their children?

Parents may hold community and egalitarian values strongly. If so, they may want schools where students of all abilities, from local neighbourhoods, can be educated together.

They may hold particular religious beliefs strongly. If so, they may want schools which reflect those beliefs.

They may hold meritocratic values strongly. If so, they may want children of higher academic ability to be educated together. And they may be predisposed to believe that their own offspring are sufficiently intelligent to qualify as potential members of the meritocracy.

They may hold class values strongly. If so, they may want their children to be educated with others from the same or similar social class, or who come from families which aspire to belong to those classes. In effect, in contemporary circumstances, this is likely to mean with children from professional and managerial families, and those from the middle or upper classes. Quite possibly, they will also want their children to have a boarding education. This, of course, can have its own intrinsic benefits, and may be used to promote a wide range of educational philosophies. However, it traditionally and effectively supports the class-based traditions of English education.

They may hold free-market values strongly. Such a philosophy can be closely associated with a belief in the importance of accumulating, holding and wielding the power of wealth. This view of the world characteristically brings with it an understanding that choice of school should be seen as a purchase of commodity. Here, lavish provision for the successful, and deprivation for the impoverished can be seen as inevitable, natural and acceptable.

Each of these interests, in their own terms, may be justified as legitimate – even though such justification can be less convincing in some cases than in others. They can, however, be accompanied by illegitimate interests. Thus, with schools which have social prestige, it is always possible that parents may choose them primarily with a view to displaying their own success or status; in effect, using their children as items of conspicuous consumption. Or, parents may choose a school which could indoctrinate; or which is clearly unsuited to the educational needs of a particular child.

Parents' interest in securing a worthwhile education for their children is predominantly to do with achieving private good. The selfish gene is in control.

But, especially for parents who hold particular sets of values, egalitarian, religious, meritocratic, class, free-market, and so on, there is a substantial and inevitable overlap with public visions of good. What parents see as, in the first instance, educationally desirable, they and others will also see as socially desirable, as desirable for society as a whole.

The sets of values which are of interest to parents can have some common elements. Nevertheless, they are seldom likely to be wholly consistent. There is, accordingly, potential for both theoretical and practical friction.

In education, the differing value systems contribute to the generation of differing, albeit in places overlapping, school systems, or more accurately sub-systems: comprehensive schools, grammar schools, secondary modern schools, public schools, schools with religious foundations, schools ranked by parental ability to pay; and so on.

These systems of school are, like the value systems they reflect and promote, more or less incompatible. But, in the true tradition of liberal democracy, ways are found, under certain circumstances, of enabling them to exist side by side, at least in name.

For those who wish to exercise right of choice, practical difficulties can arise.

Parents who want a comprehensive education may live in an area with selection. Or, conversely, parents who want a grammar school education may live in an area with comprehensives. Or parents who want education according to particular religious, social or other principles may not have access to a suitable school for financial or geographical reasons.

For a fortunate few, some of these difficulties may be soluble. A minority of families, seeking either comprehensive or selective education, may have the opportunity to choose to move to a neighbourhood which provides the schooling they would like. Or they may live on the boundaries between comprehensive and grammar/secondary modern systems. Parents seeking private education may have sufficient income or capital with which to pay fees, or they may have access to scholarships or bursaries. The great majority of parents, however, have no real choice between types of school. Of course, they are much more likely to have choice between schools of similar types, especially primary and comprehensive. But that is an issue, not so much of choice of values, as of choice between more or less good education of a certain sort.

The differing values sustaining schools can also provide moral dilemmas for parents who find themselves in a situation where choice, possibly not desired, becomes necessary. Such difficulties essentially arise where one school appears to support the values endorsed by the parents, while another appears otherwise better suited to meet the needs of the child. For political reasons, some sorts of dilemma have been better publicized than others. But they exist across the board. Parents wanting to educate a child at a fee-paying school may find that their offspring express a preference for the more democratic style of a local school. Rationalist or humanist parents may find that a neighbouring church school provides all their child requires, save for daily mass and four hours of religious education a week. Parents who want an egalitarian education may find the local comprehensives so heavily creamed that, for all practical purposes, they are secondary moderns, effectively unable to provide an adequate education for bright children. And so on.

Schools rooted in particular value systems not only educate students in those values. They have the potential, through their former students and their wider activities and networks, to help and promote the acceptance of those values in society at large.

So, not only certain parents and those immediately concerned with particular schools, and types of schools, are interested in their well-being. Those who strive to create a society arranged according to given values favour those schools which promote such values. And needless to say, they are unlikely to look benignly upon schools which support different values.

Thus, certain types of school are fought for, attacked or defended depending on whether they are likely to create or undermine a given ideal of society. The achievements, failings, merits and drawbacks of the different types of schools are all too frequently presented and assessed not so much in relation to fact, as in relation to the value placed by protagonists on the type of school being considered. Clouds of black- and rose-tinted propaganda swirl around our schools, making it unnecessarily difficult for the would-be impartial observer to perceive what on earth is going on, and – the ultimate irony – for parents to make well-informed and objective choices.

We now come to the interests of major providers of education, in particular teachers, civil servants and political ideologues.

Teachers have two major legitimate interests in education. The first lies in knowledge, and the second in pay and conditions of service. It is this latter interest which is fundamental, and on which I intend to concentrate.

Teachers have a legitimate interest in gaining knowledge of their subjects and related disciplines; of methodology; and of how to communicate to those whom they serve the purposes, procedures and outcomes of what they do. Their main concern is with the application of knowledge. But creativity is also involved. For good education, from the class-room, through curriculum planning, to school management requires a continuing, controlled process of innovation and experiment.

The interest in knowledge should be accompanied, morally, by a concern for truth. The essential interest of teachers is in the integrity of knowledge, and in truth.

The creation, growth, application and communication of knowledge originates with persons. Of course, individual thought and initiative can be valuably developed through cooperation with others. And, in a liberal society, bodies of knowledge are public, and open to debate. Knowledge develops and becomes more secure through democratic scrutiny and challenge. However, in principle, it is the individual who knows.

So, it is as individuals that teachers acquire and use knowledge. This inevitably raises the question of moral responsibility. In the social and civic milieu of education, all teachers are answerable for what knowledge they teach (subject to statutory requirements), and for how knowledge, of subject content, methodology, etc. is used.

In the first instance, teachers have a responsibility to themselves as professionals. In other words, in their moral dialogue, both internally and with colleagues, teachers always need to be considering whether they can provide good reason for what they are doing, or are planning to do.

Teachers also have a responsibility to fellow teachers. This requires that shared aims and procedures are agreed and followed. More generally, it requires that professional standards of conduct are upheld.

Teachers have what are now well-understood responsibilities to those who use and who fund the education service. Responsibility to users involves provision of full information about the curriculum, and about students' achievements in their studies. It also requires that users have sufficient evidence to judge how far educational provision (quality of teaching, of accommodation, of resources, of welfare and guidance, etc.) is adequate to promote effective learning.

Responsibility to funding agencies involves providing evidence that resources provided are being deployed so that the agreed purposes for which support is provided are pursued as efficiently and effectively as possible. It demands that the best possible results be achieved with the available provision.

Where teachers do not accept, or are denied, responsibility for knowledge there is serious danger of erosion or breakdown of education in schools and through the system.

Where teachers do not accept responsibility, they are liable to teach courses which take little, if any, direct account of the needs and interests of anyone other than themselves. They oppose accountability, being hostile to any evaluation of their work, whether by fellow teachers or through the more formal processes of inspection by those from outside the school. They are reluctant to provide more than the most minimal information to users of the educational service. They pursue, individually and collectively, an illegitimate interest in establishing an exclusive and unquestionable right to ownership and use of the knowledge in which their professionalism is grounded.

Where teachers are denied responsibility for knowledge, a curriculum is imposed on them, whether within a school, or nationally. They are consulted, individually or through those who represent them, perfunctorily, or not at all. Their involvement in assessment of student achievement is substantially taken over, or at least directed, by others. They are, in effect, treated as administrators, rather than as professionals.

And so, to the real administrators, the civil servants.

The civil service has a legitimate interest in certain aspects of the use of power, in particular in advising on the formulation of policy, and in the administration, and interpretation, of laws and regulations.

However, although, day in and day out they sit at tables where executive power is exercised, civil servants are constitutionally denied any grip on it. Nevertheless, evidence suggests that they are liable to wish that they could be in the seats where the substantive decisions are taken.

Civil servants may try to convince themselves and others that they have no interest in executive power. Indeed, to hear the almost-institutionalized contempt many civil servants routinely express for politicians individually and collectively, one might be excused for imagining that the last thing that would be in their minds would be any desire to usurp part of the governmental role.

Nevertheless, the direct use of executive power, particularly when it comes to making policy, is a continuing and ever-present illegitimate interest of the civil service. Educational civil servants, over the years, have seldom appeared to turn away from any chance to create policy. Certainly they have been seen by ministers of both Conservative and Labour administrations as eager to develop and implement their own ideas (Lawrence, 1992, pp. 61–2; Graham and Tytler, 1993, p. 12). Equally certainly, while just about observing the constitutional niceties, senior civil servants have also been ready to justify promotion by the civil service of its own thinking on what should be done in schools (Pile, 1979, pp. 35–6).

And, over the years, the officers of the education department, under its varying titles, have proved remarkably successful in getting their own way; or, to put it more tactfully, in achieving the implementation of government policies which are in harmony with their own. Thus, when the structure of the school system was the key issue, top civil servants ensured that the 1944 Education Act resulted in grammar and secondary moderns, not in comprehensives or technical schools (Annan, 1990, p. 362). Come national concern over the curriculum, the civil service early put down a marker on its interest in a subject curriculum, which downgraded the arts and gave little attention to personal and social education or citizenship (DES, 1980b; DES, Welsh Office, 1987). This was in striking contrast to the then influential thinking of Her Majesty's Inspectorate (HMI). The subsequent

National Curriculum, as legislated and implemented through governmental guidance, reflected the civil service line with considerable faithfulness (Graham and Tytler, 1993).

Civil service interests are strongly influenced, for better or worse, by the bureaucratic nature of the structure within which they operate. The relevant features of the education department would still be readily recognized by Weber. It is a hierarchy, bound by rules, in which each member is trained to occupy a closely defined role. No official may monopolize any position, and hence each is moved from job to job at fairly frequent intervals. Functions are, in principle, kept strictly separate from both the personal and political domains, a requirement which in practice frequently results in the civil service transacting its affairs behind an arras of secrecy.

Authority, within any bureaucracy, derives from the legitimate use of power. Power is used legitimately where it is exercised in accordance with rules, procedures and objectives which derive from higher order regulations and aims which the civil service accepts as rational. The exercise of rationality, in the identification and carrying out of bureaucratic responsibilities, together with the creation of structures intended to support the performance of those responsibilities, is fundamental to the nature of bureaucracy. Educational civil servants like, above all else, to see themselves as rational beings. They are inclined to perceive those outside the privileged environs of Whitehall as sometimes less than entirely rational.

In their illegitimate interest to exert direct control over the education system and the school curriculum, civil servants, in the first instance, are inclined to seek arrangements which reflect their own values and experience as bureaucrats. Accordingly, they are sympathetic to the principle of hierarchy, and tend to favour an educational system, whether layered along social or, preferably, meritocratic lines, which is pyramidically structured. When it comes to the curriculum, they like the appearance of subjects which require the exercise of reason, preferably abstract. They look with suspicion on activities requiring the development of spiritual, aesthetic, emotional or social faculties.

Civil servants can also be tempted to see considerable benefits in arrangements of the system and of the curriculum which reflect their own educational experience. Traditionally, many senior civil servants have had a classical background, and in recent years this has remained true of numbers of senior figures in the education department. The principles of such an education can dovetail nicely with the respect for rationalism and ordered rank endorsed by bureaucracy.

Civil servants frequently display an illegitimate interest in maximizing the size of their bureaux, a phenomenon that is often commented on (Marquand, 1988, p. 77). A major reason for this interest is a desire to increase the ability to exercise power. The greater the strength and reach of a bureaucracy, the greater is likely to be its capacity to flex executive muscle to good effect.

Bureaucracies can be inclined to give a low priority to respect for truth. For them, the ultimate justification of administrative action is whether it is in accordance with the organization's objectives, procedures and regulations. These may, or may not, place a high value on veracity.

A government department may expect civil servants, in pursuit of ministerial objectives, to manipulate or suppress data, or to encourage others to do so. In such cases, while civil servants are no doubt being inducted into a culture of deception, they cannot be said to be acting dishonestly on their own behalf.

In certain respects, whatever the pressures of their role as bureaucrats, and as government employees, civil servants have an interest in honest administration. In its absence, their public reputation is likely to suffer. Further, however hard government works to turn civil servants into smoothly operating, obedient functionaries, many obstinately remain creatures of conscience. As such, they have an interest in integrity.

However, civil servants can also have interests, specific to themselves, which are not best promoted by total honesty. Where they have their own policies to pursue, civil servants are adept, when operating in that no-man's land between ministerial fiat and administrative interpretation, at putting a spin on ideas which suits their own purposes. Needless to say, this is nearly always done with masterful ambiguity. It is rare indeed to catch a civil servant telling anything so indiscreet as a lie. Duncan Graham (Graham and Tytler, 1993, p. 14) put the point nicely when commenting on negotiations between the National Curriculum Council and the Department of Education; and Science: 'it was always difficult to know when civil servants were acting on behalf of their political masters and when they were acting on their own account.'

Civil servants may also attempt to restrain others from truth-telling. This is most likely to occur where truth-telling will inhibit fulfilment of bureaucratic aims, and where consequently it may undermine not only administrative efficiency, but also the power of the civil service. The long-standing tensions between the civil servants and Her Majesty's Inspectorate (HMI) are best understood in this light. The recent emasculation of HMI, and the slow erosion of its reputation for independent judgement, have in part resulted from the enthusiasm which civil servants have brought to bringing the inspectorate into line with bureaucratic, and congruent political, requirements.

Probably the crucial issue for bureaucracy, however, and the one which has the strongest influence, for better or worse, on the development, pursuit and realization of civil service interests, is the nature of the bureaucracy's objectives, and the processes by which they are decided.

Civil servants have an overriding, legitimate interest in being involved in the formulation of departmental objectives. As Anthony Woollard, a former education mandarin, has argued (*Times Educational Supplement*, 23 February 1996), they need to be managed through shared vision, and a recognition of their concerns as stakeholders.

Where this occurs, civil servants have a very reasonable opportunity to secure acknowledgment of their legitimate interests. Correspondingly, the chance that they will be anxious, or able, to pursue illegitimate interests stands to be reduced.

However, trouble arises where, as has too frequently happened in recent years, government ignores the civil service interest in participating in the development of objectives for the administration. Individual civil servants are liable to come into conflict with ministers, to be peremptorily moved, to be denied promotion, or even to resign. Civil servants as a body are inclined to become alienated, and so are more likely to follow their own agenda. In such circumstances pursuit of power, aggrandizement of bureaux, efforts to impose civil service control over system and curriculum, erosion of respect for truth, all become characteristic of educational administration. Good practice is debased.

And lastly, briefly but critically, there are the interests of the political ideologues. In the vocabulary of neo-Marxists and post-structuralists the term 'ideology' has acquired distinctly negative connotations: thus 'a system of illusory beliefs ... which serve to perpetuate a particular social formation or power structure' (Dollimore, 1989 pp. 9–10). I shall use the term in an earlier, more innocent, less value-laden sense. I take it to refer to coherent systems of ideas concerning the phenomena of social, cultural, economic or political life.

Political ideologues have two major legitimate interests in education. The first is to develop and make available systems of ideas, and related policy proposals intended to give form and substance to the underlying philosophies of political movements or parties.

From this follows the second legitimate interest: to influence political parties, both in and out of government, to act in accordance with the thinking of the ideologues. In a democracy, such influence should be developed primarily through open persuasion and debate.

It is a characteristic of ideologues, whether individually or in groups, to be utterly convinced of the rightness of their beliefs. Their cast of mind is absolutist. And this frequently leads to an intention to impose their views by authoritarian, or clandestine, means: obviously, an illegitimate interest.

The moral government of education

And now. How should government set about achieving justice in education?

The answer is that it should be guided by two major concerns:

- First, a concern to act fairly towards those users and providers with interests in education.
- Secondly, a concern to develop and manage the system justly.

So what principles should government follow if it is to act fairly towards key users and providers of education?

The predominant educational interests with which government should concern itself are those of students. Young people, whatever the power they may be able to exert from time to time, are vulnerable. In the absence of a written constitution, the less organized and the less powerful are always at risk.

In the normal course of events, parents and teachers will always do their best to protect and further the legitimate interests of those students with whom they are directly concerned. But only national government is in a position to ensure that the interests of all students in receiving a good education can be met.

Parental interests coincide with those of students insofar as both should have an overriding concern to gain access to education of quality. However, parents in particular, may have a strong interest in choice of school.

Once government is doing its best to provide for education of universally good quality it should provide for choice of school.

Systems of schools are means of reflecting and promoting particular sets of social, cultural, religious and educational values. Intrinsically, none offers a path to an education which by some universal, agreed standard is better than any other. Different types of school offer paths to different forms of education, no more, no less.

It is, however, the unique tragedy of English education that class and social pressures have so operated, over more than a century, that particular types of school have tended to enjoy higher status, to attract better resourcing and to gain greater parental support. In these circumstances, almost inevitably certain systems have come to be considered, of their nature, as better than others. But this is not so. They are simply more privileged, which is quite another matter.

The tasks of government in meeting parental interest in choice are: first, to secure a level playing-field; secondly, to ensure that any changes in the composition and balance of the whole national system enjoy substantial and majority support from those with relevant interests; and thirdly, itself to refrain from promoting by undemocratic or devious means any system its ideology may lead it to favour. Thus, government should not repress or distort information necessary for the reaching of objective conclusions about the merits or otherwise of particular types of school; and it should not impose, or unilaterally undermine, types of schools which the party it represents respectively supports or opposes.

Government in education has always found difficulty in managing appropriately and effectively the interests of providers.

As regards teachers, left-wing governments have generally been inclined to look with some indulgence on restrictive practices, in particular the desire to exert exclusive control over the curriculum. Right-wing administrations have historically been inclined, albeit for different reasons, to take a similarly *laissez-faire* approach. However, recent conservative governments have adopted a different tack entirely. While attacking illegitimate interests, they have also frequently worked to undermine the legitimate interest of teachers in knowledge, in what is taught, and how. They have frequently imposed, and at least as often they have failed to consult.

It does now appear that, on balance, the legitimate interests of teachers would best be served by the establishment of a General Teaching Council. Until such a body can be established, with status and self-regulatory powers, well-founded conditions are unlikely to exist for the development of a balanced relationship between the teaching profession and government. (There has been considerable debate over the possible benefits and drawbacks of introducing a General Teaching Council. A clear and reasoned assessment is offered by Peter Smith, general secretary of the Association of Teachers and Lecturers, in the *Times Educational Supplement*, 6 May 1994. The balance appeared to have swung in favour of establishing a Council, when it was advocated in the 1997 government White Paper *Excellence in Schools*).

As with teachers, so with bureaucracy. Government has frequently failed to deal reasonably with civil service interests. Government has veered in the decades since the 1944 Education Act from leaving the educational civil service more or less to its own devices to regarding its every action with suspicion. Particularly recently, government has made clear its view that it perceives the educational bureaucracy, certainly no less than the rest of the Whitehall machine, as, in Adam Smith's phrase, a conspiracy against the laity. Actually, it has tended to include itself in the notion of laity.

Just as government needs to consult teachers over their fundamental concern with knowledge and curriculum, so it should involve civil servants in their main concern, planning the purpose of bureaucratic activity. If government has sufficient will, ministerial continuity and consistency of policy, it should have the strength to manage the civil service, not by command and control, but through a shared sense of purpose. Only if the civil service feels that its skills and experience are trusted and its views valued (if not necessarily accepted) is it likely to work consistently for its legitimate rather than its illegitimate interests.

The final key educational provider whose interests government has to manage are those of the political ideologues. And, particularly, those of the ideologues who are in sympathy with the government of the day, and seek to influence it.

In dealing with political ideologues it is essential for the executive to distinguish the interests of party from those of government. Ministers, as representatives of a party, need to be able to draw on coherent sets of ideas and policy proposals arising from their own political philosophy. In the absence of such fuel, administrations are liable to run out of steam, and to drift.

Ministers as members of a national government, however, have to deal with the notions of ideologues as only one thread in the complex web of legitimate interests which the executive has to consider in formulating policies for the benefit of education as a whole. Whenever, in education, a democratic government is driven predominantly by ideology, rather than by a concern to promote good schools, one is likely to observe, whatever the official language, a practical neglect of the first virtues of education.

The second major concern of government should be to develop and manage the whole system justly.

It would seem that, since the system is unjust, it ought to be reformed. The difficulty is that all the familiar proposals for reform, and even the new variations on old ideas, seem likely to result in little more than simply changing existing patterns of injustice. Abolish private schools? Right of parental choice is denied. Give brighter students, irrespective of social class and ability to pay access, by whatever means, to what is seen as privileged education (as, for instance, proposed by Walden, 1996)? The educational rights of the majority remain neglected.

Currently fashionable approaches, whether from the left or right of the ideological spectrum, have in common that they accept substantial elements of the free market in education. For the right, for instance, Robert Skidelsky (1996) proposes a root-and-branch reform of the system. He wants all state schools to be established as legally independent, non-profit-making private corporations, in line with most existing private schools. On the left, New Labour, along with many others, are mainly concerned to raise standards within the system as it exists, give or take a few relatively insignificant changes.

Such approaches are destined, however good their intentions, to exacerbate, preserve or at best only marginally soften the inequities of existing arrangements. This is because of the way any market, including that in education, operates. It reinforces the strong. And not only that. Those schools with power, overtly or covertly, using whatever implements are to hand, cultural, economic, political, social, do their utmost to depress the performance, not so much of the very weak, but of those who show signs of threatening their supremacy. And, needless to say, there is a knock-on, or more accurately, a knock-down, effect.

It is this market mechanism, above all, which has enabled the strong private educational sector to preserve its privileges for generations. And this has been at the expense of the rights of the nation's children as a whole, and of the interests of the nation as a whole.

Facing this situation, there is a bitter truth to be accepted. Since we live in a liberal democracy, there is no overall policy which any government can pursue with a realistic hope of establishing a system which appears just to all.

However, there are certain strategies which any government interested in justice would be morally bound to pursue.

- In general terms, it should contribute, listen and respond to national debate concerned to secure a fairer education system. In the absence of discussion of the nature of educational justice, and of possible means of achieving it, inequity is bound to remain entrenched.
- It should develop and implement policies to deal with specific injustices, identified in national debate, and which can command significant support.
- It should encourage and facilitate cooperation between every type of school. From sharing of facilities, to increased mutual understanding and trust, there can only be benefit in helping schools to break out from the natural isolation and self-preoccupation to which they are, by their very nature, so prone.
- It should regulate the system as a whole. Schools exist, rightly, in a mixed economy. That economy should be driven predominatly by the national interest. If it is driven by the free market there is no hope of justice. Accordingly, in education, as in other areas of government, the actions of ministers and civil servants need to occur, whatever the

particular and detailed arrangements, within a statutory framework, a philosophy of politics, and a culture of power, concerned to ensure an even-handed treatment of stakeholders.

- Less formally, government should view and treat the education system inclusively. This requirement has most obviously been ignored, over many years, and by governments of all political outlooks, with regard to private education. Schools outside the state sector have somehow been regarded as apart. Yet, private and state education are inextricably intertwined. Both share the same basic principles of education, both teach to the same public examinations, both provide for the same institutions of further and higher education, both send students out to compete in the same employment market, both have many teachers and parents with experience of both systems, both exert political pressures on government to safeguard their own interests, both, through their spokespersons, from time to time, express concern over the national educational scene. No nation can be educationally successful if government fails coherently to consider all stakeholders as members of a whole.

- Finally, government should ensure that resources are distributed equitably. I refer to resources in the widest possible sense. I include not only finances, but teachers, accommodation, grounds, training, etc. Of course, just distribution of resources is not a universal panacea. Resources can be squandered. Or they can be misused, for lack of appropriate professional expertise. But it does not follow that schools can manage satisfactorily without proper resources. They are absolutely essential. And, what is more, they are something over which government has the opportunity to exert some control.

Just distribution of resources does not necessarily require sameness of provision. There may be differences which are fair. For example, the education of students who are handicapped, or who have particular gifts, may require extra resources and expenditure. Similarly, older students are likely to require a wider range of specialist subject teaching and sports facilities than younger children. Such differences, to provide for contrasting needs, are fair, provided they do not result in inequalities of regard, or of opportunity.

However, justice in education does require that schools are so funded that all students have equal access to education of quality.

Within state schools such relatively minor, but nevertheless very significant, discrepancies as may occur between types of school, individual schools and regions can in principle be put right by initiatives which lie almost entirely within the direct control of government. Where they do not take place it is, essentially, through lack of governmental will, or, worse, on account of government will.

An even more serious problem lies in the divide, discussed above, which has developed between the funds available to pay for students in the private sector and those available to pay for students in the public sector. This divide is now almost certainly greater than at any point in the post-war era. It has been calculated that to achieve parity between private and public provision would require an extra 7 pence on income tax (Robert Skidelsky, as reported in the *Guardian*, 18 March 1995).

This dramatic figure, however, raises an important issue. We do not know whether private schools are giving value for money. There is a strong case for all private schools to be regularly inspected and publicly reported on in the same way as now happens to all state schools. Only by analysing the sort of information which would emerge could a balanced view be achieved of the overall quality of private schooling, its contribution to national education, and its justifiable cost. Until such findings are available, any debate about how far educational funding viewed in relation to private and state schools needs to be levelled up, differently targeted, or redistributed, will inevitably be conducted in a mist of partial data and guesses.

In the meantime, it is clear that there can be no serious argument for the state subsidizing private education. This is not a question of principle. The health of a liberal democracy requires a thriving private education system. If it were ailing, then help from the taxpayer might be desirable. But just now the health of private schools is rude. Charitable status arrangements, and so on, are simply icing on a very rich cake. In the interests of justice, and of a good education for all, government needs to channel all the resources it has to raising general standards.

However, whatever minor measures could be taken, it is true that the current inequities of funding are simply too great to be righted in the short term. Government needs to develop long-term policies, together with related strategies, to promote equitable distribution of resources.

CHAPTER 12

The good school in the good society

So, I come to the final question to be discussed in this book. Is there any one system of schools which is more likely than another to encourage the development and thriving of good schools?

But, first, a preliminary issue. How is this question best approached?

It is, I consider, a mistake to consider systems of schools primarily in the light of one's vision of society – always, of course, assuming one has such a vision in the first place. Such an approach has proved, at best, to lead nowhere very much except towards inconclusive controversy. At worst, it results in education becoming a political football, and, arguably, must bear substantial responsibility for national failure to focus on the real problems of education. Ideology, too often, has taken precedence over pragmatism, to the detriment of the public good.

One should evaluate the merits of particular systems of schools not so much in the light of one's vision of the good society as in the light of one's vision of the good school. In other words, systems of schools should be judged primarily in relation to educational, rather than to social or political criteria. The question of whether one system of schools is preferable to another is, accordingly, a question which ought to *conclude* any discussion of the nature of good education, not to *start* it.

Put this way, the question arises in a fundamentally democratic context. It is to do with empowering and respecting persons. It asks how individual young people, in individual schools, can best be helped to give of their best. It does not ask, as happens when one enquires what system of schools can best support a particular vision of society, how young people can most effectively be fitted to play their parts in a given notion of the adult world. The latter approach betrays an implicitly organic, and authoritarian, approach to education and society.

The vision of a good school which I have described is, I believe, more likely to be realized where a particular system of schools enjoys pride of place.

To recap briefly. A good school is one which successfully reflects in its teaching and learning the qualities of respect for persons, truth, justice and responsibility. These first virtues of education are both ends in themselves and means towards achieving the aims of the school. Any school which neglects the moral and intellectual virtues is poorly placed to help students develop as whole persons, spiritually, morally, socially, culturally, artistically, mentally and physically. The practice of the educational virtues is a necessary condition for the achievement of all educational goods, whether utilitarian or idealistic.

Good schools are more likely to develop and be sustained where they are within a system of schools which itself is committed, in theory and practice, to the first virtues of education.

So, the question arises, what system of schools is best fitted to promote respect for persons, truth, justice and responsibility?

At first sight, the answer seems, to me at least, to be a system of comprehensive primary and secondary schools.

In principle:

- Here, all persons, and educational ideals of what it means to be worthwhile person, are respected.
- Here, too, the significance of differing ideas of truth is acknowledged.
- The system is grounded in justice. The rights of all students are identified and observed. Equality of regard and opportunity is practised. Equality of citizenship ensures that openness, participation and answerability occur throughout, and that democratic values are taught and observed within schools. There is no discrimination against, or in favour of, any students, on any grounds, including gender, ethnicity, ability, social background or the capacity to pay for education.
- There is active acknowledgement of a duty to uphold the principles of justice, and to encourage all concerned in education – students, parents, school staff, members of external agencies, community and political representatives, etc. – to exercise the responsibilities which arise from the rights they enjoy in, and from their commitment to, education.

Such a vision of a system of comprehensive schools is, needless to say, vulnerable to various objections.

The first objection is that, to some at least, the vision may present a picture distant from any recognizable reality. Whether or not this is so, it seems to me to be an irrelevant criticism. For a system of schools, as for a school itself, there has to be an idea of what it is, and of what it should be, capable. In the absence of such an ideal, potential remains unfocused and substantially unrealized.

A further possible objection is that other systems might equally well respect the first virtues of education. I rather doubt it. A system of meritocratic schools tends to undervalue the less able; a system of fee-paying schools to favour those who are relatively well-off financially; a system of religious schools to overemphasize religious truth; and so on, and so on. However, the fact that we have no one of these systems to the exclusion of all others means they have to compete, and so tend to have to keep their less attractive tendencies in check.

And this leads to a final, and much more serious objection to seeing a system of comprehensive schools as best fitted to support the good school.

If it is to be the only system, then almost insuperable difficulties follow.

First, right of choice is denied. Or at least it is unless society has reached the Elysian state where all are in agreement. And, of course, to deny choice is to ignore the obligation to respect persons, which is itself a first virtue of education.

Secondly, the possibility of exploring educational ideas and practices different from those sanctioned by a system of comprehensive schools is denied, or at the least, minimized. Any system of schools, including a comprehensive system which enjoys monopoly status, is liable to become lethargic, self-satisfied and unimaginative.

Thirdly, there are a range of highly specialist educational needs which even a very good system of comprehensive schools might struggle to meet. From the gifted, in different fields, to those with serious disabilities, there may be groups of students who would benefit from schooling on their own.

So, what is the solution? It is to ensure, through the achievement of democratically reached consensus, that:

- There is a properly funded and resourced system of comprehensive schools at the heart of the national educational system.
- There is, through the success of the system of comprehensive schools, no educational need for parents to purchase privilege.
- Choice is available, through safeguarding the right to existence of systems of schools, and of individual schools, which differ in approach and principle from comprehensive schools. However, there should be no right to a choice of school, or system of schools, which evidently deny or neglect the first virtues of education.
- Any very special or particular educational needs, which cannot properly be catered for in comprehensives, are met in other types of schools.

All this, taken as a whole, represents what a good, overall national system of schools, would look like. However, such a system could only exist where there was a vision of, and a determination to achieve, a good society: and a particular idea of the good society. Such a society would be one which, at its heart, respected persons, and valued truth, justice and responsibility. It would also be one which demonstrated its commitment to those values by striving to promote schools, and systems of schools, and an overall national system of schools, which enacted those values. The frustration of a liberal democracy is that visions of good schools, and of good systems of schools, and of good overall national systems of schools, and of the good society, all compete. But its great mercy, and one for which perhaps we are not always as grateful as we might be, is that it allows us all to articulate, and to strive for the realization of, our own visions.

I find it very hard to imagine why anyone should dissent from a vision of the good school grounded in respect for persons, truth, justice and responsibility. Or from the vision of a comprehensive-based national system of schools, and of a moral national community, which that entails.

But, no doubt, there are those who will disagree. I suppose I must accept that that is the glory of democracy.

References

Note: Works have been cited under the date of the edition used, with the original date of publication, where available, given at the end of the reference.

ACE (1993) *Children's Voices in School Matters*. London: ACE.
Adorno, T. (1973) *The Jargon of Authenticity*. Trans. K. Tarnowski and F. Will. London: Routledge. (First published 1965).
Alexander, R., Rose, J. and Woodhead, C. (1992) *Curriculum Organisation and Classroom Practice in Primary Schools: A Discussion Paper*. London: DES.
Amis, K. (1992) *Memoirs*. Harmondsworth: Penguin.
Anderson, E. (ed.) (1989) *The Letters of Mozart and his Family* (3rd edn). London: Macmillan.
Annan, N. (1990) *Our Age*. London: Weidenfeld & Nicolson.
Appleby, J., Hunt, L. and Jacob, M. (1994) *Telling the Truth about History*. London: W. W. Norton.
Aquinas, T. (1939) *Selected Writings*. Ed. M. C. D'Arcy. London: Dent.
Aristotle (1905) *Politics*. Trans. B. Jowett. Oxford: Clarendon Press.
Arnold, M. (1964) 'Schools and universities on the continent', in *The Complete Prose Works of Mathew Arnold*, vol. 4. Ed. R. H. Super. Ann Arbor: University of Michigan Press. (First published 1868).
Ayer, A. J. (1936) *Language, Truth and Logic* (1st edn). London: Gollancz.
Bailey, C. (1984) *Beyond the Present and the Particular: A Theory of Liberal Education*. London: Routledge & Kegan Paul.
Baker, K. (1993) *The Turbulent Years*. London: Faber & Faber.
Barthes, R. (1977) *Roland Barthes*. Trans. R. Howard. London: Macmillan (First published 1975).
Bellow, S. (1994) *It All Adds from the Dim Past to the Uncertain Future*. London: Secker & Warburg.
Bentham, J. (1931) 'Principles of the Civil Code', in *The Theory of Legislation*. Ed. C. K. Ogden. London: Macmillan.
Berlin, I. (1969) 'Two concepts of liberty', in *Four Essays on Liberty*. Oxford: Oxford University Press. (First published 1958).
Bonhoeffer, D. (1964) *Ethics*. London: Fontana. (First published 1949).
Bowra, C. M. (1957) *The Greek Experience*. London: Weidenfeld & Nicolson.
British Humanist Association (1995) *Education for Living: A Humanist Perspective*. London: BHA.
Brooks, P. (1993) *Body Work: Objects of Desire in Modern Narrative*. Cambridge, Mass.: Harvard University Press.
Browne, T. (1977) 'Religio medici', in *The Major Works*. Ed. C. A. Patrides. Harmondsworth: Penguin. (First published 1643).
Buber, M. (1961) *Between Man and Man*. London: Fontana. (First published 1947).

Burke, E. (1901) 'The reform of representation in the House of Commons', in *Works*, vol. 6. London: Bohn. (First published 1809).

Burn, A. R. (1990) *The Penguin History of Greece*. Harmondsworth: Penguin.

Calvin, J. (1949) *Institutes [of the Christian Religion]*. Trans. H. Beveridge. London: Clarke. (First published 1559).

Cassirer, E., Kristeller, P. O. and Randall, J. H. (1948) *The Renaissance Philosophy of Man*. Chicago: University of Chicago Press.

Castle, E. B. (1961) *Ancient Education and Today*. Harmondsworth: Penguin.

Chekhov, A. (1964) 'A boring story', in *Lady with a Lapdog and Other Stories*. Trans. D. Magarshack. Harmondsworth: Penguin. (First published 1889).

Clark, K. (1956) *The Nude*. London: Murray.

Coleridge, S. T. (1965) *Biographia Literaria*. Ed. G. Watson. London: Dent. (First published 1817).

Commission on Social Justice (1994) *Social Justice: Strategies for National Renewal*. London: Vintage.

Conrad, J. (1963) *Nostromo*. Harmondsworth: Penguin. (First published 1904).

Cordingley, P. and Harrington, T. (1996) *Schools, Communities, and LEAs: Learning to Meet Needs*. London: Association of Metropolitan Authorities.

Cupitt, D. (1980) *Taking Leave of God*. London: SCM Press.

Curriculum Council for Wales (1991) *The Whole Curriculum: 5–16 in Wales*. Cardiff: Curriculum Council for Wales.

Davies, B. (1982) *An Introduction to the Philosophy of Religion*. Oxford: Oxford University Press.

Davies, N. (1996) *Europe: A History*. Oxford: Oxford University Press.

Dearing, Sir Ron (1996) *Review of Qualifications for 16–19 Year Olds*. London: SCAA.

Dent, H. C. (1966) *The Education Act 1944* (11th edn). London: University of London Press.

Department of National Heritage (1996) *Setting the Scene: The Arts and the Young*. London: DNH.

Derrida, J. (1978) *Writing and Difference*. Trans. A. Bass. London: Routledge. (First published 1976).

DES (Department of Education and Science) (1980a) *A View of the Curriculum*. HMI series: Matters for Discussion 11. London: DES.

DES (1980b) *A Framework for the School Curriculum*. London: DES.

DES (1981a) *The School Curriculum*. London: DES.

DES (1981b) *The School Curriculum*. (Circular 6/81). London: HMSO.

DES (1983) *The School Curriculum*. (Circular 8/83). London: HMSO.

DES (1985a) *Better Schools*. London: HMSO.

DES (1985b) *The Curriculum from 5–16*. HMI series: Curriculum Matters 2. London: HMSO.

DES (1986) *Local Authority Policies for the School Curriculum*. Report on the Circular 8/83 Review. London: DES.

DES (1989) *National Curriculum: From Policy to Practice*. London: DES.

DES, Welsh Office (1987) *The National Curriculum 5–16*. A Consultation Document. London: DES.

Descartes, R. (1968a) 'Discourse on method', in *Discourse on Method and the Meditations*. Trans. F. E. Sutcliffe. Harmondsworth: Penguin. (First published 1637).

Descartes, R. (1968b) 'The meditations', in *Discourse on Method and the Meditations*. Trans. F. E. Sutcliffe. Harmondsworth: Penguin. (First published 1641).

DFE (Department for Education) (1995) *The National Curriculum*. London: HMSO.

Dollimore, J. (1989) *Radical Tragedy* (2nd edn). London: Harvester-Wheatsheaf.

Donaldson, M. (1978) *Children's Minds*. London: Fontana.

Donaldson, M. (1993) *Human Minds*. Harmondsworth: Penguin.

Donne, J. (1955) *Complete Verse and Selected Prose*. Ed. J. Hayward. London: Nonesuch Press. (First published 1611).

Dostoyevsky, F. (1958) *The Brothers Karamazov*, vol. 1. Trans. D. Magarshack. Harmondsworth: Penguin. (First published 1880).

Dworkin, R. (1993) *Life's Dominion*. London: Harper Collins.

Eaglesham, E. J. R. (1967) *Foundations of Twentieth Century Education in England*. London: Routledge & Kegan Paul.

Eliot, G. (1994) *Middlemarch*. Harmondsworth: Penguin. (First published 1871–2).

Eliot, T. S. (1939) *The Idea of a Christian Society*. London: Faber & Faber.

Eliot, T. S. (1951) *Selected Essays*. London: Faber & Faber.

Elliott, P. (1972) *The Sociology of the Professions*. London: Macmillan.

Etzioni, A. (1995) *The Spirit of Community*. London: Fontana.

Feintuck, M. (1994) *Accountability and Choice in Schooling*. Buckingham: Open University Press.

Foucault, M. (1970) *The Order of Things: An Archaeology of the Human Sciences*. London: Tavistock. (First published 1966).

Foucault, M. (1977) 'Nietzsche, genealogy, history', in *Language, Counter-memory, Practice*. Trans. D. F. Bouchard and S. Simon. Ithaca, NY: Cornell University Press. (First published 1971).

Frank, R. H. (1988) *Passions with Reason: The Strategy of the Emotions*. New York: W. W. Norton.

Galbraith, J. K. (1992) *The Culture of Contentment*. London: Sinclair-Stevenson.

Gardner, H. (1996) *Leading Minds: An Anatomy of Leadership*. London: Harper Collins.

Glatter, R., Woods, P. and Bagley, C. (1996) *Choice and Diversity in Schooling: Perspectives and Prospects*. London: Routledge.

Gombrich, E. H. (1956) *The Story of Art* (8th edn). London: Phaidon.

Gombrich, E. H. (1960) *Art and Illusion*. London: Phaidon.

Graham, D. and Tytler, D. (1993) *A Lesson for Us All: The Making of the National Curriculum*. London: Routledge.

Gray, J. (1993) *Beyond the New Right: Markets, Government and the Common Environment*. London: Routledge.

Hamlyn, D. W. (1970) *The Theory of Knowledge*. London: Macmillan.

Hargreaves, A., Baglin, E., Henderson, P., Leeson, P. and Tossell, P. (1988) *Personal and Social Education: Choices and Challenges*. Oxford: Blackwell.

Hargreaves, D. H. (1975) *Interpersonal Relations and Education* (Revised edn). London: Routledge & Kegan Paul.

Hargreaves, D. H. (1991) 'Coherence and manageability: reflections on the National Curriculum and cross-curricular provision'. *The Curriculum Journal*, **2**, 1, 33–41.

Harries, R. (1993) *Art and the Beauty of God*. London: Mowbray.

Havel, V. (1989) *Living in Truth*. Ed. J. Vladislav. London: Faber & Faber. (First published 1986).

Hawkes, T. (1992) *Meaning by Shakespeare*. London: Routledge.

Hayek, F. (1978) *New Studies in Philosophy, Politics, Economics and the History of Ideas*. London: Routledge & Kegan Paul.

Healey, D. (1989) *The Time of My Life*. London: Michael Joseph.

Henry, D. (1992) Child and Co. lecture, 17 June.

Hirsch, D. (1994) *School: A Matter of Choice*. London: HMSO.

Hirst, P. H. (1974) *Knowledge and the Curriculum*. London: Routledge & Kegan Paul.

Hobbes, T. (1946) *Leviathan*. Ed. M. Oakeshott. Oxford: Blackwell. (First published 1651).

Hogg, Q. (1947) *The Case for Conservatism*. Harmondsworth: Penguin.

Holbrook, D. (1961) *English for Maturity*. Cambridge: Cambridge University Press.

Holmes, E. (1920) *In Quest of an Ideal*. London: Constable.

Holmes, G. (1993) *Essential School Leadership: Developing Vision and Purpose in Management*. London: Kogan Page.

Hooker, R. (1845) 'Of the certainty and perpetuity of faith in the elect', in *Works*, vol. 3. Ed. J. Keble. Oxford: Oxford University Press. (First published 1612).

Hughes, M., Wakeley, F. and Nash, T. (1994) *Parents and their Children's Schools*. Oxford: Blackwell.

Hume, B. (1991) Address to Catholic Secondary Head Teachers in the Archdiocese of Westminster, London Colney, 24 September.

Hume, D. (1978) *A Treatise on Human Nature* (2nd edn). Ed. R. Selby-Bigge. Oxford: Clarendon. (First published 1739).

Hutton, W. (1995) *The State We're In*. London: Cape.

Joseph Rowntree Inquiry Group (1995) *Income and Wealth: Report*. York: Joseph Rowntree Foundation.

Jowett, B. (1905) *Aristotle's Politics*. London: Oxford University Press.

Jowett, S. (1995) *Allocating Secondary School Places*. Slough: NFER.

Keenan, B. (1993) *An Evil Cradling*. London: Hutchinson-Vintage.

Ker, I. (1990) *John Henry Newman*. Oxford: Oxford University Press.

Keys, W. and Fernandes, C. (1993) *What Do Students Think About School?* Slough: NFER.

Koestler, A. (1964) *The Act of Creation*. London: Hutchinson.

Kogan, M. (1975) *Education Policy-Making: A Study of Interest Groups and Parliament*. London: Allen & Unwin.

Kung, H. (1978) *On Being a Christian*. Glasgow: Fount.

Laing, R. D. (1960) *The Divided Self*. London: Tavistock.

Lane, R. (1991) *The Market Experience*. Cambridge: Cambridge University Press.

Langford, G. (1978) *Teaching as a Profession*. Manchester: Manchester University Press.

Lao-Tzu (1922) *Tao Teh King*. Trans. I. Mears. London: Theosophical Publishing.

Lawrence, I. (1992) *Power and Politics at the Department of Education and Science*. London: Cassell.

Lawton, D. (1973) *Social Change, Education Theory and Curriculum Planning*. London: Hodder & Stoughton.

Levi-Strauss, C. (1966) *The Savage Mind*. London: Weidenfeld & Nicolson. (First published 1902).

Locke, J. (1947) *An Essay Concerning Human Understanding*. London: Dent. (First published 1690).

Lorenz, K. (1966) *On Aggression*. Trans. M. K. Wilson. London: Methuen.

Lowry, H. F. (ed.) (1932) *The Letters of Mathew Arnold to Arthur Clough*. Oxford: Oxford University Press.

MacIntyre, A. (1985) *After Virtue: A Study in Moral Theory* (2nd edn). London: Duckworth.

MacIntyre, A. (1988) *Whose Justice? Which Rationality?* London: Duckworth.

MacNeice, L. (1935) *Poems*. London: Faber & Faber.

MacPherson, C. B. (1977) *The Life and Times of Liberal Democracy*. Oxford: Oxford University Press.

MacQuarrie, J. (1972) *Paths in Spirituality*. London: SCM Press.
Mack Smith, D. (1983) *Mussolini*. London: Granada.
Mansfield, K. (1977) *The Letters and Journals: A Selection*. London: Allen Lane.
Marquand, D. (1988) *The Unprincipled Society*. London: Cape.
Marshall, T. H. (1950) *Citizenship and Social Class and Other Essays*. Cambridge: Cambridge University Press.
Maslow, A. H. (1954) *Motivation and Personality*. New York: Harper & Row.
McLellan, D. (ed.) (1977) *Selected Writings*. Oxford: Oxford University Press.
Meijer, W. A. (1995) 'The plural self: A hermeneutical view on identity and plurality'. *British Journal of Religious Education*, **17**, 2 (Spring), 192–9.
Midgley, M. (1995) *Beast and Man* (revised edn). London: Routledge.
Mill, J. S. (1979a) 'On Liberty', in *Utilitarianism*. Ed. M. Warnock. Glasgow: Collins/Fount. (First published 1859).
Mill, J. S. (1979a) 'Utilitarianism', in *Utilitarianism*. Ed. M. Warnock. Glasgow: Collins/Fount. (First published 1861).
Montaigne, M. (1991) *The Complete Essays*. Trans. M. A. Screech. Harmondsworth: Allen Lane, the Penguin Press. (First published 1580).
Mortimer, J. (1983) *In Character*. Harmondsworth: Penguin.
Murdoch, I. (1992) *Metaphysics as a Guide to Morals*. London: Chatto & Windus.
Murphy, J. (1971) *Church, State and Schools in Britain 1800–1970*. London: Routledge & Kegan Paul.
National Curriculum Council (1989) *The National Curriculum and Whole Curriculum Planning: Preliminary Guidance*. York: NCC.
National Curriculum Council (1990a) *The Whole Curriculum: Curriculum Guidance 3*. York: NCC.
National Curriculum Council (1990b) *Education for Economic and Industrial Understanding: Curriculum Guidance 4*. York: NCC.
National Forum for Values in Education (1996) *Consultation on Values in Education and the Community*. London: SCAA.
Newell, P. (1991) *The UN Convention and Children's Rights in the UK*. London: National Children's Bureau.
Newman, J. H. (Cardinal Newman) (1982) *The Idea of a University*. Ed. M. J. Svaglic. Notre Dame: University of Notre Dame Press. (First published 1852).
Northern Ireland Curriculum Council (1990) *A Guide for Teachers*. Belfast: NICC.
OFSTED (1994) *Access and Achievement in Urban Education*. London: HMSO.
OFSTED (1995) *The Annual Report of Her Majesty's Chief Inspector of Schools: Standards and Quality in Education 1993/4*. London: HMSO.
O'Keefe, D. (1993) *Truancy in English Secondary Schools*. London: Department for Education.
Owusu, K. (1986) *The Struggle for Black Arts in Britain*. London: Comedia.
Parfit, D. (1985) *Reasons and Persons*. Oxford: Oxford University Press.
Pascal, B. (1966) *Pensées*. Trans. A. J. Krailsheimer. Harmondsworth: Penguin. (First published 1670).
Paton, H. J. (1958) *The Moral Law*. London: Hutchinson.
Perkin, H. (1989) *The Rise of Professional Society: England since 1880*. London: Routledge.
Peters, R. S. (1956) *Hobbes*. Harmondsworth: Penguin.
Phenix, P. (1964) *Realms of Meaning*. New York: McGraw-Hill.
Pile, W. (1979) *The Department of Education and Science*. London: Allen & Unwin.
Plato (1951) *The Symposium*. Trans. W. Hamilton. Harmondsworth: Penguin.
Plato (1955) *The Republic*. Trans. H. D. P. Lee. Harmondsworth: Penguin.
Popper, K. (1959) *The Logic of Scientific Discovery*. London: Hutchinson. (First published 1934).

Popper, K. (1966) *The Open Society and its Enemies*, 2 vols (5th edn). London: Routledge & Kegan Paul. (First published 1945).

Popper, K. (1983) 'Truth and approximation to truth', in *A Pocket Popper*, ed. D. Miller. Glasgow: Collins/Fontana. (First published 1960).

Pring, R. (1984) *Personal and Social Education in the Curriculum*. London: Hodder & Stoughton.

Rahner, K. (1966) *Theological Investigations*, Vol. 5. London: Darton, Longman & Todd.

Rawles, J. (1972) *A Theory of Justice*. Oxford: Oxford University Press.

Ribbins, P. (ed.) (1993) *Delivering the National Curriculum: Subjects for Secondary Schooling*. Harlow: Longman.

Ricoeur, P. (1988) *Time and Narrative*, Vol. 3. Chicago: University of Chicago Press.

Rieff, P. (1966) *The Triumph of the Therapeutic*. Chicago: University of Chicago Press.

Rieff, P. (1975) *To My Fellow Teachers*. Chicago: University of Chicago Press.

Robinson, K. (1989) *The Arts in School: Principles, Practice, Provision*. London: Gulbenkian. (First published 1982).

Robson, G. (1996) 'Religious education, government policy and professional practice, 1985–1995'. *British Journal of Religious Education*, **19**, 1, 13–23.

Rogers, C. (1967) *On Becoming a Person*. London: Constable.

Rorty, R. (1991) *Essays on Heidegger and Others*, Vol. 2. Cambridge: Cambridge University Press.

Ross, M. (ed.) (1989) *Readings in Aesthetic Education*. London: The Falmer Press.

Rousseau, J.-J. (1953) *The Confessions*. Trans. J. M. Cohen. Harmondsworth: Penguin. (First published 1781).

Rousseau, J. J. (1967) *Julie ou la nouvelle heloise*. Paris: Garnier-Flammarion. (First published 1761).

Ruddock, R. (1972) *Six Approaches to the Person*. London: Routledge & Kegan Paul.

Runcie, R. (1990) Address to the Headmasters' Conference, 18 September.

Russell, B. (1946) *The Problems of Philosophy* (19th impression). London: Oxford University Press. (First published 1912).

Russell, B. (1954) *History of Western Philosophy*. London: Allen & Unwin.

Russell, B. (1957) *Why I Am Not A Christian*. Ed. P. Edwards. London: Allen & Unwin.

Sartre, J.-P. (1948) *Existentialism and Humanism*. Trans. P. Maret. London: Methuen. (First published 1946).

Schools Council (1968) *Enquiry 1: Young School Leavers*. London: HMSO.

Schumpeter, J. A. (1976) *Capitalism, Socialism and Democracy* (5th edn). London: Allen & Unwin. (First published 1942).

Schwarzschild, L. (1986) *Red Prussian: Life and Legend of Karl Marx*. Trans. M. Wing. London: Pickwick Books. (First published in UK 1948).

Scott, P. (1984) *The Crisis of the Universities*. London: Croom Helm.

Selbourne, D. (1994) *The Principle of Duty*. London: Sinclair-Stevenson.

Seminar, University of Cambridge Department of Education and King Abdulaziz University, Jeddah (1993) *Religion and Education in a Multicultural Society: An Agreed Statement*. Cambridge: University of Cambridge Department of Education.

Simon, H. A. (1969) *The Sciences of the Artificial*. Cambridge, Mass.: MIT Press.

Singer, P. and Cavaliaeri, P. (1994) *The Great Ape Project*. Basingstoke: St Martin's Press.

Skidelsky, R. (1996) *A Question of Standards: Raising Standards through Choice.* London: Politeia.

Skilbeck, M. (1982) *A Core Curriculum for the Common School.* London: University of London Institute of Education.

Smith, A. (1986) *Wealth of Nations.* Books 1-3. Ed. A. Skinner. Harmondsworth: Penguin. (First published 1776).

Smith, T. and Noble, M. (1995) *Poverty and Schooling in the 1990s.* London: Child Poverty Action Group.

Social Affairs Unit (1984) *Trespassing?* London: Social Affairs Unit.

Solow, R. (1990) *The Labour Market as a Social Institution.* Oxford: Blackwell.

Sophocles (1947) *The Theban Plays.* Trans. E. F. Watling. Harmondsworth: Penguin.

Stark, W. (ed.) (1952) *Jeremy Bentham's Economic Writings.* 3 vols. London: Allen & Unwin.

Steutel, J. and Spiecker, B. (1997) 'Rational passions and intellectual virtues: A conceptual analysis', *Studies in Philosophy and Education,* **16**, 59-71.

Strachey, L. (1934) *Eminent Victorians.* London: Chatto & Windus.

Strawson, P. F. (1959) *Individuals.* London: Methuen.

Tate, N. (1995) Address to Christian Education Movement Teachers' Conference, June.

Taylor, A. J. P. (1965) *English History 1914-1945.* London: Oxford University Press.

Thatcher, A. (1990) *Truly a Person, Truly God.* London: SPCK.

Thompson, M. (1993) *Pay and Performance: The Employee's Experience.* Brighton: Institute of Manpower Studies, University of Sussex.

Thucydides (1972) *The Peloponnesian War.* Ed. M. I. Finley, trans. M. Warner. Harmondsworth: Penguin.

Tillich, P. (1953) *Systematic Theology.* vol. 1. Welwyn: Nisbet. (First published 1951).

Tomlinson, J. (1992) 'Retrospect on Ruskin: prospect on the 1990s', in *Continuing the Education Debate,* ed. M. Williams, R. Daugherty and F. Banks. London: Cassell.

Turgenev, I. S. (1898) *A Lear of the Steppes, and Other Stories.* Trans. C. Garnett. London: Heinemann. (First published 1873).

Walden, G. (1996) *We Should Know Better.* London: Fourth Estate.

Walzer, M. (1985) *Spheres of Justice.* Oxford: Blackwell.

Weil, S. (1952) *The Need for Roots.* Trans. A. F. Wills. London: Routledge & Kegan Paul. (First published 1949).

Weldon, T. (1946) *States and Morals.* London: Murray.

West, A. (1993) *Choosing a Secondary School.* London: Centre for Educational Research.

Weston, P., Barrett, E. and Jamison, J. (1992) *The Quest for Coherence.* Slough: NFER.

White, J. P. (1973) *Towards a Compulsory Curriculum.* London: Routledge & Kegan Paul.

White, J. P. (1982) *The Aims of Education Restated.* London: Routledge & Kegan Paul.

Wiener, M. J. (1985) *English Culture and the Decline of the Industrial Spirit 1850-1980.* Harmondsworth: Penguin.

Willetts, D. (1992) *Modern Conservatism.* Harmondsworth: Penguin.

Williams, R. (1962) *Culture and Society.* Harmondsworth: Penguin.

Williams, R. (1965) *The Long Revolution.* Harmondsworth: Pelican.

Willis, P. (1990) *Moving Culture: An Enquiry into the Cultural Activities of Young People.* London: Gulbenkian.

Wordsworth, W. (1936) *Poetical Works*. Ed. E. de Selincourt. London: Oxford University Press. (First published 1801).

Young, J. Z. (1951) *Doubt and Certainty in Science*. London: Oxford University Press.

Index

Adorno, T.   16
aims   8, 127
Alexander, R.   92
Amis, Kingsley   1
Annan, Noel   40, 72, 145
Appleby, J.   90
Aquinas, St Thomas   20, 34, 76, 102
arete   36
Aristotle   20, 26, 76, 95, 100
Arnold, Matthew   39, 42
Arnold, Thomas   80
art   50–1, 75
arts education   80–1
Ashbery, John   16
Athens *see* Greece, ancient
Augustine, St   20, 32, 34, 67, 76, 102
Austin, J. L.   61
Ayer, A. J., *Language, Truth and Logic*   68

Bacon, Francis   76
Baker, Kenneth   94
Barthes, Roland   16
Bellow, Saul   81
Bentham, Jeremy   44, 104
Berlin, Isaiah   39
Better Schools (DES)   93
Board Schools   82
Boesky, Ivan   44
Bonhoeffer, Dietrich   33–4, 100
Bowra, C. Maurice   36, 75, 95
Bradley, A. C.   91
Brecht, Bertolt   15
British Humanist Society   55
Brooks, Peter   24–5
Browne, Thomas, 'Religio medici'   33
Bruner, Jerome   50
Buber, Martin   12, 27
Burke, Edmund   106, 113
Butler, R. A.   83

Calvin, John   32
capitalism   43, 44, 45, 113
Chekhov, A.   22
child psychology   48
child-centred education   55, 56
choice   54, 139–43, 149, 150, 156
Christianity: the Christian person   32–4;
   influence on education   54, 58, 78; notion
   of a person   101, 102; respect and   10;
   responsibility   112; society   102; status
   in religious education   83, 85; truth   67,
   70, 71, 76
church schools   82
Church of Scotland   106
Chuter-Ede, Baron (James Chuter Ede)   83
City Technology College   88

civil service   145–8
Civitas Dei   13
Clark, Kenneth (Lord Clark)   35–6, 39, 81
classicism   34–8, 49, 58, 101–3
Cobbett, William   87
cognitive psychology   51
coherence theory   67, 68, 69, 70
Coleridge, Samuel Taylor   39, 50
Commission on Social Justice   113, 135
communitarianism   107, 110
communities, schools as responsible   126,
   127, 132
comprehensive schools   58, 79, 139, 142,
   143, 155–6, 157
Comte, Auguste   64
Conrad, Joseph, *Nostromo*   15–16
consciousness   16, 20, 24, 61
Copernicus, Nicolas   13
Cordingley, Philippa   137
correspondence theory   67, 68, 69
county schools   82
creativity   49, 50–1, 56, 57, 80
Cupitt, Don   33
curricular crisis of identities   12–17
curriculum, the true: the battle of the
   truths   74–89; the way forward   97–8;
   the whole curriculum   89–97
Curriculum Council for Wales   93

Darwin, Charles   13
Darwinism   64, 96
Davies, B.   70
Davies, N.   90
Dawkins, Richard   23, 82, 85
Dearing, Sir Ron   86; *Review of
   Qualifications for 16–19 Year Olds*   47
democracy   101–5, 109–14, 116, 119, 120,
   123, 129, 151, 153, 156, 157
Department for Education   88
Department of Education and Science   91,
   92, 94, 145, 147
Department for Employment   88
Department of National Heritage   81
Derrida, Jacques   16–17, 65
Descartes, René   14, 20, 38, 68, 76
Dewey, John   104
divine revelation   71
Dollimore, J.   15, 19, 148
Donne, John   32
Dostoevsky, Fyodor   105
Dulwich College   136
Durkheim, Emile   64
duties in democratic institutions   123–4
Dworkin, Ronald, *Life's Dominion*   11

Eaglesham, E. J. R.   87

Eckhart, Johannes 34
Education Act (1870) 82
Education Act (1902) 82
Education Act (1944) 82–5, 139, 145, 150
Education (No. 2) Act (1986) 92
Education for Economic and Industrial Understanding (National Curriculum Council) 47, 87
Education Reform Act (1988) 8, 48, 83, 84–5, 88, 92, 93, 96, 97
Eliot, George, *Middlemarch* 15, 46
Eliot, T. S. 32, 96
Elliott, Philip 42–3
Engels, Friedrich 62, 63, 66
English literature 90–1, 96
Enlightenment 20, 38, 46, 76, 80, 82, 101
equality 120–3, 127–8, 155
ethology 26
Eton College 139
Etzioni, Amitai 107
Euripides 35
evaluation 132, 144–5

falsification theory 69, 71
first virtues of education 5–9, 98, 154–5
Forster, E. M. 73
Foucault, Michel 16; 'Nietzsche, genealogy, history' 25
Frank, Robert H. 46
free markets 43, 44, 45, 57, 101, 110, 111, 120, 142, 150
free will 19–20, 33, 61
Freud, Sigmund 16

Galileo Galilei 13
Gardner, H. 127
GCE/GCSE 135–6
gender 25
General National Vocational Qualification 88
General Teaching Council (proposed) 149
geography 80, 86
God: 'death of' 33; and *homo creator* 49; as Spirit 34
Golding, William 32
Gombrich, E. H. 50, 51, 81
the Good 67, 75–6, 78
good and evil 19–20, 33
the good school: defined 1–2, 154–5; fields of education 3, 5; in the good society 154–7; purposes 8; a vision of the good school 2–9
government: as an institution 134; the moral government of education 148–53; societies and government 99–107
Graham, Duncan 136, 145, 146, 147
Gray, J. 45
Greece, ancient 34–8, 54, 75, 77–8, 95, 103, 107

Hadow Report, 1926 87

Hailsham, Lord (Quintin Hogg) 44
Hamlyn, D. W. 61
Hargreaves, A. 80
Hargreaves, David 26, 92
Harries, Richard, Bishop of Oxford 49
Harrington, Tim 137
Havel, Vaclav 20
Hayek, Friedrich 111
headteachers 127
Healey, Denis 14, 86
Hegel, Georg Wilhelm Friedrich 13–14, 61, 65, 66, 100, 108; *Logic* 62; *Philosophy of History* 61, 62; *Philosophy of Law* 61
Hegelianism 66
Heidegger, Martin 16
Henry, Sir Denis 44
Her Majesty's Inspectorate (HMI) 92, 93, 94, 145, 147
Heraclitus 37
Hirsch, Donald 140, 141
history 80, 86, 90
Hobbes, Thomas 20, 25, 99–100, 107, 108, 116
Holbrook, David 50
Holmes, E. 87
Homer 20, 36
Hooker, Richard 70
Hughes, M. 141
humanism 13, 40–2, 55–6, 112
Humboldt, Alexander, Baron von 38
Hume, Cardinal Basil 32
Hume, David 14, 67, 124
Hurd, Douglas 113
Hutton, Will 43
Huxley, Aldous 34, 40
Huxley, Sir Julian 40

ideals 52, 53, 54, 55, 56, 57
imagination 49, 50, 51, 56, 57, 70
individualism 39, 105, 106, 112–14, 120
inequality 121, 134–7
institutions: government as an institution 134; schools as just 126, 127, 132

Jagger, Mick 14
Jefferson, Thomas 106
Johnson, Samuel 19
Jung, Carl Gustav 16
justice 5–8, 99, 107–12, 115–21, 123, 124, 126–33, 148, 151–3, 154–7; and the national system of education 134–7

Kant, Immanuel 10, 20, 38–9, 106, 110
Keenan, Brian 22–3
Ker, Ian 70
Keynes, John Maynard, 1st Baron 40
Kierkegaard, Sören 33
Koestler, Arthur 50, 51

Laing, R. D. 16

Lane, Robert, *The Market Experience*   46-7
Langford, Glenn   23
language   16-17, 65, 69
Lao-Tzu, *Tao Teh King*   105-6
'The Law in Education Project'   128
Lawson, Nigel   45
leadership   127, 130-2
Leavis, Frank Raymond   15
Lenin, Vladimir Ilyich   66
Levi-Strauss, Claude   16, 64
liberty, right to   120
local education authorities (LEAs)   92, 135, 136, 140
Locke, John   20, 24, 25, 67
Lorenz, Konrad   26

McDonald's   60
MacIntyre, Alasdair   6, 28, 29, 110, 112, 120
McLellan, D.   16, 62, 63
MacNeice, Louis, 'Snow'   15
Macpherson, C. B.   104
MacQuarrie, John   34
maintained schools   82, 127, 135-6
management   127, 130-1, 132, 133
Mansfield, Katherine   22
Marquand, David   25, 105, 146
Marx, Karl   13, 16, 64, 65, 66, 108; 'Eleven theses on Feuerbach'   62; 'Preface to a critique of political economy'   63
Marxism/Marxists   16, 63, 64, 100, 108, 109, 117
Maslow, A. H.   41
mathematics, in ancient Greece   78
Meijer, Wilna   28
Midgley, Mary   23, 26
Mill, James   104
Mill, John Stuart   38, 50, 83, 104, 106; *Utilitarianism*   112
mind/body dualism   25
mixed education   141
Montaigne, Michel Eyquem de   14
Moore, G. E.   40
moral and intellectual qualities *see* justice; respect for persons; responsibility; truth
Mozart, Leopold   73
Murdoch, Iris   11, 16, 20, 66, 68, 72, 98
Mussolini, Benito   101

National Association for the Promotion of Technical Education   86
National Curriculum   54, 128; and the civil service   146; development   93; and religious education   90; revision of   86
The National Curriculum 5-16 (DES)   84
National Curriculum Council   91, 92, 93, 128, 136, 147
National Curriculum Orders for Art and for Music   81
National Forum for Values in Education   3, 97, 128

national system of education: interests and   137-48; justice and   134-7
natural selection   13
neo-Platonism   76, 79
New Labour   151
Newman, Cardinal John Henry   40, 70, 95
Newsom Report, 1963   87
Niebuhr, Reinhold   102
Nietzsche, Friedrich Wilhelm   20, 65
Northern Ireland Curriculum Council   93

Oakeshott, Michael   30
objectives   130-1, 132
Officer Training Corps   118
OFSTED   85, 136
Organisation for Economic Cooperation and Development   140

Parfit, Derek   14
Parmenides   37
Pascal, Blaise   14, 34
pastoral care   55
Paton, H. J.   10, 38
Perkin, Harold   96
personal school   52-8; aims, curriculum, pastoral care   53-7; aspirations   53; school nature and ethos   57-8
persons: centred person   13-17, 19-20; Christian person   31-4, 101, 102, 105, 112; classical person   34-8, 101, 102, 103, 105; economic person   42-7, 102, 103, 104, 112; humanist person   40-2, 102-5, 112, 123; ideal   41-2; overall approach of schools   18-19; person as narrator in a quest   27-30; rational person   38-40, 102, 103, 105, 112, 123; religious   123; respect for *see* respect for persons; the school's working model of a person   48-51; what a person is   20-7
Peters, R. S.   107
Picasso, Pablo   51
Pico della Mirandola   27
Pile, W.   145
Pindar   35
planning   130, 131
Plato   20, 35-8, 46, 75-6, 78, 95, 100, 108; *The Republic*   35; *The Symposium*   37; *Timaeus*   22
Platonism   54, 67, 70, 76, 78, 86, 89
Popper, Karl   37, 49, 61, 66, 67, 69, 71, 108
practical education   86-9
Pravda newspaper   64
Praxiteles   36
Pring, Richard   23
private education   136, 150-3
Protestantism   101
Przysucha, Rabbi von   12
public schools   87, 118, 139; curriculum   78-9, 80

The Quest for Coherence (National Foundation for Educational Research) 93

Rahner, K. 33
rationalism 38–40, 103, 112, 123, 146
Rawles, John 5, 110, 111, 119–22, 134
reason 24, 38, 40, 49, 62, 70
reductionism 25–6
religious education 82–6, 90, 128
Renaissance 13, 14, 15, 19, 76, 78
respect for persons 5–8, 10–11, 12, 21, 23, 31, 52, 58, 97, 133, 154, 155, 157
responsibility 5, 6, 7, 9, 97, 99, 107, 108–9, 112–19, 123–33, 144–5, 155, 156, 157
Ribbins, P. 95
rights of students 120–4, 127
Rogers, Carl 40, 41–2
romanticism 20, 39, 49
Rousseau, Jean-Jacques 20, 26, 40, 41, 46, 72; *Confessions* 24
Rowntree Foundation 135
Ruddock, Ralph 24
rules 129
Runcie, Robert 59
Russell, Bertrand 40, 62, 67, 83

sanctification 33–4
Sartre, Jean-Paul 20
Saussure, Ferdinand de 16
school councils 129–30
Schools Council 84; 'The practical curriculum' 88
Schools Council Curriculum Projects 80
Schools Council Religious Education Curriculum Projects 84
Schools Curriculum and Assessment Authority (SCAA) 3, 85, 90, 128
science: in the curriculum 79–80, 88; scientific truth 91
Scott, Peter 96
Scott inquiry 60
Selbourne, David 106
selective education 142, 143
self-knowledge 22
senior management 130, 131, 132
'seven liberal arts' 78
sexuality 25
Shakespeare, William 15, 91
Singer, P. and Cavaliaeri, P. 23
single-sex education 141
Skidelsky, Robert 150–1, 152
Smith, Adam 43, 44, 150
Smith, Peter 149
Social Affairs Unit 87
social anthropology 26, 48
social capital 113
social psychology 26, 48
social sciences 80
sociology 64–5
Socrates 36

Sophocles, *Antigone* 34
soul 33, 34, 39
Southwark, London borough of 136
specialist educational needs 156
Spencer, Herbert 64
the state: the Greek city state 103; reality and 61, 62
Strachey, L. 80
Strawson, P. F. 24
structuralism 16, 17, 65, 66
structure 127

Taylor, A. J. P. 83
teachers: evaluation 132, 144–5; legitimate interests in education 144, 149; performance 133; responsibilities 144–5
technical education 86
technology 88
Thatcher, A. 21
Thatcher, Margaret (Baroness) 106, 113
Thatcherism 96
Thucydides 35, 107
Tillich, Paul 70
Tomlinson, John 106
Toryism 106
truanting 139
truth 5–8, 154–7; the attack on truth 59–66; the battle of the truths 74–89; ideas of truth 67–73; logical 91; scientific 91; and subject areas 90–1, 95; transcendent 91; and Goodness 37; way forward 97–8; whole curriculum 89–97
Turgenev, Ivan Sergeevich 90–1
Tytler, D. 136, 145, 146, 147

Übermensch 20
underperformance 135–6
United Nations Convention on the Rights of the Child 120–1

values 68–9, 72, 141–3
vocational courses 88

Walden, G. 151
Weber, Max 146
Weil, Simone 34, 122
Weldon, Tom 100, 101
West, A. 141
The Whole Curriculum (National Curriculum Council) 93
Wiener, Martin 42–3, 80
Willetts, David 44, 120
Williams, Raymond 26, 62, 63, 122
Wittgenstein, Ludwig 16, 67
Woollard, Anthony 147
Wordsworth, William, *Lyrical Ballads* 81
work: and the Dearing *Review* 47; role of 46
worthwhile educational practices 3–4, 5, 8

Young, J. Z. 50